Asian Flashpoint

Security and the Korean Peninsula

WITHDRAWN

edited by

Andrew Mack

Allen & Unwin
in association with the
Department of Internat
RSPacS, ANU, Canbe

First published in 1993

Allen & Unwin Australia Pty Ltd.
9 Atchison St., St Leonards, NSW 2065, Australia.

Department of International Relations, RSPacS,
Australian National University, Canberra ACT 0200, Australia.

National Library of Australia
Cataloguing-in-Publication entry:

   Asian Flashpoint: security and the Korean peninsula.

   ISBN 1 86373 401 5.

   1. National security – Korea. I. Mack, Andrew, 1939– .
   II. Australian National University, Dept of International Relations
   (Series: Studies in world affairs; no. 5)

355.03300519

Printed by ANU Printery, ANU, Canberra ACT 0200, Australia

Table of Contents

iv

Notes on Contributors

Byung-joon Ahn, Department of Political Science, Yonsei University, Seoul, Republic of Korea.

Paul Bracken, School of Organisation and Management, Yale University, New Haven, Connecticut, USA.

Gennady Chufrin, Institute of Oriental Studies, Moscow, Russia.

James Cotton, Political Science Department, University of Tasmania, Australia.

Aidan Foster-Carter, Department of Sociology at the University of Leeds, UK.

Peter Hayes, Nautilus Research, Berkeley, California, USA.

Norman Levin, Rand Corporation, Santa Monica, California, USA.

Kyongsoo Lho, Korean Institute of International Studies, Seoul, Republic of Korea.

Chung-in Moon, Department of Political Science, University of Kentucky, Lexington, Kentucky, USA.

Andrew Mack, Department of International Relations, Australian National University, Canberra, Australia.

Satoshi Morimoto, Nomura Research Institute, Tokyo, Japan.

Ye Ru'an, China Institute of International Studies, Beijing, People's Republic of China.

Abbreviations

AECL	Atomic Energy Canada Ltd
ASEAN	Association of South East Asian Nations
CBM	Confidence-Building Measure
CFA	Combined Field Army
CFC	Combined Forces Command
CIS	Commonwealth of Independent States
CSBM	Confidence- and Security-Building Measure
CSCE	Conference on Security and Cooperation in Europe
CWC	Chemical Weapons Convention
DMZ	Demilitarised Zone
DPRK	Democratic People's Republic of Korea
EASI	East Asian Strategic Initiative
FBR	Fast Breeder Reactor
GNP	Gross National Product
GWe	Gigawatt-electric
HWR	Heavy Water Reactor
IAEA	International Atomic Energy Agency
IRBM	Intermediate Range Ballistic Missile
JNCC	Joint Nuclear Control Commission
KAERI	Korean Atomic Energy Research Institute
KEPCO	Korean Electric Power Company
KMRR	Korean Multipurpose Research Reactor
KSN	Korean Standard Nuclear unit
Kt	Kiloton (nuclear explosive equivalent)
KWP	Korean Workers Party
LWR	Light Water Reactor
MAPLE	Multipurpose Applied Physics Lattice Experiment
MIA	Missing in Action
MOX	Mixed Oxide Fuel
MTCR	Missile Technology Control Regime
MWe	Megawatt-electric
MWt	Megawatt-thermal
NAM	Non-Aligned Movement
NATO	North Atlantic Treaty Organisation
NFZ	Nuclear-Free Zone
NIC	Newly Industrialised Country
NPT	Nuclear Non-Proliferation Treaty
NSSS	Nuclear Steam Supply System

PHWR	Pressurised Heavy Water Reactor
PIE	Post-Irradiation Examination
POL	Petroleum, Oils and Lubricants
Pu	Plutonium
PWR	Pressurised Water Reactor
ROK	Republic of Korea
SEZ	Special Economic Zone
SGN	Societe Generale pour les Techniques Nouvelles
SLOC	Sea Lanes of Communication
UNCMAC	United Nations Command Military Armistice Commission
UNDP	United Nations Development Program

Acknowledgements

Thanks are due to Lynne Payne, Mary-Louise Hickey, Barbara Owen-Jones and Robin Ward of the Department of International Relations at the Australian National University, Canberra, for editorial work and preparation of the manuscript. Sue Gerrard and Jena Hamilton assisted with typing. Thanks are also due to the Cartography Unit of the Research School of Pacific Studies, ANU.

Special thanks are given to the Northeast Asia Program for assistance in funding the March 1992 workshop held at the ANU at which the original versions of the chapters in this volume were presented.

Neither the workshop nor this volume would have been possible without the generous support of the W. Alton-Jones Foundation of the United States.

Preface

This monograph had its genesis in a workshop on 'Security and the Korean peninsula in the 1990s' run by the Department of International Relations at the Australian National University, 26–27 March 1992. The papers have subsequently been revised and the introductory chapter discusses the most recent developments—up to mid-November 1993.

In planning the monograph we wished to explore the various security dilemmas on the peninsula from a variety of different perspectives. Consequently there are chapters by distinguished Japanese, Chinese, Russian, Australian and American analysts. There are also three chapters by South Korean scholars which focus primarily on inter-Korean relations. Two North Korean analysts from the Foreign Ministry's Disarmament Research Institute also attended the workshop and provided valuable commentary on a number of papers. However, since their formal presentations were simply short statements of North Korean government policy they have not been included in this volume.

In addition to different national perspectives of security issues on the peninsula there are separate chapters examining a range of other issues, including South Korea's nuclear program, the prospects for conventional arms control and confidence-building measures between the two Koreas, and the political economy of Korean security in regional context. A recurrent theme in a number of chapters is the question of the survivability of the regime in North Korea—an issue of considerable relevance following the collapse of most other communist states around the world and the growing crisis in the North Korean economy.

The project which gave rise to this monograph was made possible by a generous grant from the W. Alton Jones Foundation.

1   Security and the Korean Peninsula in the 1990s

ANDREW MACK

In late 1993, the security situation on the Korean peninsula remains both uncertain and highly problematic, in part because the end of the Cold War has created both new opportunities and problems for the region. The US–Soviet competition, which was a determinate factor in most regional security equations, is now a rapidly fading memory. In its wake have come changes which would have been inconceivable less than five years ago. South Korea has established diplomatic relations with both Moscow and Beijing, and North Korea has been abandoned by the new Russia, and is being kept at a distance by a rapidly modernising China.

America's role in the region is also changing. Without a Soviet Union to contain, the US is having to redefine both its regional role and its relationships with its alliance partners. The fact that the central rationale for a US forward military presence in Asia has disappeared is causing concern among US allies about Washington's long-term commitment to the region. Alliance relationships, particularly in the case of Japan and Korea, are being complicated by sometimes bitter trade frictions.

The arms build-up in Northeast Asia has not slowed since the end of the Cold War—if anything it has increased. In part this reflects the rapid rates of economic growth which characterise the region, and which tend to drag defence spending upwards regardless of external threats, but it also reflects the fact that the region is still characterised by a unique combination of deeply held historical animosities and a range of unresolved territorial and sovereignty disputes.

Of particular security concern is the spectre of nuclear proliferation in the region. China is already a nuclear power—and the only one in the world which is not observing a nuclear testing moratorium. Although China joined the Nuclear Non-Proliferation Treaty (NPT) regime in

1

1992, the US is still concerned about Chinese nuclear technology transfer to countries like Pakistan, Iran and Algeria. The Chinese, together with the North Koreans, are also the major Third World exporters of ballistic missiles.

Taiwan has sought to acquire technologies necessary for the manufacture of nuclear weapons in the past, but was forced to desist under strong US pressure. There is concern that Taiwan may be continuing with its nuclear weapons research program. In 1988, a Taiwanese nuclear scientist, Colonel Chang Hsien-Yi, who had been Deputy-Director of the military's Chungsan Institute of Science and Technology, informed the US that Taiwan was continuing to seek to make nuclear weapons. US officials later said that Taiwan had been secretly building a plutonium extraction facility but that it had now been closed down.[1]

Japan remains firmly committed to the NPT regime, but is also committed to a program of fast and fast breeder nuclear power reactors. Tens of tons of plutonium will be produced for this program, a fact which causes considerable regional concern, even though the Japanese plutonium is not weapons grade.[2] A minority of 'Japanese Gaullists' within the Japanese security community believes, like the late President de Gaulle, that the US is not a reliable ally and that Japan should have its own independent nuclear deterrent. If North Korea acquires nuclear weapons, support for the nuclear option in Japan would likely grow rapidly.

South Korea sought to acquire nuclear weapons technologies in the mid-1970s and again in the early 1980s. It has considerable nuclear expertise as a consequence of its large nuclear power program, and a large potential source of fissile material in the spent fuel from its reactors. There is a sizeable body of opinion within the Korean political and security communities which believes that the South should acquire its own independent nuclear deterrent. This is *not* the view of the present government, however, and the government's position is unlikely to change as long as the alliance relationship with the US remains firm.

But it is North Korea which has been at the centre of proliferation concern in Northeast Asia in the 1990s. The US argues that the North's nuclear program is the most serious security threat in the region, certainly it is the dominant security issue on the Korean peninsula.

---

[1] *Arms Control Reporter*, Section 602, 11 March 1988.

[2] Plutonium derived from the spent fuel of power reactors is 'weapons usable', but the process of weaponisation is both more difficult and dangerous than with the weapons grade plutonium produced by research reactors like those in North Korea.

Background

North Korea, which has operated a small nuclear research program since the 1960s, started construction of a large research reactor in the early 1980s. It acceded to the NPT in 1985, under considerable pressure from Moscow. However, it was not until 1989 that international concern about the nuclear complex at Yongbyon north of the DPRK capital began to grow. There were a number of reasons for this.

First, the North had refused to sign a nuclear safeguards agreement with the International Atomic Energy Agency (IAEA). NPT signatory states have a legal obligation to sign a safeguards agreement within eighteen months of acceding to the Treaty. Without such an agreement the IAEA was unable to inspect the North's nuclear facilities to verify that the North was not making nuclear weapons.

Second, the 30 megawatt research reactor at Yongbyon was unnecessarily large for research purposes and was capable of producing 7–8 kilograms of weapons grade plutonium a year—enough for one small nuclear weapon. The reactor is fuelled by locally mined uranium and moderated by graphite—also local in origin.

Third, US satellite photographs had revealed the existence of a nuclear fuel reprocessing plant—necessary to transform spent reactor fuel into plutonium, the fissile material for nuclear weapons. Since the North had no capability to build fast breeder reactors (which use plutonium as a fuel), the clear implication was that the reprocessing plant was part of a nuclear weapons program. There was also photographic evidence that nuclear weapons detonators had been tested.

Fourth, there were reports from North Korean defectors and, later, from the KGB, confirming that the North was seeking to build nuclear weapons.

Confronted with increasingly insistent demands that it meet its international legal obligations, the North argued that it could not sign a safeguards agreement because the American 'nuclear threat' against it had been increased. It demanded that the safeguards agreement be amended to contain clauses which would effectively require the US to give an undertaking not to use nuclear weapons against it, and that US nuclear weapons be withdrawn from the South. Both demands were rejected by Washington and Seoul.

For reasons which are still not clear, but which almost certainly related to the growing rift between Moscow and Pyongyang at that time, the North's position on the nuclear issue changed in 1991. On 31 December, North and South Korea signed a 'Joint Declaration for Denuclearisation of the Korean Peninsula' in which they undertook not to 'test, manufacture, produce, receive, possess, store, deploy, or use nuclear weapons'. They also agreed not to 'possess facilities for nuclear reprocessing or uranium enrichment',[3] i.e., they committed themselves not to use their nuclear power and research programs to produce fissile material that could be used in nuclear weapons.[4]

On 7 January 1992 the North finally signed a safeguards agreement with the IAEA. South Korea simultaneously announced that the huge annual US–ROK 'Team Spirit' exercise, which the North had long denounced as a highly provocative 'nuclear war exercise' would be cancelled in 1992. During 1992, the nuclear complex at Yongbyon was subjected to six IAEA inspections and discussions about a separate North–South nuclear inspection regime commenced in the Joint Nuclear Control Commission.

A number of questions about the North's nuclear program remained unresolved, and the CIA was still suspicious, but, in general, international concern about the North's nuclear program diminished considerably in 1992. The controversial Yongbyon reactor was at last under safeguards, as was the reprocessing plant—which inspections had revealed was far from complete anyway.

But towards the end of 1992 the mood of optimism began to sour. After eight meetings of the North–South Joint Nuclear Control Commission (JNCC) there had been no real progress. Seoul had pushed hard for an intrusive regime of 'special inspections'. It wanted the right to inspect *any* suspicious site in the North at short notice. The North refused, arguing that any questions about *its* nuclear facilities were being resolved by IAEA inspections, and that the real issue the JNCC should focus on was the inspection of US 'nuclear bases' in the South. By early January 1993, there was a total impasse, for which each side blamed the other.

These were not the only reasons for concern. In December 1992, Russian security forces had physically prevented 36 senior weapons scientists from flying to Pyongyang, where they had been hired for large salaries. Western suspicions that the North might still be working on a nuclear weapons program were reinforced by a claim by Yevgeny Primakov, Director of the Russian Foreign Intelligence Service—successor to the KGB—that Pyongyang was 'on the threshold of developing nuclear bombs'. In February 1992, the new CIA chief, James Woolsey, stated there was a 'real possibility' that the North had secreted enough material from its own nuclear program for at least one nuclear weapon.

---

3   This does not, however, prevent either side from acquiring plutonium from overseas *or* sending their own spent reactor fuel for reprocessing overseas. This was a rather odd and worrying omission. If the concern was to avoid the introduction of fissile material to the peninsula, its importation should have been banned as well.

4   The agreement did not, however, call on external powers to refrain from using, or threatening to use, nuclear weapons against the two signatory states as had been the case with the South Pacific Nuclear Free Zone (SPNFZ) treaty of 1985.

The current crisis grew out of the repeated refusal of the North Koreans to permit IAEA inspectors access to two suspicious undeclared facilities at Yongbyon. The IAEA believed that the facilities were spent nuclear fuel repositories—which should have been declared by the North. The North claimed that they were 'military objects' which had 'nothing to do with the nuclear problem' and denounced the demands for special inspections as 'brigandish' acts of spying. It claimed that the IAEA was bowing to sinister US pressures, threatened to quit the NPT,[5] and warned that any attempt to impose inspections could plunge the peninsula into 'a holocaust of war'.[6] The IAEA, of course, has a perfect right to demand a special inspection of 'military objects', if it believes that they may conceal illegitimate nuclear activities.[7]

Responding to the North's defiance, the IAEA's Board of Governors gave the North an ultimatum: accede to inspections by 25 March or face 'further measures'. The North again refused. On 9 March, the 1993 'Team Spirit' exercise began and North Korea declared a state of 'semi-war'. On 12 March, it announced that it was withdrawing from the NPT, and its withdrawal would take effect on 12 June, after the required three months notice. This was an extremely serious development. Once outside the NPT there would be no legal impediment to the North making as many nuclear weapons as it wished. Even more worrying was the prospect that, having stockpiled sufficient weapons for its own use, the North could then sell either weapons grade plutonium, weapons technology, or even the weapons themselves to states such as Iraq, Libya and Iran.

On 12 May, after a period of intensive consultations, the UN Security Council adopted resolution 825 which called for the DPRK to reconsider its decision to withdraw from the NPT, to respect its non-proliferation obligations and abide by the safeguards agreement. Shortly afterwards bilateral talks with the US started and the North announced that it had 'suspended' its withdrawal from the NPT.

Interpreting the North's behaviour

How should the North's persistent stalling on the nuclear issue, the failure to sign an IAEA safeguards agreement for more than six years, the subsequent failure to agree to an inspection regime with the South, and

---

5 'North Korean Ambassador Threatens "Countermeasures" Against IAEA Inspection', BBC *Summary of World Broadcasts* (henceforth *SWB*) FE/1615 A1/1 17 February 1993 and Patrick Worsnip, 'Switzerland: North Korean Envoy Says Nuclear Accord with IAEA in Peril', Reuters, 22 February 1993.

6 See Douglas Busvine, 'Austria: IAEA Discusses North Korean Nuclear Sites', Reuters, 22 February 1993.

7 Part of the North's sensitivity on this issue may arise from the fact that it is the first state ever to be subjected to an IAEA 'special inspection'.

the refusal to allow the IAEA to inspect the two suspect sites at Yongbyon, be interpreted?

Many analysts believe that, despite the stalling, Pyongyang *is* prepared to give up its nuclear program, but that it is seeking to extract the maximum price from the US in the process. According to these analysts the US interests in preventing Pyongyang from 'going nuclear' gave the North's 'nuclear card' considerable leverage and led directly to the US–DPRK talks in the northern summer of 1993. Since Pyongyang had always sought to deal with the US rather than Seoul, or the IAEA, Washington's agreement to hold talks was indeed a diplomatic coup for the North.

During the various US–DPRK meetings which stretched into the autumn of 1993, it is clear that the US did canvass a range of significant concessions with the North. These included:

• permanent cancellation of the US–ROK 'Team Spirit' exercise;

• a so-called 'negative security guarantee' for Pyongyang, meaning a US undertaking not to use nuclear weapons against the North;

• a US commitment to signing a mutual non-aggression agreement with the North;

• US support for the introduction into the North of modern light water power reactors to replace the existing graphite-moderated research reactors;

• the possibility of US diplomatic recognition of North Korea (which would have paved the way for recognition by Japan and other countries too);

• and the possibility of a formal peace treaty ending the Korean war.

In return the North agreed to submit to 'full and impartial' IAEA safeguards, and that the long-stalled North–South nuclear talks would be restarted. Hopes that this might lead to genuine progress were swiftly dashed, however. Legalistic as ever, the North found ample pretext to avoid meeting its commitments. It refused to agree to IAEA demands to inspect two suspect nuclear facilities at Yongbyon on the grounds that the IAEA was *not* being 'impartial'. It was, claimed Pyongyang, acting at the behest of the US and on information provided by 'partial' US intelligence agencies. 'Western forces' were accused of having 'instigated and manipulated the IAEA Secretariat to attain their sinister political purpose'.[8] The North continued to claim that the suspect sites at Yongbyon were military facilities, and not nuclear as the 'biased' IAEA had claimed. There were therefore no grounds for them to be inspected.[9]

---

[8] Cited in BBC *SWB*, Asia–Pacific, 8 November 1993.

[9] The North's claim that the suspect sites are non-nuclear military sites is quite untrue. Their obvious nuclear role was revealed by US military satellite

Attempts to revive the North–South talks also failed, primarily because the North insisted on two preconditions First, that Seoul agree to halt all 'nuclear war exercises' (i.e., 'Team Spirit' and some lesser US–ROK exercises); second, that the South stop what was described as 'international cooperation'—a reference to the policy coordination between Seoul, Washington and Tokyo on the nuclear issue. Both demands were unacceptable, as the North must have known they would be.

By now, it seemed clear that Pyongyang did not intend to meet either its commitment to allow IAEA inspections, or to make progress on North–South talks. In September, the US suspended the third of the planned mid-level meetings.[10] In the weeks that followed there were more worrying developments.

In October, the annual South Korean Defence White Paper reported that the North was now in 'the final stage' of making a bomb.[11] Shortly afterwards, Hans Blix, Director General of the IAEA, said that the DPRK's refusal to admit even routine inspections of its declared facilities meant that batteries and film in the IAEA's on-site monitoring equipment at Yongbyon could run out. Without its nuclear operations being monitored the North could divert nuclear materials to bomb production without being detected.[12]

Also in October, the South Korean Science and Technology Minister suggested that if there was no progress in resolving the nuclear issue with the North, the South should consider reviewing its 1991 commitment to the denuclearisation of the peninsula. According to a report in the Seoul newspaper, *Choson Ilbo,* the implication of the Minister's statement was that the South should acquire its own reprocessing facilities, which were banned under the terms of the 1991 agreement.[13] With plutonium 'on tap' so to speak, the South could 'go nuclear' very rapidly.

---

photographs which were shown to the IAEA Board of Governors. Inspection of the nuclear waste located at the two sites is crucial to determine the extent to which the North has reprocessed spent reactor fuel into weapons grade plutonium. The fact that plutonium has been produced is not in doubt; the quantities diverted are still not known. Even if the suspect sites were military facilities this does not exempt them from special inspections.

[10] Low level talks continued in New York, however.

[11] Peter Hartcher, 'North's N-Plant: Threat to Trade', *Financial Review*, 18 October 1993

[12] Lim Yun-suk, 'South Korea: IAEA Chief Says His Worries Grow Over N. Korea', Reuters, 19 October 1993

[13] There is apparently no support for this option in the Blue House, but within sections of the bureaucracy, parliament and the public, the idea that South Korea should have its own reprocessing facility, and hence fissile material for nuclear weapons should they be needed, has a considerable appeal. Since the 1991 denuclearisation accord is not a treaty it could be negated simply by issuing another declaration.

In sections of the US intelligence community, there is apparently growing concern that the North Koreans may be planning to launch a conventional attack against the South. According to one report, citing 'Western intelligence sources', the North has added three submarines, 20 000 ground troops and some 100 tanks to its inventory. It has tested a new 1000 km missile, the Rodong-I, and is developing another, the Rodong-II, with an even greater range. It has also 'tripled the frequency of fighter training exercises despite an acute national fuel shortage'.[14] In November, a top Defense Department official in Washington warned that the North had deployed 70 per cent of its 1.2 million troops, 'right up close to the border. Heavy artillery and multiple-launch rocket systems have been moved close to the Demilitarised Zone'.[15]

US Defense Secretary Les Aspin threatened in a November visit to Seoul to push for UN sanctions unless Pyongyang cooperated with IAEA inspectors. Meanwhile the prospect of military strikes against the Yongbyon nuclear facilities is back on the media agenda in both Washington and Seoul. On 8 November, shortly after US media reports that the Pentagon had prepared contingency plans for cruise missile strikes against Yongbyon, President Clinton declined to comment on whether or not pre-emptive strikes against the North were an option. He did, however, claim that the DPRK nuclear issue was on top of the international agenda. North Korea, he stated, 'cannot be allowed to develop a nuclear bomb'.[16] On 10 November, South Korean President Kim Yong Sam stated that 'North Korea's nuclear development should be stopped by all means'.[17]

Pyongyang's response was predictable: 'Answering dialogue with dialogue, war with war, is our stand', declared Vice Marshall Kim Kwang-chin, Vice Minister of the People's Armed Forces.[18] Pyongyang had also been denouncing the South Korean military build-up in characteristic prose:

From the fact that they have a craze for preparing for a war...one can clearly see that the South Korean rulers are warmongers, who are even more bellicose than military gangsters in the past.[19]

---

14 Hartcher, 'North's N-Plant'.

15 Ambrose Evans-Pritchard, 'N-Bomb Fears as North Korea Threatens War', *Sunday Telegraph*, 7 November 1993.

16 Cited in 'N-Arms Clinton Warns North Korea', *Sydney Morning Herald*, 9 November 1993.

17 Lee Se-wan, 'South Korea: S. Korea Prepares for Any Eventuality With North', Reuters, 10 November 1993 [emphasis added].

18 KCNA News Agency, Pyongyang, cited in BBC *SWB* Asia–Pacific, 4 November 1993.

19 'North Korea: South's Air Force Chief's Remarks on Arms Buildup Denounced', cited in BBC *SWB*, Asia–Pacific 18 October 1993.

The tense situation which exists at the time of writing may be defused by a further round of carefully staged concessions by the North, or it may not. Those analysts who believe that the North's central objective is to use its 'nuclear card' to gain as many concessions as possible from the US may be correct. But to reap the rewards, the North, sooner or later, has to actually play its card.

From its long talks with US and South Korean officials, the North must by now recognise that if it *did* provide credible guarantees that it has abandoned the nuclear option, it could gain almost all of its demands very swiftly. 'Team Spirit' would never be held again, trade with, and investment from, the South would flourish, and it would recover billions of dollars of reparations from Japan. Aid and investment from international institutions like the World Bank would be forthcoming, and possibly even diplomatic recognition from Washington.

This suggests an obvious question. Given that the rewards are there for the picking, given the reality of the deepening crisis in the North's economy, given the daunting prospect of UN-imposed economic sanctions, plus the possibility of military strikes against its nuclear facilities, why *doesn't* the North play its 'nuclear card'?

It may be that the regime is simply irrational, as some American observers have suggested. It may also be that Pyongyang is playing a delicate and dangerous game of brinkmanship and that it is still probing to see if it can extract any further concessions from Washington before playing its card. These are all superficially plausible explanations, but they ignore one critically important possibility. Pyongyang may see nuclear weapons, not as a 'card' to be bargained away, but as a vital strategic asset that must be maintained at almost any cost.

Why the North needs a bomb

The rationale for a North Korean bomb is compelling given the DPRK's security mindset. The reasons are obvious enough:

- nuclear weapons would provide a countervailing deterrent against US nuclear threats. These threats still exist in the form of the 'nuclear umbrella' held over South Korea, 'nuclear umbrella' being another way of saying that under certain circumstances, the US would use nuclear weapons against North Korea;

- nuclear weapons will act as a deterrent against the threat to the North posed by the overwhelming conventional military superiority that the South will achieve at some time during this decade (some observers believe that the South is already clearly superior);

- nuclear weapons will compensate the North for the loss of its nuclear ally, Russia;

- and nuclear weapons will ensure that North Korea is taken seriously as a major player in the region, even though its economy may be in crisis.

The possibility that the North Koreans might have *genuine* perceived security fears is rarely taken seriously by US and South Korean officials. Yet it is hardly surprising that Pyongyang would want a countervailing deterrent against the nuclear threats which the US has directed against it for decades. Nor is it surprising that it should feel the need for a 'strategic equaliser' against the growing perceived threat from the ROK's conventional forces and the 36 000 US troops deployed just across its border. And if the DPRK and the USSR had staged huge annual exercises comparable to the US–ROK 'Team Spirit' (exercises which clearly were a rehearsal for war), can anyone doubt that South Korea would have found them highly threatening.[20] Even repressive totalitarian states can have genuine security fears.

But while the regime may perceive a security imperative to acquire nuclear weapons, most analysts believe that there is also a countervailing economic imperative to secure outside assistance—trade, aid and investment—for its crisis-ridden economy. To gain that economic assistance the regime has to give credible assurances that it has given up its nuclear ambitions. Optimists believe that the economic imperative to acquire external assistance is greater than its security interest in acquiring nuclear weapons—and it is this fact which gives the US and the ROK their

---

[20] The apparent inability of America and South Korean analysts to put themselves in North Korea's shoes is also evident in the response to the recent reported build-up in the North. US officials have speculated that build-up is being undertaken because the North is planning to attack the South, possibly to deflect attention from the crisis at home, or because Kim Jong-Il is irrational enough to want to start a war he cannot win. It does not appear to have occurred to these analysts that the North may be preparing, not to launch an unprovoked attack, but to *defend* itself from attack from the US and/or the South. During the past two years there have been repeated suggestions, from officials as well as commentators, that 'the military option' might be used against the North. In 1991, the then South Korean Defense Minister twice canvassed the idea of military strikes against Yongbyon. This was never a serious option for Seoul and Washington as long as the nuclear facilities there were under IAEA safeguards. But it is not clear that the somewhat paranoid North Koreans would have recognised this. Indeed the North may ultimately be correct in its worst case assumption. If the US cannot get an international consensus on sanctions, if dialogue fails and the North quits the NPT, the military strike option *may* be considered seriously in Washington. As noted above, once out of the NPT, it would be perfectly legal for the North to produce as many nuclear weapons as it could. When the second, 200 megawatt reactor comes on stream at Yongbyon, it will produce enough plutonium for quite a large number of bombs each year—sufficient to provide a DPRK deterrent *and* to export to countries like Iran, Iraq and Libya.

bargaining edge. Pyongyang, it is assumed, will trade its nuclear option in order to secure its economic future.

But if the economic imperative *were* more salient than the security imperative, one would have expected the North to have indicated a price for giving credible assurances it was not making nuclear weapons. It should also have indicated an in-principle willingness to submit to a highly intrusive verification regime, the *sine qua non* for progress on every issue. Yet Pyongyang has done neither. It has steadfastly and with total consistency rejected the idea of a 'challenge' or 'special' inspection regime. It has not shown the slightest willingness to allow the IAEA to inspect the two suspect nuclear facilities at Yongbyon, despite nearly a year of intensive pressure. During the abortive North–South Joint Nuclear Control Commission talks in 1992, the North consistently rejected demands by the South for a regime of 'special inspections'.

The 'challenge' inspection issue is of critical importance because the post-Gulf War experience with Iraq has reminded the international community that regular IAEA inspections of *declared* facilities cannot, by definition, reveal clandestine nuclear weapons activities. Only if an intrusive challenge inspection regime is in place is there any hope of uncovering clandestine facilities.[21]

But while this evidence may suggest that the North is determined to continue with its nuclear weapons program, it does not explain *how* Pyongyang thinks it will be able to cope unaided with what is undoubtedly a growing crisis in its economy. Indeed the North's problem is not simply the extant economic crisis, but the prospect that UN sanctions may be imposed as well. The North is in a no-win situation. The choice it confronts is not to decide what is the best option, but what is the least-worst.

The crisis in the DPRK economy

The crisis in the North's economy, which is described in some detail by a number of contributors to this volume, is not in doubt. In 1993, the DPRK economy shrank for the fourth year in succession. The nation's GNP is now less than a tenth the size of South Korea's. There is insufficient oil to meet national needs following the Russian supply cut-off in 1991, and some estimates suggest that industrial production is

---

[21] It is possible that the North would not even have permitted the regular IAEA inspections of 1992 had it realised the extent to which the Agency could detect the diversion of nuclear materials. In 1992, IAEA chemical analysis of samples of nuclear material from Yongbyon revealed that the North had in fact produced plutonium over a period of four years and had lied when it claimed that it had only produced 'a tiny amount' of plutonium in one year. Subsequent to being caught out, the North has persistently denounced the IAEA for lacking 'impartiality'.

down by as much as 40 per cent. Grain production has been declining, and the North has to import food grains. Food shortages have been reported and the population has been urged to make do with just two meals a day.

But the fact that the nation is in deep trouble economically does not mean that the *regime* cannot survive politically, at least for a considerable period. The population will certainly not welcome a decline in living standards, but dissatisfaction does not necessarily translate into active opposition, especially in a state which is so ready and able to repress dissent. The regime blames its economic difficulties on the 'imperialists and reactionaries' who seek to bring down socialism. This argument may have some credibility in the North. At least part of the North's economic problems *do* result from the oil cut-off imposed by the Russians, *and* to the refusal of the Japanese to discuss reparations until the nuclear issue is resolved, *and* to the restrictions on trade and investment by the South, etc.

A decline in living standards does not mean a threat to physical survival, or a threat to regime survival. Between 1980 and 1988 nineteen Latin and Central American economies suffered declines in their per capita GNP—in some cases by as much as a quarter. Yet no governments were overthrown for this reason.[22] In June 1993, the Bank of Korea estimated that the DPRK's per capita income was $US943, considerably greater than that of China or Vietnam.[23] Even if living standards declined by 50 per cent, North Koreans would still be materially better off than most Chinese and Vietnamese. Moreover the populace is being prepared for the worst, with the regime constantly stressing the growing external threat and the need to return to the psychology of the struggle against Japanese colonialism.

The North is also working hard to compensate for the single most serious economic problem it confronts—the lack of oil. The oil crisis was triggered in 1991 by the Russian insistence that, in future, Russian oil had to be paid for in hard currency, which the North did not have and could not borrow. In 1992, China also demanded that the DPRK pay for Chinese-supplied oil in hard currency. But the Chinese have apparently relented and are again willing 'to accept barter trade'[24] for the oil which is provided. Nevertheless the decline in oil consumption has been dramatic—from 2 520 000 tons in 1990, to 1 520 000 tons in 1992, according to South Korean sources.[25] While undoubtedly very serious,

22 Paul Kennedy, *Preparing for the Twenty-First Century*, Harper Collins, Toronto, 1993, p. 203.

23 Cited in Young-ho Park, 'Will North Korea Survive the Current Crisis', *Korean Journal of National Unification*, vol. 2, 1993, p. 113.

24 Hartcher, 'North's N-Plant'.

25 Seung-yul Oh, 'Economic Reform in North Korea: is China's Reform Model Relevant to North Korea', *Korean Journal of National Unification*, vol. 2, Summer 1993, p. 128.

the oil crisis needs to be seen in perspective. The regime only relies on oil for 10 per cent of its total energy supply (coal provides 70 per cent; hydro-electricity, 16 per cent, and 'other', 4 per cent). This is one of the lowest levels of dependency in the world.[26]

To reduce its dependency on imported oil, the North is relying increasingly on coal (of which it has massive supplies) as the major energy source. Oil-fired power stations are being replaced by coal-fired stations, and diesel-powered locomotives are being retired as the rail electrification program is expanded. New coal mines are being opened up to meet the growing demand and a number of new, large-scale hydro-electric power stations are being constructed.[27] Prospecting for oil in North Korean waters has been underway for some years and, according to Western sources in Pyongyang, there is a reasonable chance that the North may uncover considerable reserves. The North's nuclear power program, however, is on hold. Russia will not provide the technology it contracted to provide in the 1980s until the nuclear inspection issue is resolved.

If the North succeeds in its substitution program it may be able to reduce its dependence on imported oil to a manageable level. If, in addition, it discovers oil in its offshore waters, oil dependency and shortage will cease to be a problem.

In the absence of sanctions, the North continues to trade internationally, causing additional international concern with its sales of missiles to mid-East states like Iran. The foreign currency earned from trade is insufficient for all of the North's needs, but the regime also receives considerable economic assistance from Japan. Subventions from, and trade with, the pro-Pyongyang, *Chosensoren*, the 200 000 strong General Association of Korean Residents in Japan, generate circa $US650 000 million a year according to one source.[28] Total DPRK trade volume dropped by 16.7 per cent between 1990 and 1991, but by a mere 2.2 per cent in 1992.[29]

Given the above, the regime may well believe that it can survive economically and politically without giving up its nuclear option. Whether it could continue to do so under a tough sanctions regime is a different question.

---

[26] Bon-Hak Koo, 'North Korea Close to the Brink', *Korean Journal of Defense Analysis*, vol. 1, no. 1, Summer 1993, p. 103.

[27] Some reports suggest that DPRK coal production declined considerably between 1991 and 1992. See Park, 'Will North Korea Survive', p. 114.

[28] Ben Hills, 'North Korea: the Scariest Place in the World', *Age*, 18 October 1993. The US has been pressuring Tokyo to stop the flow of resources to the DPRK.

[29] Park, 'Will North Korea Survive', p. 114.

Will sanctions be applied, and would they work?

In the autumn of 1993, the North was repeatedly warned that if no progress was made on the nuclear issue the matter would be referred to the UN Security Council with a demand that economic sanctions be imposed.

However, there are a number of difficulties with the sanctions option. First, it is not at all clear how China would vote on a Security Council sanctions resolution, and neither Japan nor South Korea are very enthusiastic. The Chinese have long argued that sanctions against the North would be counterproductive, although they have not gone so far as to say that they would actually veto a sanctions resolution at the Security Council. In October, however, the Chinese ambassador to Japan said flatly 'We can't agree to sanctions' and reiterated China's long held view that the nuclear issue should be resolved by dialogue.[30] This is also the clear preference of Japan and South Korea.

However, the fact that the Chinese say they oppose sanctions does not mean they would *necessarily* veto a sanctions resolution at the UN. The costs to Beijing of so doing would be considerable. Already strained relations with the US would be worsened, increasing the chances that China would lose its 'most favoured nation' trading status in 1994, and Beijing's increasingly important economic relationship with South Korea would be jeopardised.

But Beijing also confronts potential costs if sanctions *are* imposed. Chinese officials have argued that the effects of sanctions could put China in a 'most disadvantageous position'.[31] Beijing is deeply concerned about the political and security consequences of a sudden collapse of the regime in the North which sanctions might precipitate. The resulting chaos—with a real possibility of extensive civil violence—could lead to massive refugee flows across the long common border and into China.

If it was clear that Beijing would veto a sanctions resolution, the US would be unlikely to take the issue to the Security Council. It would still be possible to push for a sanctions regime outside the UN framework, but this would lack both legitimacy and efficacy. Since China is the North's major trading partner, a sanctions regime which excluded it would not be very efficacious.

It is also clear that within the South Korean political system many officials and politicians have serious reservations about sanctions. From Seoul's perspective sanctions would need to be just effective enough to persuade the North to change its policy, but not so effective as to cause the regime to collapse precipitately. But lack of reliable knowledge about the balance of political forces in Pyongyang would make it impossible for

---

30 'Japan: China Opposes UN Sanction Against North Korea', Reuters, 27 October 1993.
31 ibid.

policy-makers to have any confidence about the likely impact of sanctions on the regime.

Seoul's waking nightmare is a sudden and precipitous collapse of the regime in the North. The German model of 'reunification by absorption' following the collapse of the communist regime would pose extraordinary costs on the South and be fraught with grave political, social and security problems.[32]

This points to a fundamental difference in interests between the US and South Korea. The primary US interest is in checking nuclear proliferation. North Korea's nuclear program poses a serious threat to the non-proliferation regime, both as a producer of nuclear weapons and as a potential exporter of nuclear weapons, technology and materials. The surest way to destroy the North's nuclear weapons program is to bring down the regime. The sudden collapse of the North, which Seoul fears, would suit US anti-proliferation interests very well.

While the South shares the US goal of stopping the North's nuclear program it also wants to avoid the collapse of the DPRK regime. The South would prefer a gradual process during which the North's economy is opened up and developed—the 'perestroika without glasnost' development model. Variants of this model are being practised in China and Vietnam. Ultimately, according to the optimists' scenario, the decentralisation of economic power leads to a decentralisation of political power and the emergence of a more affluent and pluralist North Korea which would facilitate a process of gradual reunification.

The imposition of sanctions is based on the somewhat crude notion that economic privation causes pain, and that if sufficient pain is applied the victim will concede to whatever demands are being made. The theory assumes that the party which is hurt is the party which makes decisions. This is often an unwarranted assumption. In Iraq it was not Saddam and the decision-making elite who suffered from the effect of sanctions, but the powerless majority. And the Iraqi experience is not a particularly encouraging one for the proponents of sanctions. Sanctions have been imposed on Iraq for more than two years with a near total cut-off of oil exports and the regime has suffered a humiliating military defeat. But Saddam remains in power and has still not succumbed to the UN's demands.

The effect of sanctions on North Korea would be very similar. Ordinary North Koreans who have no say in politics would bear the costs of sanctions; the elite decision-makers would not. It is possible, of course,

---

[32] South Korea would be in a much more difficult position than West Germany if the communist regime collapsed suddenly. East Germany's population was relatively small compared with that of the West; North Korea's population is approximately half that of South Korea. The income per capital gap between the two Germanies was also much less than that which exists between the two Koreas.

to argue that the pain which sanctions inflict on the populace will cause them to revolt against the regime which caused the sanctions to be applied in the first place. There are several problems with applying this argument in the North Korean case, however.

First, it is not at all clear that the regime *would* be blamed for the imposition of sanctions. The only information which the average North Korean has about the outside world comes from the state—there is no 'other side of the story'. Unlike the situation in East Germany where citizens could visit West Germany, send letters, make phone calls and watch West German television, North Koreans can have no contact at all with the outside world. *All* their information comes from the regime.

Lack of information, plus the pervasive 'womb to tomb' ideological indoctrination of the populace, suggests that the mass of North Koreans may well believe the regime's claim that it is the imperialists who are to blame for the sanctions. There would surely be some citizens who doubted this but, given the vast networks of informers and the massive repressive apparatus at the disposal of the regime, it is not clear they could do anything about it.

If this analysis is accepted then it follows that the Kim regime could well believe, and with good reason, that it can survive sanctions without either too much hardship or political cost to itself—at least for as long as it takes to complete a modest arsenal of nuclear weapons (say five years). With sufficient hidden 'bombs in the basement', the North could then dismantle its nuclear facilities, invite inspections and demand that sanctions be dropped. The existence of the clandestine weapons could subsequently be hinted at obliquely and in private—thus providing the deterrent the North needs—while being denied indignantly in public.

I have suggested that the threat which sanctions may pose to the regime in the North may not be as serious as some observers seem to believe. It is also the case that the *benefits* of giving up the nuclear option may not be as attractive as is assumed either—again from the point of view of regime survival.

In giving up its nuclear option the North would be 'rewarded' by external economic assistance—aid, trade, investment. But, as several chapters in this book suggest, the economic opening which such assistance will demand may pose a serious long-term threat to regime security. External funding, technology and expertise inevitably bring knowledge of the outside world with them. In particular, since South Korea would be a major investor and trading partner, North Korean citizens would learn a great deal about life in the South. In the process they would discover that they had been systematically lied to for decades. Moreover the sorts of reforms which would be necessary to reverse the decline of the North's economy would involve a devolution of economic power away from the state. Creating sources of economic power independent of the government would inevitably, if not immediately, lead to some devolution of political power with obvious risks to regime security.

What this suggests is that *from the perspective of regime security* the economic 'rewards' for giving up the nuclear option may not appear sufficiently attractive for the North to abandon the nuclear option. That the regime is keenly aware of the risks of economic *détente* is not in doubt.[33]

Conclusion

The logic of the foregoing analysis suggests few grounds for optimism with respect to security on the Korean peninsula. If my reasoning is correct we may expect the North to offer, as it so frequently has in the past, various non-critical concessions—for example, to re-admit IAEA inspectors for routine inspections. But we would also expect total intransigence in the face of demands for the sort of intrusive verification regime which will be necessary if the international community is to have any real confidence that the North's nuclear ambitions have been abandoned. This is not an encouraging prospect.

Are there any other initiatives which might forestall the North's nuclear ambitions? I suggested earlier that the North's nuclear program was primarily a product of the regime's perceived security fears. These related to American nuclear threats, the South's growing conventional power and the defection of the North's nuclear ally, Russia. Economic rewards, no matter how generous, cannot assuage the North's security concerns; these must be addressed directly. What might this mean in practice?

The following 'reassurance' measures suggest themselves:

- an unconditional US commitment that it would not use nuclear weapons against the North—this is the so-called 'negative security guarantee' and would require Seoul to give up its 'nuclear umbrella' protection;

- the permanent cancellation of the provocative annual US–ROK 'Team Spirit' exercise;

- and a unilateral and verifiable commitment by the South that it will not seek to acquire military superiority over the North.

Would such a package, some elements of which are already on offer, assuage the North's security concerns sufficiently for it to give up its

---

33 The Special Economic Zones and schemes like the Tumen river project in the remote north of the country are intended to provide economic benefit while insulating the North Koreans involved from the rest of the populace. But, as argued in a later chapter, the impact of such schemes will be too small to turn the economy around.

nuclear program? It would address some of the North's security anxieties, but not all of them:

- nothing can compensate the North for the loss of its nuclear-armed ally, Moscow;

- although the North has long demanded a 'negative security guarantee' from the US, it is not clear why it would prefer to rely on a mere promise that its arch enemy would not use nuclear weapons against it, rather than the reality of a countervailing nuclear deterrent, the effect of which is independent of US intentions;

- and the assurances do not include a long-standing DPRK demand for withdrawal of US forces from South Korea. This is deliberate. Without a continued US military presence in the South it would be impossible to gain ROK agreement for the removal of the US 'nuclear umbrella', or a unilateral ROK commitment not to seek conventional military security over the North.

Writing nearly a year ago I observed of the 'reassurance' approach that:

> Given the present impasse, the risks attendant in the current situation and the absence of attractive alternatives, the reassurance approach is surely worth trying. In the meantime, and because optimism about the current situation is hard to sustain, the international community needs to start thinking hard about what it will mean to live with the reality of a nuclear-armed Korea.[34]

In late 1993, the security future of the peninsula appears, if anything, more pessimistic. The international community confronts a very real dilemma. On the one hand, the costs of sanctions, or of simply continuing the existing policies of economic denial, may not be sufficient to coerce the regime to give up the bomb. On the other hand, the inducements currently on offer are unlikely to tempt the North to relinquish its nuclear 'security blanket' voluntarily.

The military option remains untested but it suffers four obvious defects. First, it is, by definition, impossible to hit unknown targets and it is difficult to believe that the somewhat paranoid North has not taken the obvious precaution of keeping a large part of its nuclear program hidden. Second, 'surgical strikes' against Yongbyon could unleash a very unsurgical war against the South. The South and the US would almost certainly prevail, but the costs could be very high—300 000 plus according to some estimates. Seoul is only 25 miles from the border where North Korean troops, artillery and armour are massed. Third, it would be a

---

34   Andrew Mack, 'The Nuclear Crisis on the Korean Peninsula', *Asian Survey*, vol. XXXIII, no. 4, April 1993, p. 359.

gross violation of international law and would not be supported by Seoul, Tokyo or Beijing. Fourth, it would release clouds of deadly radioactivity.

One bold, but politically difficult to implement, alternative would be to accede to a number of the North's key demands *unilaterally*. The US and the ROK could offer the North a package which cancelled 'Team Spirit'; invited the North to inspect any US 'nuclear base' it cared to designate;[35] gave an undertaking not to use nuclear weapons against the North; and provided a verifiable guarantee that the South would not seek offensive conventional military superiority. No immediate reciprocation would be demanded, but it would be made clear that the continuation of the concessions after a fixed period, say six months, would be dependent on an unambiguous and verifiable commitment by the North to progress in resolving the nuclear issue. Further inducements—for example, diplomatic normalisation—would be offered, but again would be contingent on acceptable progress.

Such a package would be difficult to sell in parts of the security community in both Washington and Seoul, where it would surely be denounced as rewarding North Korean intransigence. The case for trying such an approach is partly a negative one: that the other strategies which have been tried thus far have not succeeded, and that there are very obvious problems with the strategies which have been proposed but not yet tried.

The reassurance package offers both North and South the possibility of breaking away from the endless, acrimonious and legalistic arguments which poisoned the atmosphere of the North–South JNCC negotiations. Being without immediate strings the package is more likely to be perceived by the North as an unambiguously conciliatory move than a competitive gambit. In the past the North has responded positively to such overtures—for example, in agreeing to sign the IAEA safeguards agreement immediately after 'Team Spirit' was cancelled in 1992.

The package is non-confrontational. It offers inducements not threats—and threat-based strategies have a very poor track record in persuading the North. Most important of all it focuses on positive inducements which are appropriate, i.e., it addresses the North's security concerns, rather than its economic problems.

Would such an approach work? It is impossible to say. But since all of the concessions can be taken back if there is no progress, the security costs of implementing them would be negligible. And if there is only a small chance of realising the prize—a nuclear-free Korea—the minimal risks would be well worth taking.

---

[35] There are no nuclear weapons now deployed in South Korea.

2 US Interests in Korean Security in the Post-Cold War World

NORMAN D. LEVIN

Introduction

Writing about US interests in Korean security in the post-Cold War world at the present time is easier said than done. For one thing, the focus of the US government has been almost wholly on the effort by North Korea to develop nuclear weapons. Given Pyongyang's continuing refusal to agree to an adequate inspections regime, this understandably hinders any government effort to re-examine US interests and security policies more broadly. Moreover, the scope and pace of change over the past few years have been so dramatic and the future in some areas so uncertain, that it has been difficult to make projections about anything. This is particularly true with respect to future US security policies given the current fluidity in American attitudes toward the outside world and the growing domestic debate over desirable long-term goals and national objectives.

Before addressing the future, therefore, this chapter looks at the historical record and reviews the factors that have affected US calculations in the past. It then examines the current mood in the United States and assesses how the dramatic recent global changes affect these past calculations. The chapter concludes with an assessment of likely directions in US policy over the coming three to five year period.

The postwar US security role in Korea

Looking at the past, the record of the US security role in Korea has been—on the surface at least—somewhat chequered. There has been no consistent pattern, no clear and constant definition of US security interests, and no adequate public articulation of US policy. As a result, US policy has had over the years a quality of ambivalence and vacillation.[1] This may be seen in the lack of wartime planning for Korea's liberation from Japanese colonial rule and chaotic postwar occupation, the exclusion of Korea from the US defence perimeter and total US withdrawal in 1949, the reintervention and dominant US role in the 1950s and 1960s, the US force drawdowns in the late 1960s and early 1970s under the 'Nixon Doctrine', the abortive plan under President Carter to withdraw all American ground forces from South Korea in the latter 1970s, and the revitalisation of the US security presence and role under President Reagan in the 1980s.

Yet, except for the total US withdrawal in 1949, this surface vacillation is a bit deceiving. Throughout the past four decades there has been a sustained US commitment to the defence of South Korea and clear cut actions by all American administrations to support that commitment. These include: a substantial US military presence in the Republic of Korea (ROK); a demonstrated willingness and ability to rapidly reinforce that presence; a sustained flow of US weapons and technology to South Korea, which permitted a significant modernisation of ROK military forces; and a broad range of measures to bolster South Korea politically and economically, including sustained support for the Seoul government's efforts to reduce tensions with, and foster change in, North Korea.

The Bush administration, like its predecessors, firmly adhered to this consistent US commitment. Although the administration withdrew a small number of support troops as part of its response to the Nunn–Warner amendment, it has strongly reaffirmed the US defence commitment to South Korea. It has also laid out a gradual and open-ended process under the Pentagon's East Asian Strategic Initiative (EASI) program for further US force reductions that are linked explicitly to North Korean behaviour. This was evident in Secretary of Defense Cheney's announcement in November 1991 suspending further US force reductions pending resolution of the nuclear issue.[2] The Bush administration also took advantage of the growth in South Korean capabilities. US forces, which once played a leading role in the defence of South Korea, now play a more 'supporting' role. Important steps include: the appointment of a senior South Korean military officer to head the Ground Component Command of the Combined Forces Command (CFC) and another ROK general officer as the senior member of the United Nations Command Military Armistice Commission (UNCMAC); the disestablish-

---

1   For more detailed treatment of this theme, Norman D. Levin and Richard Sneider, 'Korea in Post-War US Security Policy', in *The US–South Korean Alliance*, eds Gerald Curtis and Sung-joo Han, Lexington Books, Lexington, 1983, pp. 31–64.

2   *New York Times*, 22 November 1991. See *Korea Newsreview*, 30 November 1991, pp. 4–6 for a more extensive account.

ment of the US–ROK Combined Field Army (CFA); and the increase in the South Korean component of defence burden-sharing.[3] Finally, the administration has taken numerous steps to support the process of North–South dialogue, while making clear that any future improvements in US–DPRK (Democratic People's Republic of Korea) relations hinge—among other things—on a satisfactory resolution of the nuclear issue.[4]

A number of factors account for this underlying continuity in US policy. The one most commonly emphasised was the US Cold War rivalry with the former Soviet Union. This emphasis is certainly right and understandable. Indeed, new information coming out of the former USSR about Soviet involvement in Korean War activities makes clear how right the Truman administration was to respond in global terms to North Korea's unprovoked attack on South Korea.[5] But a number of other factors have also been important in accounting for the underlying continuity.

One is the historic US interest in preventing the rise of a hostile power or group of powers able to dominate Asia. In the first half of this century, this meant playing balance of power politics to prevent domination of the region by Japan, Russia, or the imperial powers. In the second half of the century, it meant essentially containing Soviet or Chinese communism. This historic US interest has existed independent of the USSR and has always given US policy toward Korea an important regional dimension.

Second, and related to this, is Korea's inherent strategic importance as the fulcrum of major power interest in Northeast Asia and the relative lack of change over the years in the objective conditions on the Korean peninsula. These conditions include the physical division of the peninsula into two distrustful and antagonistic systems, the longstanding commitment of one of those systems—North Korea—to bring the entire peninsula under its control, the ongoing development by North Korea of a range of means and capabilities to achieve this goal, and the inability of the ROK to defend itself against large-scale North Korean attack without US assistance. Also included is historically difficult relations between the

---

3 General Robert RisCassi, 'Shifts and Disparities in the Two Koreas', *Army*, October 1991, pp. 118–24.

4 Other US concerns that have been emphasised include: North Korea's export of missiles; Pyongyang's support of terrorist activities; resolution of the Missing in Action (MIA) issue; and an improvement in the human rights situation in North Korea. Although none of these have been described as 'preconditions' for expanded US–DPRK interactions, an absence of movement on these issues hinders progress, as does continued North Korean anti-US propaganda and lack of genuine interest in confidence-building measures.

5 In addition to longstanding reports of Stalin's encouragement of Kim Il Sung's decision to launch a military attack on South Korea in an effort to bring the entire peninsula under his control, the recent reports suggest active Soviet advice on the handling of American POWs and other issues. See *New York Times*, 25 September 1992.

two Koreas and the major regional powers. In this context, maintaining stability on the Korean peninsula has been closely linked to maintaining stability throughout the region.

Third is the broader US interest in fostering the spread of market-oriented economies and democratic political systems. This interest is rooted in the American belief, generally confirmed by history, that an open, democratic world is a safer, more prosperous and secure world, for America and the world at large. Active and sustained US involvement in Korea furthers this interest—as the ROK's progress toward a more fully democratic polity and open economy testifies. The US objective of supporting Korean unification essentially on South Korean terms will also further the spread of democratisation and market-oriented economies. Together these factors have underpinned support in the United States for a sustained role in Korean security.

Effects of global trends and recent changes

If it is true that a number of factors have contributed to the underlying continuity in postwar US policies, it is also true that the dramatic changes of the past couple of years are increasingly calling these policies into question. Three broad trends and one more recent development seem most relevant to a consideration of future US roles in Korea.[6]

The first was the disintegration of the Soviet Union. The effect of this development in the United States is hard to exaggerate. Among other things, it has left the United States without either a global rival or clear external threat, created widespread uncertainty about long-term US goals and weakened public support for continued American assumption of a heavy international burden. The end of the Cold War also significantly worsened North Korea's strategic situation, as well as its political and, especially, economic difficulties. This has helped counter somewhat the continuing concern in US political and military circles about the military imbalance on the Korean peninsula.

The effect of the second broad trend, the relative shift of economic power to the Pacific and change in the economic balance of power between the US and key Asian countries, has been only slightly less dramatic. In 1960, the combined national products of Japan, China, South Korea, and Taiwan were roughly half those of West Germany, France, and the United Kingdom; by 1980 they had overtaken these three European powers. The combined Gross National Product (GNP) of these four Asian countries could surpass that of the United States as early as

---

6   For more elaborate treatment, see Norman D. Levin, 'Prospects for US–Japan Security Cooperation: The Mutual Security Treaty and Beyond', in *Japan's Emerging Global Role*, eds Daniel Unger and Paul Blackburn, Lynne Rienner Publishers, Boulder, Co., 1993.

the end of this decade.[7] The per capita GNP of Japan already exceeds that of the United States. Although this trend has not forced a total reappraisal of American world views, it has significantly strengthened the image of Asian countries as rivals, rather than as security partners, and exacerbated public anxieties about US pre-eminence and long-term economic competitiveness.

The third trend is the increasing primacy of domestic considerations. The effect of this trend has been to strengthen insular tendencies in the United States—including a political backlash against foreign aid and overseas spending—and heighten political pressures for cutbacks in US military spending. Current US plans already project that the military shares of GNP and of the Federal budget will fall over the next five years to 3.4 per cent and 16 per cent respectively—the lowest levels in over 50 years.[8] These reductions could be even more substantial which would place even greater pressures on US forward deployments and rapid rein-forcement capabilities. Meanwhile, a larger debate continues in the United States over the wisdom, not simply of reducing, but dramatically restructuring, US military forces to reflect a policy of selective US engagement overseas.

These broad trends are bolstered, to a certain extent, by a more recent development: the apparent shift in North Korean thinking away from reunification on North Korean terms, to regime preservation. This shift, reflecting North Korea's awareness of its weakening international posi-tion, has generated new policy departures in Pyongyang.[9] These depar-tures include North Korea's decision to join the United Nations, sign the safeguards accord with the IAEA (International Atomic Energy Agency), and explore possibilities for economic cooperation with South Korea, as well as Pyongyang's efforts to normalise relations with Japan and per-suade the US to expand its interactions with North Korea. Such policy changes have increased fluidity on the Korean peninsula and stimulated interest in arms control, confidence-building, and tension reduction measures. South Korea's successful policies of 'Nordpolitik', especially

---

[7]   Charles Wolf, et al., *Long-Term Economic and Military Trends, 1950-2010*, N-2757-USDP RAND, April 1989, p. 7.

[8]   Statement of the Secretary of Defense, Dick Cheney, before the Senate Armed Services Committee in Connection with the FY 1993 Budget for the Department of Defense, 31 January 1992, and Secretary Cheney's similar statement before the House Budget Committee on 5 February 1992.

[9]   See *Foreign Broadcast Information Service (FBIS)*, 'DPRK Moving to Opt for Independence Over Unity', *Trends*, 8 January 1992, pp. 18–21, for North Korea's explicit acknowledgement of its weakening position. For a broader treatment of the North Korean policy shift, see Rhee Sang-Woo, 'North Korea in 1991—Struggle to Save Chuch'e Amid Signs of Change', *Asian Survey*, January 1992, pp. 56–63. Rhee sees North Korea's central thrust as having shifted from pursuing unification to defending the North Korean system against the threat of absorption by South Korea.

its dramatic breakthrough in relations with China, are likely to intensify
this development, with North Korea becoming even more isolated and
receptive to new policy approaches which would help maintain the North
Korean regime and system.

Prospects

The implications of these trends and recent developments do not all point
in a single direction. Clearly, we have entered a new era, one of
decreased danger of global military conflict. But it is equally clearly an
era of significantly increased fluidity and uncertainty. Not surprisingly,
there is considerable ferment today in the United States about how to
respond to the new conditions. It is unlikely that this ferment and debate
will be resolved quickly. We are likely to live with continued debate and
uncertainty for some time to come. This will undoubtedly affect US
policies toward Korea, just as it affects American policies elsewhere. But
it seems safe to say that the post-Cold War world will not simply be the
Cold War world with minor modifications and that US policies will, over
time, adjust accordingly.

At the same time, however, it is important to recognise some important elements of continuity affecting US security policies in Asia. These
include: a continuation—and perhaps intensification—of historic animosities and regional rivalries; unresolved territorial disputes and ethnic
tensions; a continuing build-up of sophisticated weapons and military
capabilities; and the absence of any region-wide security or alliance
system. Other likely continuities include the growth in US economic
interactions in the region, as both Asian economic dynamism and US
global economic interests foster increased economic interdependence, and
the growing importance of US alliance relationships for addressing a
range of 'new order' issues including environmental deterioration, international terrorism, and the rise of regional troublemakers. The continuing dangers on the Korean peninsula—highlighted by North Korea's
continuing refusal to allow a full-scale IAEA inspections regime, but
reflected more broadly in the potential for North Korea's violent
disintegration—bolster these regional continuities and ameliorate, in the
short term at least, the effects of the dramatic global changes.

One further fact might also be added: the changes in basic US
interests are not as dramatic as the changes in the global environment.
This may seem somewhat counter-intuitive but it reflects a global reality:
while a country's policies can change rapidly in response to changing
conditions, its fundamental national interests tend to have a more
enduring quality. Assuming the kinds of continuities identified above, the
United States is likely to continue to pursue—albeit with the smaller and
restructured military forces which are appropriate to an altered threat
environment—its historic interests. These include preventing the creation

of conditions that could lead over time to domination of the region by a hostile power or group of powers; assuring US access to and through the region, including a place at the political table; and fostering the spread of market-oriented economies open to US exports and the growth of democratic values and institutions. But two new interests are likely to receive much greater emphasis than in the past: strengthening US competitive economic capabilities; and controlling nuclear, ballistic missile, and other advanced weapons proliferation.

US interests in Korean security will reflect these broad global and regional interests. Preventing nuclearisation of the Korean peninsula will remain a top US priority, and no significant improvement in US–North Korean relations will be possible until this issue is satisfactorily resolved. The United States will also continue to have an interest in maintaining stability on the peninsula and preventing perceptions of a vacuum of power from growing more broadly in the region. The numbers and kinds of military forces deployed for this purpose may, however, change over time in response to changing threat conditions and the growth in South Korea's own military capabilities. Decisions about the ultimate size and nature of the US military presence and role in Korea will almost surely continue to be linked to North Korean behaviour, whatever administration is in power in Washington. Finally, the US will continue to have an interest in reducing tension on the Korean peninsula and in supporting the peaceful reunification of the two Koreas. Indeed, now that it is clear that a reunited Korea need neither accommodate communism, nor be politically 'neutral', unification can contribute to precisely the kind of stability that the United States has been trying to foster in the region for decades.

Given such interests, the United States will maintain its defence commitment to South Korea. The US will also seek to sustain close US–ROK relations, with a continuing effort being made to establish greater balance and responsibility-sharing in bilateral security relations. Some forward-deployed forces will be maintained, as will the capability to reinforce those forces if necessary. These deployments will remain as long as North Korea remains a threat to South Korean and regional security. There is nothing magic about the number of troops the US has in Korea today. These numbers can, and undoubtedly will, change over time, reflecting the US conviction that deterrence and defence can be maintained with a different mix of US and South Korean forces and responsibilities. But a continued US forward presence plays important environment-shaping and hedging roles which the United States will almost surely continue. Indeed, it is not inconceivable that we could see some continued US military presence in Korea even beyond unification, should Koreans themselves seek such a presence, with the US role taking on an even more explicitly regional dimension. US security policies are likely to continue to emphasise a range of other traditional components as well, including the importance of continued military exercises to sustain joint US–ROK combat capabilities, force modernisation, and increased South Korean responsibility-sharing.

If and when the nuclear issue in North Korea and other US concerns are satisfactorily addressed, Washington will be willing to explore new approaches toward arms control and tension-reduction on the Korean peninsula. The central responsibility, however, will almost surely remain with the two Koreas themselves, with the United States continuing to play a positive but supporting role. US policies in the post-Cold War world will continue to support the two incipient processes of political dialogue and regional economic integration, with the ultimate objective being to link a unified Korea into the 'Western' club of nations.

In short, we can anticipate change and evolution in US policies as the United States adjusts over the course of the 1990s to a new global and regional environment, but there will be no dramatic change in fundamental US interests. The US defence commitment to South Korea will continue and decisions about US military force levels will continue to be linked to developments in North Korea. The peaceful unification of the Korean peninsula, involving essentially the extension of the South Korean system to the entire peninsula, will remain the long-term goal of US policy. And the United States will remain actively engaged in regional security.

Meanwhile, the national debate in the United States over long-term goals and appropriate national strategies will continue. In particular, the United States will face the challenge of balancing its interest in strengthening American economic competitiveness with its equally strong interest in avoiding a slide toward protectionism. In Korea, apart from the nuclear issue, the key challenge will be to manage successfully the almost inevitable transition to unification in ways that contribute to a stable and prosperous region. For both of these challenges US leadership will be essential.

3 Russian Interests in Korean Security in the Post-Cold War World

GENNADY CHUFRIN

Dramatic domestic events in the Soviet Union in 1991 caused fundamental political, economic and structural changes. The once powerful
unitary state was replaced by a galaxy of sovereign republics. The big-
gest, of course, is Russia which inherited roughly 70 per cent of the total
territory and population, and a comparable share of the raw materials,
industrial and agricultural potential of the former Soviet Union. Russia's
share of the Soviet legacy of strategic nuclear, as well as conventional,
weapons is even higher.

And although the new sovereign republics have declared their intention to conduct their own independent foreign policy, the international
community rightly expects Russia to be the principal guarantor of the
fulfilment of the responsibilities and obligations which flow from the
treaties and agreements concluded by the former Soviet Union on political, economic and security issues. These include the non-proliferation of
nuclear weapons, the reduction of conventional armed forces and the
repayment of foreign debts. International recognition of Russia's new
status was demonstrated by the United Nations and its Security Council
when Moscow's request to take up the seat of a permanent member in the
Security Council left vacant by the Soviet Union was acceded to without
any ado.

Retaining the role of a global power (though on a much reduced scale
and in a different manner to the role played by the Soviet Union), Russia
also inherited from its predecessor many interests and concerns in the
Asia–Pacific region. These interests, however, coincide only partially
with former Soviet interests in this area, while the manner and means of
their implementation are expected to be very different from the past.

29

First, there is an obvious geopolitical difference between Russia and the former Soviet Union that dictates a fundamental change in Russian political, economic and strategic priorities from those of the USSR. Thus Russia today has to work out its 'Eastern' policy, not only with regard to Japan, China, the situation on the Korean peninsula, and in Southeast Asia, but also with regard to the former Soviet Central Asian Republics which are now independent and with which Russia maintains highly extensive and diverse relations which it does not wish to jeopardise.

Russia also announced its intention to place a high priority on its relationships with its immediate neighbours, particularly Japan and China, while relegating relations with more distant Asia–Pacific countries to the next echelon.

Second, economic interests were given a clear preference over other issues—including security considerations—in Russian policy towards Asia–Pacific countries. A set of laws was enacted by the Russian parliament to facilitate trade with the region and to promote regional investment in Russia's economy. It was in this context that in January 1992, Vladivostok was declared an 'open city'. Various moves are now underway to create a 'free trade zone' in the neighbouring maritime province. Another important change in Russian foreign economic policy was the discontinuation of economic assistance on liberal terms to former Soviet allies in the Asia–Pacific region.

Third, Russia pledged to defend its security interests in the Asia–Pacific region, mostly by political means, while maintaining its armed forces on the level stipulated by principles of 'defensive sufficiency'. In its relations with other Asia–Pacific countries on security issues, Russia expressed its intention to focus on bilateral negotiations rather than stressing such ambitious proposals as an Asian collective security system which had generated so much suspicion in the past.

Such are the basic guidelines of Russian foreign policy in the Asia–Pacific as declared by the new Russian leadership after the formal dissolution of the Soviet Union. Whether they will become a working policy remains to be seen. Russia remains confronted by political and economic problems which raise questions about the ability of the new Russian leadership to conduct consistent domestic and foreign policies.

Taking the above into account, we may now analyse Russian foreign policy towards the two Koreas, as well as towards the United States, Japan, China and other Asia–Pacific countries with interests in developments in this part of Northeast Asia.

* * *

The Soviet Union was the principal trading partner of the Democratic People's Republic of Korea (DPRK) from the time it became an independent state. Although USSR–DPRK bilateral trade started to decline in

1988, in 1990 the Soviet Union's share in the total trade of the DPRK was still over 45 per cent. However, North Korea's share of Soviet foreign trade was never significant, remaining at about 1 per cent of the USSR's overall trade turnover. During most of the 1980s Soviet–North Korean trade grew at a very high rate. In the 1980–1988 period it grew almost threefold (from 572.1 million roubles to 1601.7 million roubles). Soviet sales to the DPRK increased by 270 per cent, from 287.9 to 1062.2 million roubles, in this period. As a result the trade imbalance, which had almost always been in favour of the USSR, reached staggering proportions by the end of the 1980s. In 1981–1985 the negative balance amounted to 149.2 million roubles; in the next five years it reached 1850.7 million roubles.

The primary cause of this imbalance was the unsatisfactory performance of North Korean exporters who failed to fulfil the terms of their contracts, violating dates of delivery and failing to supply commodities if they could sell them elsewhere for hard currency. Soviet exporters also confronted problems in the face of the growing political and economic crisis in their own country. However, the evolving pattern and structure of Soviet–North Korean trade tilted more and more in favour of the DPRK, which received such much-needed commodities as crude oil, industrial machinery, transport equipment and spares, without providing adequate and timely payment for them.

In principle, payments for merchandise trade between the USSR and DPRK should have been settled annually. Prices were fixed in roubles every five years and mutual payments were to be settled in so-called transferable roubles. However, even the reformed system, which was similar to that which existed in the now defunct Comecon, grew less and less effective and North Korean debt to the Soviet Union reached 2.5 billion roubles in 1990.

Clearly this system of payment had to change and from 1991 Moscow demanded that all bilateral transactions be concluded on the basis of world prices with payments in hard currency. The only exception was Soviet supplies of crude oil to the DPRK which were agreed to be repaid on a barter basis with a specially indicated list of commodities.

However, this agreement failed since neither side showed any particular interest in fulfilling its provisions. North Korea failed to pay for the delivery of 50 thousand tons of crude oil; in response the Soviet side refused to proceed with further deliveries of 250 thousand tons of crude oil despite a signed contract which committed it to do so. North Korean authorities continued to delay the repayment of debts to the Soviet side and only 20 per cent of the due amount was actually paid in 1991.

The deepening crisis of both Soviet and North Korean economies, as well as lack of mutual trust between Soviet and North Korean trade partners, resulted in an overall fall of bilateral trade which, in the first six months of 1991, amounted to only 452 million roubles. This was 35 per cent less than in the first six months of 1990. Trade exchanges were limited to a few commodities only (crude oil, coking coal, steel wire and cars from the Soviet side and magnesite bricks, Kyanite, refractory bricks and clothing from the North Korean side). Only a year or two previously, Soviet–North Korean bilateral trade had included at least 50 commodities.

According to current estimates it is highly unlikely that this situation will improve in the near future. Indeed it is safe to predict that trade between North Korea and Russia will be further reduced. In anticipation of these negative trends, in 1991 the DPRK signed separate trade agreements with Byelorussia, Kazakhstan, Kirgizia, Turkmenia and Tadzhikistan. This will, however, make little difference to the overall situation.

The dramatic reduction of trade in 1991 between North Korea and the former constituent republics of the Soviet Union was accompanied by a sharp contraction of other forms of economic relations between them.

Thus, although in 1990 Moscow had extended a 15 million dollar credit to the DPRK to finance imports of Soviet equipment for the construction of a large Pyongyang power station, it became clear in 1991 that this credit was insufficient to cover the increased costs of equipment. Since North Korea could not mobilise additional funds to finance the required imports from any alternative sources, the construction of the power station was frozen.

Financial difficulties experienced by North Korea also caused a serious disruption in the operation of the largest Soviet–North Korean joint venture—the 'Hychhon-Gorky' industrial enterprise built to produce milling machines.

Similarly the non-payment by Pyongyang for the services of Russian engineers who conducted surveys at the proposed construction site of a new nuclear power station caused a complete stoppage of that work. In this particular case the reason for the stoppage was probably not entirely financial, however.

In 1990, the Soviet government changed its position on the problem of denuclearisation of the Korean peninsula. It withdrew its unconditional support of the DPRK's stance on the issue, and publicly called on the North Korean government to accept its obligations under the Nuclear Non-Proliferation Treaty (NPT) by opening its nuclear facilities to international inspection. Although Moscow stopped short of endorsing the American demand to close down the North Korean nuclear fuel reprocessing plant at Yongbyon, the change of stand was significant.

The present Russian government has assumed the same position on the nuclear issue as the last Soviet government. It welcomed the mutual non-aggression agreement signed in Seoul on 13 December 1991 during the fifth round of prime ministerial talks between the DPRK and the Republic of Korea (ROK). Among other things this provided for mutual inspection of nuclear facilities and nuclear storage sites. Commenting on the agreement a spokesman of the Russian Ministry of Foreign Affairs said that:

> ...the results of the Seoul meeting following the reported removal of US nuclear weapons from the South raise hopes that Pyongyang will soon sign a nuclear safeguard agreement thus contributing to the progress in de-nuclearisation of the Korean peninsula.

The Russian government also welcomed the second agreement reached by the DPRK and ROK at Panmunjom on 31 December 1991, and endorsed by the prime ministers of the two countries a few days later. This called for a nuclear weapon-free zone on the Korean peninsula and banned the testing, manufacturing, possession, storage, deployment or use of nuclear weapons by both countries.

The Russian government made a special point of expressing its satisfaction when, in early January 1992, Pyongyang announced that the DPRK reached a formal agreement with the International Atomic Energy Agency (IAEA) on the issue of holding inspections of North Korean nuclear facilities.

In March 1992, during an official visit to Seoul of the Russian Foreign Minister, Andrei Kozyrev, it was officially announced that Russia had completely stopped financial and technical assistance to Pyongyang for the construction of nuclear power stations. Moscow responded favourably to the US–ROK negotiations held in Seoul at the beginning of January 1992 during an official visit of President Bush there. It welcomed the US–ROK offer to cancel the joint US–ROK 'Team Spirit' military exercises in 1992 if the DPRK fulfilled its obligations outlined by the NPT provisions. The negotiations were also interpreted in Moscow as marking a significant change in the US strategy regarding its direct military presence on the Korean peninsula—a sensitive area given the closeness of the Russian border to the exercise areas.

For all practical purposes the US–ROK negotiations also removed the possibility of a US military strike against the North Korean nuclear facilities, a possibility widely discussed in the international, as well as in the Russian, press prior to President Bush's visit to Seoul. Russia, as a successor to the Soviet Union, technically remained a military ally of the DPRK and any open military conflict between Washington and Pyongyang would have put Moscow in a rather awkward position, not dissimilar to that in which the Soviet Union had found itself during the Gulf crisis.

It was to be expected therefore that many voices were raised at that time, outside and inside the Russian government demanding that Russia unilaterally abrogate the Soviet–North Korean Treaty of Friendship of 1961. So doing would relieve Moscow from the obligations it contracted to the DPRK at the height of the Cold War.

Today, after some heated discussion, a more balanced point of view seems to be gaining strength among the Russian political leadership.

Proponents of this view argue that Russia should remain a party to the Treaty, using its relationship with Pyongyang as leverage to prevent the North Korean leadership from taking any adventurist steps. In a more fundamental sense the 1961 Treaty is regarded as a legal framework for building a new relationship between Russia and the DPRK under radically changed conditions—conditions which might require modification of some of the Treaty's provisions.

Proponents of maintaining the Treaty argued that its significance lay not only in the fact that it constituted a basis for a multi-dimensional bilateral relationship, but also because it served as part of a sophisticated system of international agreements regulating security issues in Northeast Asia. Thus, a hasty abrogation of the Soviet–North Korean Treaty would have not only a negative bilateral impact, but also negative international repercussions.

One should not forget in this context that the Treaty serves as a basis not only for political, economic and cultural relations between the Soviet Union and the DPRK, but also for their relations in such sensitive areas as military cooperation, arms transfers, modernisation of weapons systems, etc. Obviously many of the reasons for past cooperation between Moscow and Pyongyang no longer apply. But there remain areas of common interest—including the denuclearisation of the peninsula and a reduction of the ongoing North–South arms race in conventional weapons.

It is well known that during recent years the two huge Korean armies which confront each other across the 38th parallel, have received large quantities of sophisticated military equipment, including the latest models of combat aircraft from their principal suppliers. The ROK acquired F-16 aircraft from the USA; the DPRK purchased MIG-29 fighters, SU-25 bombers and SA-5 surface-to-air land-based missiles from the Soviet Union. It is worth noting also that in the 1980s the defence expenditures of the ROK grew faster than those of the DPRK and that this has caused the military balance in principal conventional weapons to tilt towards the South. Thus during the last decade, while the total number of tanks in North Korea increased by about 35 per cent, in the South they grew by 82 per cent. The number of jet fighters increased in the North in the same period by 7 per cent and in the South by 26 per cent, and the total number of warships of different classes (excluding coastal patrol and support ships) increased by 47 per cent and by 80 per cent respectively.

Although the DPRK still retains numerical advantage over the South in some categories of weapon systems, as well as in the overall size of ground forces, this advantage is now more of a quantitative than a qualitative nature.

That change in the military balance between the two Korean states, as well as the increased capacity of the ROK to provide for its own defence, has been attested to by independent observers. A rough parity in conventional arms was achieved between the two Korean states by the beginning of the 1990s, thus opening unprecedented opportunities for an intra-Korean dialogue on many issues, including that of mutual security.

It is therefore expedient to review the military commitments previously made to the ROK and the DPRK, by the United States and the Soviet Union (now Russia) respectively. Thus, while the US government announced plans to withdraw some of its troops from the territory of South Korea by 1993, and to transform the role of American troops still remaining there from one of leadership to one of support, the Soviet Union (now Russia) decided to disengage itself from active military support of Pyongyang.

The scaling down of the Soviet/Russian–North Korean security relationship was motivated by the overall change in the political atmosphere in Northeast Asia, as well as by the emergence of military parity between the DPRK and the ROK. However this change in Soviet/Russian policy towards the DPRK needed counterbalancing steps to reassure Pyongyang. It would have been highly detrimental to the security situation in the region if Pyongyang felt itself abandoned in the face of a real or perceived military threat coming from the South.

It was therefore advisable for Russia not only to retain the existing Soviet–North Korean Treaty as an important political instrument to allay Pyongyang's fears, but also to conclude a Treaty on good neighbourliness and cooperation with the ROK as originally proposed during former Soviet President Mikhail Gorbachev's visit to South Korea in April 1991. Gorbachev and President Roh Tae-woo had decided to hold the next round of Soviet–South Korean negotiations leading to the conclusion of this Treaty in Moscow, but the dramatic political changes in the Soviet Union caused these negotiations to be postponed.

The new Russian government has indicated its interest in resuming these negotiations, and the conclusion of a Russian–South Korean Treaty on good neighbourliness and cooperation will actively involve Russia in the security of the whole of the Korean peninsula.

Russia's security relations with the two Korean states should be based on upholding normal political relations with each of them. Such an approach will also serve Russia's foreign policy goals in this part of the Asia–Pacific, i.e., the avoidance of military conflict and the preservation of stability on the Korean peninsula. It could be argued that since the end of the Korean War, Soviet policy also aimed at preventing the confrontation between the DPRK and the ROK from developing into another open military conflict. However, the principal difference between the past Soviet policy on Korea and the present Russian one may be not so much in their proclaimed goals, but in the means of their achievement. While Soviet policy-makers considered military assistance to the DPRK as security-enhancing, nowadays such an approach is seen as outdated, and non-military methods—either political or economic or a combination of both—are regarded by the Russian leadership as far more appropriate.

This does not mean that the possibility of a military conflict between the two Korean states is totally excluded from Russian strategic analysis. Obviously such a worst-case scenario, however slight and remote, could turn out to be correct. One possibility is that the transition of power in Pongyang from Kim Il Sung to Kim Jong Il could be violent. This could, in turn, create serious instability in the North and might provoke intervention from the South, possibly in collaboration with the United States. Russia would then face an unpleasant dilemma—either to withhold assistance to its ally, thus violating its international obligations, or become involved in a military conflict which would probably be very unpopular domestically.

To avoid such a possibility it has been in the best interests of Russia to help both Korean states to move towards ratification, and subsequent implementation, of agreements signed by them in Seoul in December 1991. In the short-term Russia's stance may worsen its chances of ever being repaid any of the debts it is owed by North Korea. Any meaningful rapprochement between the DPRK and the ROK will mean that all resources available in the North will be diverted to North–South economic cooperation. But in the long-term such cooperation may suit Russian interests quite well.

First, if such a scenario becomes a reality, the possibility of military conflict between the two Korean states will be effectively nullified. Second, North–South economic cooperation will facilitate the implementation of what, for Russia, are potentially attractive projects, such as the construction of a $3 billion port on the Tumen River near the Russian border. An agreement between the DPRK, the ROK, China and Mongolia to complete the construction of this port and to create a 'free trade zone' in this area was signed in Pyongyang in November 1991. Russia may also receive a 'peace dividend' from North–South rapprochement if and when plans for the construction of a trans-Korean gas pipeline to bring natural gas from Russia to Japan are implemented. Third, improvement of economic relations between the DPRK and the ROK may pave the way for their political rapprochement and, eventually, for their peaceful unification. A unified Korea, if history is any guide, will probably become a natural ally of Russia, thus improving its present geopolitical environment in Northeast Asia and its bargaining position *vis-à-vis* Japan.

4 Historic Transformation of the Korean Peninsula and China's Concerns

YE RU'AN

From confrontation to rapprochement

As a result of the Korean War and the ensuing Cold War between East and West, Seoul and Pyongyang have confronted each other for more than four decades, and the Korean nation has suffered from protracted separation and estrangement. With inter-Korean political and security issues complicated by big-power involvement, the conflict between the two Koreas has been one of the longest-lasting and most intractable regional 'hot spots' in the post-World War II period. Persistent tensions on the peninsula have, over the years, posed a threat to peace and stability in the Asia–Pacific region—and to Northeast Asia in particular.

Seeking national reunification, the Korean people on both sides of the 38th Parallel had made a number of efforts at reconciliation including the 4 July 1972 North–South Joint Statement. But then and subsequently, conditions were not ripe, either domestically or internationally. The Korean conflict remained log-jammed until the outset of the 1990s when the last glacier of the Cold War in Asia began to melt. Let me briefly record the accelerating pace of events in Korea and in international relations revolving around the Korean question:

(i) 3–7 September 1990, the North–South Prime Ministerial meetings were inaugurated, but interrupted for the US–ROK annual military exercise in Spring 1991; at the end of that month the Soviet Union, preceded by several East European countries, established diplomatic relations with South Korea.

(ii) 20 October 1990, an Agreement was reached between China and South Korea to set up trade offices in Seoul and Beijing.

(iii) 17 September 1991, the DPRK and the ROK were simultaneously admitted into the UN as full members.

(iv) 27 September 1991, President Bush announced the withdrawal and elimination of all US land-based tactical nuclear weapons deployed worldwide, including, implicitly, those in South Korea. Before and after that, both sides of Korea produced proposals for a nuclear-free zone on the Korean peninsula.

(v) 13 December 1991, the North and South Prime Ministers signed the Agreement on Reconciliation, Non-aggression and Exchanges and Cooperation.

(vi) 18 December 1991, South Korea announced that it had no US nuclear weapons on its territories, and the United States issued a statement indicating its willingness to permit inspections of its military facilities in South Korea.

(vii) 31 December 1991, North and South Korea signed the Joint Declaration of the Denuclearisation of the Korean peninsula.

(viii) 7 January 1992, the spokesman of the South Korean Defense Ministry declared that the US and the ROK were to suspend the 1992 Team Spirit military exercise. On the same day, the DPRK Foreign Ministry said in a statement that the government had decided to sign a nuclear safeguards agreement with the IAEA in the near future and that it would accept the latter's inspections of its nuclear facilities. (The North actually signed on 30 January.)

(ix) 22 January 1992, then US Under Secretary of State, Arnold Kanter, and Assistant Secretary of State for East Asian Affairs, Richard Solomon, met with Kim Rong Chung, North Korean Party Secretary for External Affairs in New York, the highest-level contact of its kind between the United States and the DPRK since World War II.

(x) 19 February 1992, the three inter-Korean agreements on reconciliation, denuclearisation and establishment of a sub-committee for high-level meetings came into force upon exchange of the texts of the agreements signed by the two Prime Ministers.

(xi) There have been a number of consultations between Japan and the DPRK on establishing diplomatic relations.

These unprecedented developments in the inter-Korean relationship, and in relations between the big four powers on the one hand, and the two parts of Korea on the other, have ushered in a new historical phase which gives real hope for ending the political and military confrontation on the Korean peninsula. It is now possible to imagine the peaceful reunification of Korea, and growing regional cooperation, which will enhance the prospects for peace and stability in Northeast Asia.

Referring to the two agreements on reconciliation and denuclearisation, President Kim Il Sung argued that they are a milestone, an epoch-making event that will bring about peace and reunification to Korea. Then President Roh Tae-woo noted that the agreements opened up a new era for the Korean nation. There are several reasons for these historical political breakthroughs on the peninsula.

First, the two governments in North and South Korea have adjusted and readjusted their policies in the light of changing domestic and international circumstances. In a series of prime ministerial meetings, both sides have shown flexibility, acting in a spirit of mutual understanding and mutual accommodation. Through continued contact and dialogue, the two sides have begun to gradually reduce mutual suspicions and build mutual trust.

Second, the two sides recognise that neither can prevail over the other through the use of force and that the only way to reunify the Korean nation is to settle outstanding disputes through dialogue and consultation. Moreover, both Pyongyang and Seoul feel keenly that the high military expenditures that have been devoted to military confrontation over the decades are an increasing heavy burden on their economies. Continued military confrontation and an arms race will disadvantage both sides in a world in which the economic factor is becoming increasingly important in international competition.

Third, a key factor that has propelled the positive developments on the peninsula is the timely and sensible decision-making by the top leaders of both sides based on a realistic assessment of the situation on the peninsula and the international environment pertaining to the Korean question. President Kim was advanced in age, while President Roh was in the last year of his term of office when they started the process of rapprochement. Both are eager to make their mark on history by contributing to a fundamental improvement in North–South relations and advancing the nation towards reunification.

Last, but not least, the favourable international environment serves as a catalyst to the North–South rapprochement. The 'Big-Four'—the US, Japan, China and Russia—and the world community at large, want to see a genuine easing of tension on the peninsula and have sought improved relations with both North and South. The disintegration of the Soviet Union eliminated the source of the confrontation and rivalry between the two superpowers in Asia and the Pacific and their respective Korean allies. Superpower rivalry constituted the root cause of instabilities and conflicts in the region. The end of the Cold War enabled the Bush initiative to withdraw US tactical nuclear weapons deployed in South Korea; most will be destroyed. The admission of the two parts of Korea into the United Nations has provided extraordinary opportunities for both Koreas to expand contact with the world community, while enabling the UN and the 'Big-Four' in particular, to promote closer ties with both North and South.

Security issues on the Korean peninsula

With the political settlement of the Cambodian question in place, the Korean peninsula is the only major flashpoint left in the Asia–Pacific region. Security on the peninsula is not only a matter of survival and development for the 70 million Korean people, it is also vital to peace and stability in Northeast Asia. In the author's view, there are several major issues concerning security on the Korean peninsula, and the nuclear issue is only one of them.

North–South reconciliation

This is the fundamental issue for Korean security. Without genuine North–South reconciliation and mutual trust there is no security to speak of, even if the nuclear issue no longer exists. I concur with former US Secretary of State James Baker when he said '[t]he key to reducing tensions on the peninsula—and ultimately to the reunification of Korea—is an active North–South dialogue...The Koreans themselves must traverse the road to peace and reunification'.[1]

In this connection, the Agreement on Reconciliation, Non-aggression and Exchange and Cooperation is of paramount importance, because the principal articles stipulate in clear-cut terms the provisions that offer the surest guarantee for security on the peninsula. These require the two sides to 'eliminate the political and military confrontation', to promote the 'mutual recognition of and respect for the other side's system', to respect the principles of 'non-interference in each other's internal affairs', and the 'non-use of force against each other' and to 'settle all differences and disputes through dialogue and consultation'. Since the agreement came into force as of 19 February 1992, security will be ensured as long as both parties abide by it in good faith.

The nuclear issue

From October 1989, James Baker and the US officials of the Departments of State and Defense began speaking publicly—and in increasingly explicit terms—of the dangers of the North Korean nuclear program.[2] Some individuals even threatened to destroy the North Korean nuclear facilities by military means, or proposed that international pressure be brought to bear upon North Korea. However, no one can deny that the US tactical nuclear weapons in South Korea, no matter how many, posed a threat to the North. This threat was the main reason for the North's refusal to sign a safeguards agreement with the International Atomic

---

[1]   Address at Japan Institute for International Studies, 'The United States and Japan: Two Global Partners in a Pacific Community', 11 November 1991.

[2]   Don Oberdorfer, 'North Korea Seen Closer to A Bomb', *Washington Post*, 23 February 1992.

Energy Agency (IAEA) which would have led to inspections of its facilities. In retrospect, it is clear that the withdrawal of all US nuclear weapons from South Korea (made public by the South Korean government in late December 1991) was necessary for progress to be made on the nuclear issue. In response, the DPRK not only signed a safeguards agreement with the IAEA but also the Joint Declaration of the Denuclearisation of the Korean peninsula with the South.

It seems to me that there still exists mutual suspicion that should be removed. Speaking to the House Foreign Affairs Committee of US Congress, CIA Director, Robert Gates, accused North Korea of deliberately stalling inspections in order to hide parts of its nuclear weapons program despite the North's repeated statement that it has neither the intention nor the capability to develop nuclear weapons. Suspicion has been mutual. Kim Il Sung reportedly told then South Korean Prime Minister, Chung Won Shik, that he could not know whether there were any nuclear weapons in South Korea, or whether they had in fact been removed. However, since denuclearisation of the Korean peninsula is in the interest of all parties and since the bilateral and multilateral mechanisms to permit verifiable denuclearisation are now available, the nuclear issue can in principle now be resolved.

Inter-Korean disarmament and the US military presence in South Korea

Over one million men in uniform confront each other daily across the 150-mile demilitarised zone (DMZ). Some 39 000 US forces are also based in the South. This confrontation is the historical legacy from the Korean War and the decades-long cold war on the peninsula which followed. Before the major breakthrough between North and South Korea, the US Department of Defense had made a plan for a phased reduction of the US military presence in South Korea. Troop levels were to be cut to 36 000 by the end of 1992, and further reduced to 30 000 by 1995. But in November 1992, then US Defense Secretary, Dick Cheney, announced that the second-phase reduction would be postponed until the threat of North Korea's nuclear weapons program and its uncertainties were removed.

As North and South move toward national reconciliation and eliminating military and political confrontation, disarmament and arms control measures should be on the negotiating agenda. According to Article XII of the Agreement on Reconciliation, such measures as elimination of weapons of mass destruction, notification of large-scale troop movements and military exercises and other confidence-building measures (CBMs) are to be taken up by a joint North–South military commission to be set up within three months upon the enforcement of the agreement.[3]

---

3   This commission has yet to be created. (Ed.)

It is the author's view that deep force reductions by both North and South will contribute to peace, security and economic development on the peninsula and that the United States should speed up, rather than delay, its force withdrawal from Korea in the light of new circumstances.

Normalisation of relations between the 'Big-Four' and North and South Korea

Russia and China now both have diplomatic relations with both Pyongyang and Seoul. However, Moscow's greatly improved relations with Seoul have been at the expense of its relations with Pyongyang. As written in the Agreement on Reconciliation, both Pyongyang and Seoul have a special relationship—not a state-to-state relationship. The fact that many countries maintain diplomatic relations with both Koreas, i.e., that they treat both states as if they were states, is a phenomenon in international relations. But most of these countries do not play a major role in the security of the Korean peninsula.

Under the new circumstances on the peninsula and in the relations between the Koreas and the countries on their periphery, the normalisation of relations between the 'Big-Four' and the two parts of Korea will, I believe, contribute to peace and security on the peninsula. The talks between Japan and the DPRK have thus far not led to any breakthrough; China and South Korea as well as Russia and South Korea, have established relations; and the United States and the DPRK have continued with relatively low-level and informal official contact. These three sets of relationships are somewhat interrelated. The key to further progress lies in the normalisation of the US–DPRK relations where, in addition to the nuclear issue, the transformation of the Armistice Agreement into a peace treaty and the withdrawal of the US forces and military bases in South Korea are the key issues. The 'Big-Four' should do everything possible to help facilitate the peaceful reunification of Korea and cooperate in ensuring security on the peninsula.

China and Korea

The dramatic recent events indicate that the situation on the Korean peninsula is now at a historic conjuncture poised to move from confrontation to reconciliation, from war to peace and from division to reunification.

China is now, and will be for many years, or decades, concentrating its efforts on national reconstruction. It needs an external environment of lasting peace, particularly on its periphery. Korea, North and South, is China's close neighbour. Security and stability on the Korean peninsula is naturally important for China's security and affects its security environment. Consequently, the Chinese government has, on several occasions, expressed its appreciation of the positive developments on the Korean peninsula and particularly the significant progress in North–South relations.

China's interest in security on the peninsula lies, for the short and near term, in a further relaxation of tension and improvement of relations between the 'Big-Four' and the two parts of Korea and in the longer term in the peaceful reunification of Korea.

Politically, China supports the principles of self-determination, peaceful reunification and national solidarity as endorsed by both North and South. Before reunification is realised, China will maintain and develop good-neighbourly relations with both the DPRK and ROK on the basis of the Five Principles of Peaceful Coexistence. As for reunification, China will respect the choices made by the Korean people in whatever form and by whatever means and strictly abide by the principle of non-interference in Korea's internal affairs.

Militarily, Chinese leaders have stated in clear-cut terms that China does not want to see the development of nuclear weapons by either side in Korea. This approach is in keeping with the consistent position of the Chinese government on nuclear non-proliferation. In view of the positive developments noted above, there are good prospects for achieving a nuclear weapons-free zone in Korea. China fully supports this and will undoubtedly undertake not to use or threaten to use nuclear weapons against such a zone.

Conventional disarmament is absolutely necessary for enhancing security on the peninsula. As President Kim Il Sung said to Chung Won Shik in early 1992, to ensure peace in Korea it is imperative for both sides to take effective measures to cease the arms race between them and make arms reductions. The pace of arms reduction on the peninsula will, by and large, depend on the degree to which the three agreements between North and South are implemented in good faith.

The economic factor in contemporary international relations is of growing importance and has become a major dimension of security. Close economic ties and increasing interdependence between states on both the bilateral and the multilateral level would enhance security in a broader sense.

China has maintained close economic relations with the DPRK over the decades. In recent years trade between China and South Korea has grown rapidly ($US5.8 billion in 1991 and an estimated $US8.0 billion in 1992). North–South reconciliation and economic cooperation will not only strengthen the economic capacity of both countries, but promote economic cooperation in the Asia–Pacific—particularly in Northeast Asia. As far as China is concerned such a development will help ensure a more favourable and secure environment to its northeast.

Enhancing security on the Korean peninsula also calls for consistent diplomatic efforts by North and South Korea and other concerned countries, and especially the 'Big-Four'. It is in the best interests of China to support the Korean people in their pursuit of reconciliation and reunification by implementing the agreements signed, and improving the relationship between the 'Big-Four' and the two Koreas. Given the great diversity within the region and the fact that there is no regional security mechanism in Northeast Asia, neither a CSCE-type security cooperation process, nor the 'two-plus-four' formula for German reunification are really applicable in the case of Korea. Nor can the United Nations help much with the settlement of the Korean question, because the UN was directly involved in the Korean war at the outset. Perhaps it is better to deal with security issues concerning Korea through bilateral channels augmented by exploratory multilateral dialogues and discussions.

Conclusion

The signing of the Agreement on Reconciliation, Non-aggression and Exchanges and Cooperation marks a historical turning-point in inter-Korean relations and creates new opportunities for solving the Korean question. The positive developments on the peninsula described above will contribute to peace, stability, security and prosperity in Northeast Asia. Given the intricacy and complexity of the issues involved—a legacy of decades of tension and confrontation—there will be twists and turns in the process of reconciliation and reunification. Dealing with these will take considerable time and call for painstaking and patient effort. The reconciliation of the two Koreas and their subsequent peaceful reunification is in the best interests of China, because it needs a peaceful and stable environment for its own national reconstruction. All countries and parties concerned with the Korean question should seek to facilitate further rapprochement in the Korean situation and refrain from doing anything that will hinder the peace and reunification process on the peninsula.

5 Japan's Interests in Security on the Korean Peninsula in a Post-Cold War World

SATOSHI MORIMOTO

Overview of Northeast Asia

Area stability

Since the end of the Vietnam War, the Asia–Pacific region has been relatively peaceful and stable in comparison with other regions. The Asia–Pacific nations are now facing a lower level of potential threat than at any time in the last three centuries. The major factors that contribute to this stability are mainly deterrence by the US presence and steady economic development.

In the security realm, the American role is critical. American involvement and leadership are indispensable to any undertakings which seek to reduce tension, enhance political stability and promote arms control in the Asia–Pacific region. Only the United States offers a nuclear guarantee to its allies in the region.

As a pillar of US policy in the Asia–Pacific region, the US–Japan security arrangement greatly contributes to the peace and stability throughout the region. The US–Japan security arrangements add credibility, particularly in the eyes of other Asian regional states, to Japan's policy of military restraint. Japan's policy of maintaining an exclusively defensive force posture in terms of its weapon system acquisitions and the scope of operations of its military forces is reassuring to countries in this region. The key requisite for the maintenance of this policy is the continuation of the alliance with the United States.

Economic development is also an important determinant of the domestic political stability of the nations. Economic interdependence among Asian and Pacific nations is becoming deeper and broader in scope.

45

As long as the US presence is maintained and economic growth continues, the Asia–Pacific region, as a whole, can be expected to remain stable.

Strategic environment

It is important to realise that, in geopolitical and military terms, the Asia–Pacific region has a very different strategic environment from that of Europe. Asia–Pacific states differ from Europe in political and cultural orientation, force structure, threat perception and strategic concern. Asia–Pacific alliance structures, unlike those of the North Atlantic Treaty Organisation (NATO) states, are basically bilateral, while the focus of security concern is essentially maritime. In Europe the central security focus was the East–West confrontation across the Central Front. Consequently, the European Conference on Security and Cooperation in Europe (CSCE) process, and European-derived confidence- and security-building measures (CSBMs) would not fit the conditions of the Asia–Pacific region well. It is thus neither reasonable nor realistic to seek to apply the European theory to Asia. The one exception to this is the Korean peninsula, where concentrated land forces confront each other across a front not dissimilar to the Central Front in Europe and where arms control concepts, including CSBMs, may be applied.

Regional instability

The end of the Cold War and collapse of the Soviet empire has had a positive impact on Northeast Asia. It has lead to the reduction and/or withdrawal of former Soviet forces—in particular from the Sino/CIS borders, to the re-establishment of diplomatic relations between South Korea and Russia, the democratisation of Mongolia, etc.

However, potential instability in China, North Korea's nuclear program, conflict within the Russian Federation and territorial disputes in the region, are all potential causes of regional instability.

Thus Northeast Asia could succumb to instability by the end of the 1990s although the rest of the Asia-Pacific region may be expected to remain stable.

New challenges and implications

Northeast Asia

Northeast Asia, where the US, the Koreas, the Russian Federation, China and Japan confront each other, is the most important sub-region in the Asia–Pacific region. However, security in the sub-region is currently undergoing profound changes. Threats to regional security could originate from the following factors:

a. the security consequences of the Soviet break-up;
b. a reduction in the US presence;
c. security problems posed by other nations.

The Russian Federation

The Russian Federation is likely to continue as a political entity for the foreseeable future. Russia has inherited the major elements of the Soviet armed forces, including nuclear weapons, and remains a military giant. The withdrawal of Soviet forces from Mongolia and Vietnam's Cam Ranh Bay has been completed, as has the major reduction in forces deployed in the Russian Far East. However, the modernisation of the weapon systems in Russia's Far East forces continued after the end of the Cold War and Russia still has an enormous stockpile of military equipment in the Asia–Pacific region.

Russia's domestic turmoil and instability does not imply any direct threat to Northeast Asia, not least because the Russian population in the Far East is small and widely dispersed. In the long-term, Russia will play a significant role in Asia because of its great raw material resources in the region. In order to develop these resources, investments will be needed from other industrialised Asia–Pacific nationals. If its economy revives, Russia may revive its military capability, including sea lanes of communication (SLOCs), in order to more effectively defend its national interests.

US presence

The US is reducing its troop levels in the Asia–Pacific according to a Pentagon plan announced in 1990. However, there is growing recognition among countries within the region that the presence of US forces is stabilising.

Korean peninsula

As for the Korean peninsula, the political and military confrontation across the demilitarised zone (DMZ) persists. The global current of the East–West reconciliation has been permeating the region since mid-1990 and is symbolised by the establishment of diplomatic relations between South Korea and the former Soviet Union and China, the first South–North Prime Ministerial meetings since the division of the Korean peninsula and the admission of both Koreas to the United Nations.

In this context, the possibility of North Korea developing nuclear weapons has become an issue of growing international concern. While a safeguard agreement between the International Atomic Energy Agency (IAEA) and North Korea was eventually signed in January 1992, Pyongyang has persisted in delaying its implementation by attaching various conditions to it. It is important for Japan, which has initiated negotiations with North Korea to normalise relations, to confirm that the North Koreans will adhere fully to their obligations under the Nuclear Non-Proliferation Treaty, which Pyongyang joined in 1985. If North Korea is indeed developing nuclear weapons, it would not only pose a threat to the global non-proliferation regime but also to the security of Japan and that of the Asia–Pacific region as a whole.

The relationship between Japan and South Korea

Japan and South Korea have what is basically a good relationship. President Roh's visit to Tokyo in May 1990, Prime Minister Kaifu's visit to Seoul in January 1991, and Prime Minister Miyazawa's visit to Seoul in January 1992, all contributed towards ending what was a long and unfortunate phase of the relationship between Japan and the Republic of Korea (ROK).

Kaifu's visit

During Prime Minister Kaifu's 1991 visit an agreement was reached on three principles which would guide the Japan–Korea relationship in the future. These principles were future-oriented and stressed cooperation. The two governments agreed to:

a. promote exchanges, cooperation and mutual understanding with the aim of strengthening the partnership between Japan and Korea;

b. seek cooperatively to promote the achievement of peace, reconciliation, prosperity and liberation in the Asia–Pacific region;

c. pursue cooperative means of settling various global problems.

Diplomatic relations

Since the late 1990s, some structural changes in the peninsula have been evident with the establishment of diplomatic relationships between South Korea and Russia and China; Prime Ministerial meetings between South Korea and North Korea; and the fact that both Korean nations have joined the United Nations, all conduce towards stability on the peninsula. Japan confidently expects that South Korea will play an active role in the Asia–Pacific region as well as in global political and economic areas.

As for the unification of Korea, Japan expects that South Korea will take positive initiatives towards unification and the unified nation will share common values such as freedom, democracy and a market economy system.

Stability of the peninsula

The stability of the peninsula has far-reaching implications for the security of Japan and here Japan believes that it will benefit from a continued US military presence in the region.

It has also become apparent that both security dialogues and cooperation between the US, South Korea and Japan are important for the stability of this region. Talks between American, Japanese and South Korean policy planning officials began in 1991 and have continued. Japan and the ROK have also initiated both a dialogue between defence experts and an exchange of information and intelligence. These contacts are expected to be further developed which will further contribute to defence cooperation in the future.

The relationship between Japan and North Korea

The normalisation of diplomatic relations with North Korea is one of the two postwar problems for Japan that remains unsettled; North Korea is the only one of Japan's neighbours with which Tokyo has no diplomatic relations. A series of talks between the two governments have been held since 1990. There are two major issues at stake with respect to normalising diplomatic relations between Japan and North Korea.

First, North Korea is seeking war reparations from Japan. It also argues that Japan continued to damage North Korea in the post-World War II period, and is demanding compensation for the 45-year postwar period as well. Japan, on the other hand, maintains that the problems which resulted from the 36 years in which the Japanese ruled Korea should be settled as an issue of property rights and claims. Japan also argues that the state of postwar Japan–North Korea relations were attributable to the Cold War. They should be understood in terms of the global East–West confrontation—a confrontation complicated by the situation on the Korean peninsula and by the policies of North Korea. For none of this does Japan admit any responsibility.

Second, Japan, together with the US and South Korea, is pressing North Korea for a prompt implementation of the Safeguard Agreement it signed with the IAEA. It is most unlikely that full diplomatic relations will be established until the nuclear issue in North Korea is resolved.

Conclusion

Stability in Northeast Asia would be enhanced by:

a. the continuation of the US military presence in South Korea and Japan;

b. the complete abandonment by North Korea of its nuclear weapons program and the opening of the country to the international community as a result of South–North dialogue and reconciliation;

c. the maintenance of China's political stability and its continued commitment to economic reform;

d. the continued economic development of the region as a whole;

e. the management of regional conflict and the combat of proliferation of weapons of mass destruction;

f. the resolution of the Northern Territories dispute between the Russian Federation and Japan, and the negotiation of a peace and friendship treaty between the two states.

Regarding the security of the Asia–Pacific region as a whole, some nations have argued for the institution of a process similar to that of the CSCE. Japan has pointed out the differences in the geopolitical conditions and strategic environment between the Asia–Pacific region and Europe and has argued that it is more important to ensure regional stability via existing mechanisms of cooperation, focusing on economic cooperation.

On the other hand, the current concern of many Asian countries is to what extent the United States will reduce its presence in the region, how much influence the former Soviet Union has in this region, and in this context, what kind of role Japan intends to play in the region, and whether it will expand this role to include military activities.

Japan believes that further enhancement of mutual trust between Japan and other Asia–Pacific countries is an indispensable task. To achieve this task it is important that Japan adheres firmly to its policy of not becoming a major military power. Japan should be sensitive to the fears and concerns that Asia–Pacific countries may have regarding Japan and take initiatives to participate in political dialogue with these countries on these issues, so that it can deepen its mutual trust with these countries. Such sentiments prompted Foreign Minister Nakayama to propose at the ASEAN Post-Ministerial Conference in July 1991 that the conference be used as a forum for political dialogue in order to attain mutual reassurance among the friendly countries. This proposal has now been adopted.

The Korean peninsula continues to be an area of serious tension. However, as a consequence of the US presence in South Korea and self-constraints maintained by the countries concerned, these tensions have not resulted in armed conflict.

The long-term stability of the peninsula will also depend on the cooperation, not just of the two Koreas, but of the other key actors in Northeast Asia. This process must embrace expanded economic cooperation and interdependence as well as multilateral security dialogues between the key players.

6 The Republic of Korea and the Nuclear Issue

PETER HAYES

This chapter examines the dynamics of nuclear proliferation on the Korean peninsula south of the Demilitarised Zone.[1] First, I review the status of the Republic of Korea's (ROK) nuclear power fuel cycle and its capabilities in nuclear weapon or dual-capable technologies. Second, I consider the ROK's propensity to construct a nuclear weapon by the year 2000. This entails analysing an array of possible motives for and against proliferation. I conclude the chapter by examining the possible contribution of a regional nuclear-free zone to the non-proliferation of nuclear weapons in Korea.

ROK's first bomb program

In 1970, President Park Chung Hee set up two *ad hoc* working groups to study how the ROK's arms industry could be upgraded. The Weapons Exploitation Committee investigated the nuclear weapons option and recommended to Park that the ROK proceed down the nuclear path. He reportedly decided to act on this recommendation in late 1971 or early 1972.[2]

---

[1] Proliferation in the North is scrutinised in a companion essay, 'Moving Target. Korea's Nuclear Potential', Department of International Relations, Australian National University, Canberra, March 1992. The reader is also referred to my earlier study of the ROK's nuclear technological and industrial base. See 'South Korea', in *International Nuclear Trade and Nonproliferation: The Challenge of the Emerging Suppliers*, ed. W. Potter, Lexington Books, Lexington, 1990, pp. 293–329.

[2] S. Meyer, *The Dynamics of Nuclear Proliferation*, University of Chicago Press, Chicago, 1978, p. 172.

President Park acted primarily in response to US President Richard Nixon's announcement that the US would withdraw the 7th Infantry Division from the ROK in order to implement his Guam Doctrine and to bolster US forces fighting in Vietnam. Park's decision was taken in spite of the continued presence of other US ground forces, such as the 2nd Infantry Division, and an estimated 600–700 US nuclear weapons stationed in Korea.

Sensitised by the Indian nuclear explosion in 1974, Washington became suspicious about the ROK's nuclear program. ROK negotiations to purchase a reprocessing plant from France had been under way since 1972, and was well known to the United States.[3] When the French–ROK deal became public in June 1975, Seoul maintained that the technology was needed for energy security, and to match the Japanese Tokai Mura reprocessing plant. In fact, the ROK had planned to acquire a reprocessing capability since 1968, but fuel security was a secondary consideration.

After questions were raised within the London Nuclear Suppliers' Group, France renegotiated the agreement with the ROK so that equipment it supplied could not be replicated for two decades. On 22 September 1975, a safeguards agreement between the IAEA, France and the ROK entered into force.[4]

By now, however, the United States was convinced that the ROK's reprocessing program was motivated by a desire to use plutonium for military purposes rather than nuclear fuel cycle needs. In March 1975, Washington intervened strongly in Seoul and demanded that the South give up its program. Washington threatened to withhold Eximbank funding of the ROK's second nuclear power reactor which had been ordered from a US supplier. US officials also insisted that the French, Canadians, and Belgians discontinue their involvement in the reprocessing deal. Henry Kissinger finally stopped the ROK program by informing President Park that the US would cancel its security commitment to the ROK if the South persisted with its nuclear weapons program.

During the Carter administration, the United States and the ROK again clashed on the nuclear weapons issue. As part of the campaign to reverse President Jimmy Carter's policy of withdrawing troops and nuclear weapons from the South, a number of South Korean academic and official statements suggested that the ROK would seek to acquire

---

3   Reprocessing plants can extract plutonium of spent nuclear reactor fuel. The plutonium extracted can be used as fuel in reactors—or as fissile material for nuclear weapons.

4   M. Reiss, *Without the Bomb. The Politics of Nuclear Non-Proliferation*, Columbia University Press, New York, 1988, p. 92.

nuclear weapons should the United States complete its announced withdrawal.[5]

In 1978, an influential communication was made privately by a ROK general to a senior US State department official with non-proliferation responsibility who was visiting Seoul. The general indicated that the ROK would not hesitate to renege on its Non-Proliferation Treaty (NPT) commitment if US nuclear weapons were removed from South Korea.

Later that year the Carter administration reversed its withdrawal policy, but the ROK has continued to seek dual-capable technologies, in particular ballistic missiles and nuclear-fuel reprocessing capabilities. In 1979, for example, the ROK tried to acquire the US Atlas Centaur IRBM which could fire a W-38 nuclear warhead over a range of 7000km with an accuracy of one mile.[6]

The ROK continued its ballistic missile research and development program until about 1980 when it was discontinued for lack of finance. In 1984, South Korea tried again to obtain reprocessing technology from Canada for mixed-oxide fuel (MOX) production. This attempt was based on cooperative research on plutonium recycling with Canada's AECL (Atomic Energy Canada Limited) begun in 1982, and extended by agreement in December 1983 to a second phase. Washington persuaded Ottowa to cancel its cooperation with Seoul, a move which the South Koreans resented as an unwarranted American interference into what they viewed as a legitimate nuclear power technology.[7]

ROK's nuclear technology base

Since 1975, the ROK has acquired an array of nuclear weapon-related technological potentials via its nuclear power program. The 'technological creep' embodied in the power program has endowed the ROK with a near-nuclear option. In extreme circumstances, that option could be exercised by crash development of a crude nuclear device in about nine months. I will outline this technological capability in terms of the

---

5   For details, P. Hayes, *Pacific Powderkeg. American Nuclear Dilemmas in Korea*, Free Press, New York, 1990, p. 72.

6   It remains unclear whether the missile software, designs and hardware that the ROK had sought were in fact transferred. See Rep. A. Beilenson, Letter to US Secretary of State, 20 August 1979; released under US Freedom of Information Act request to author.

7   US Department of Energy, briefing paper on US/ROK Joint Standing Committee on Nuclear and Other Energy Technologies, 26 February 1986, p. 1; this document is still classified; press reports covered the altercation although Canadian denials as reported are misleading. See P. Taylor, 'Ottowa Denies US Killed A Deal', *Globe and Mail*, Toronto, 16 October 1984, p. 5.

ROK's nuclear reactor program; its nuclear fuel cycle localisation program; its nuclear research and development program; and, in spite of recent disavowals, the continuing ROK desire to acquire reprocessing technology.

The nuclear reactor program and technological independence

The ROK currently operates nine nuclear power plants with a total generating capacity of 7.3 GWe and an average plant capacity of 0.8 GWe (see Table 6.1 and Figure 6.1). These plants are predominantly pressurised water reactors (PWRs), either directly or indirectly supplied by the US. One of the plants is a Canadian-supplied pressurised heavy water reactor (PHWR).[8] The ROK has another 2.5 GWe of plant capacity under construction, or on order. This capacity will be made up of two PWRs and one additional PHWR. By the end of the decade the ROK should have nearly 10 GWe of assured nuclear generation capacity.

The ROK nuclear power program was premised on maximising self-sufficiency in the material and services required to design, construct, and operate the nuclear fuel cycle. Initially, the ROK could not achieve the ambitious goals it set for itself, producing locally only 28 per cent of the Nuclear Steam Supply System (NSSS) of units reactor 9 and 10 rather than the targeted 83 per cent in 1985.[9] By 1988, self-sufficiency had reached 66 per cent in nuclear fuel production, 57 per cent in materials production, and 71 per cent in design engineering. In the reactor field it had reached 70 per cent for systems analysis, 75 per cent for reactor construction design, and 100 per cent for operation.[10] The Korean Electric Power Company (KEPCO), anticipates that Korean Standard Nuclear (KSN) power plants 1 and 2 will be 79 per cent domestically designed and contain 72 per cent Korean equipment and material when they enter service in 1995–96.[11]

The ROK's nuclear power plants have operated at an average 70 per cent load factor during the 1980s. They represented about 36 per cent of total generation capacity and supplied about 50 per cent of the ROK's electricity in 1990.[12] The Program suffers, however, from the wide diversity of models and suppliers which makes it hard for KEPCO to

---

8   The French plant is a licensed version of what was originally a US PWR design (PHWR).

9   'Koreans Strive for Self-Reliance in Nuclear Plant Construction', *Nucleonics Week*, 19 December 1985, pp. 9–10.

10   Yu Yong-won, 'Korea Must Obtain Nuclear Armament Capability', *Wolgan Choson*, Seoul, October 1991.

11   'South Korea Pursuing Nuclear Self Reliance', *Nucleonics Week*, 30 June 1988.

12   A. MacLachlan, 'Korea Planning to Build Series of Standard PWRs', *Nucleonics Week*, 19 October 1989, pp. 1, 10.

Table 6.1 Nuclear power plants in South Korea

Plant	Net MWe	Site	Type	NSSS	T-Gen	A-Gen	Const	OpDate
KNU1	556	Kori	PWR	W	GEC	Gilbert	W	4/78
KNU2	605	Kori	PWR	W	GEC	Gilbert	W	7/83
KNU3	629	Wol-sung	PHWR	AECL	NEI-Parsons	Canatom-AECL	AECL	4/83
KNU5	895	Kori	PWR	W	GEC	Bechtel	Hyundai	9/85
KNU6	895	Kori	PWR	W	GEC	Bechtel	Hyundai	4/86
KNU7	900	Yeong-kwang	PWR	W	W	Bechtel	Hyundai	8/86
KNU8	900	Yeong-kwang	PWR	W	W	Bechtel	Hyundai	6/87
KNU9	943	Uljin	PWR	Fra	Alsthom	Fra/Alsthom	Dong ah/KHIC	9/88
KNU10	943	Uljin	PWR	Fra	Alsthom	Fra/Alsthom	Dong ah/KHIC	9/89
Under construction or tender								
KSN1	900	Yeong-kwang	PWR	KHIC/C-E	KHIC/GE	Kopec S&L	-	3/95
KSN2	900	Yeong-kwang	PWR	KHIC/C-E	HKIC/	Kopec S&L	-	3/96
--	679	Wol-sung	PHWR	AECL	KHIC	?	?	?

Notes: Until a nomenclature change, KEPCO used to refer to every one of its plants with the prefix KNU + numeral, with the oldest unit known as KNUU1. But no KNU-4 existed because only one unit at the Wolsong site was ever built. Plants are now referred to by site name plus a unit number (e.g., Kori 1 through 4, etc.). The two most recent PWR orders are also referred to by designator KSN which stands for Korea Standard Nuclear power plant, the ROK's future reference design for standardised plants.

Source: J. Payne, 'South Korea: Planning for Self-Reliance', *Nuclear News*, December 1987, p. 59; *Nuclear News*, November 1989, p. 75; *Nucleonics Week*, 1 February 1990, p. 18; *Nuclear Engineering International*, June 1990, p. 25; 'Canadian Firm to Design Nuclear Power Stations', *Yonhap Radio*, 23 December 1991, in FBIS-EAS-91-247, 24 December 1991, p. 18.

Figure 6.1 Nuclear power sites in South Korea

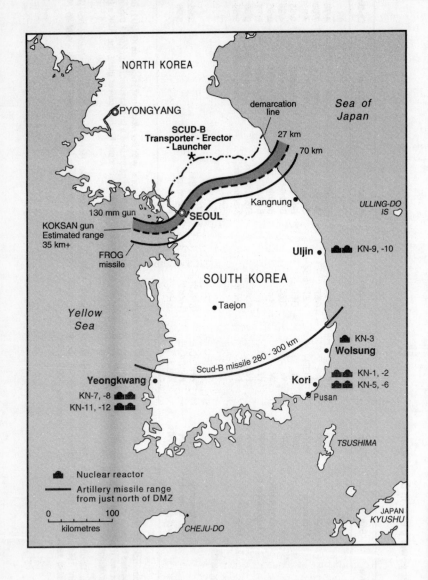

Source: J. Payne, 'South Korea: Planning for Self-Reliance', *Nuclear News*, December 1987, p. 59; *Nuclear News*, November 1989, p. 75; *Nucleonics Week*, 1 February 1990, p. 18; *Nuclear Engineering International*, June 1990, p. 25; 'Canadian Firm to Design Nuclear Power Stations', *Yonhap Radio*, 23 December 1991, in FBIS-EAS-91-247, 24 December 1991, p. 18.

improve availability and to reduce cost. The ROK therefore intends to standardise its designs and to localise the capability to produce almost all components and services for future PWRs built in (or exported from) Korea.[13] To this end, contracts for KSN-1 and 2 require the US company Combustion Engineering to transfer critical design engineering technologies to Korean counterparts. The Korean Atomic Energy Research Institute (KAERI) will play an important role in this technology transfer as Combustion Engineering will endow it with the computer codes, documents, drawings and procedures for designing reactors on its computers.[14] The basic strategy (outlined in Figure 6.2) has had three phases, moving from 'turnkey' operations in the 1970s, to local component manufacture in the 1980s, to technological independence in the mid-1990s.

Korea plans to order at least six more standardised PWRs like KSN-1 before the year 2000. In 1991, a KEPCO official estimated that the ROK would need another eighteen reactors by 2006 to meet an electricity demand growth of 15 per cent per year.[15] One report on the long-run outlook of Korea's nuclear program estimated that the ROK will build another 50 nuclear reactors by 2025 (to provide 40 per cent of projected electricity demand in that year).[16]

Increasing technological self-reliance has been a central element in the ROK's *dirigiste* industrialisation and import substitution strategies.[17] Nowhere has this been more evident than in the ROK's electric power sector.[18] If the ROK were to ever decide to again seek to produce a nuclear weapon, this policy of maximising technological independence in all aspects of the nuclear fuel cycle would be essential to success. Otherwise, it would be susceptible to denial of technology, fuel, and spare parts from supplier states. If imposed today, sanctions would cripple the ROK's electricity supply within a couple of years.

---

[13] 'Korea: Standardization is the Key', *Nuclear Engineering International*, March 1990, pp. 51–2.

[14] 'Korea: Moving Nearer to Self-Reliance', *Nuclear Engineering International*, September 1987, p. 45.

[15] 'Korea Plans Continued Dependence on Nuclear Power, Says KEPCO Chief', *Nucleonics Week*, 20 June 1991, p. 18.

[16] *Nuclear Engineering International*, January 1990, p. 7.

[17] J. Enos and W. Park, *The Adoption and Diffusion of Imported Technology. The Case of Korea*, Croom Helm, New York, 1988.

[18] Lee Jinjoo and H. Sharan, *Technological Impact of the Public Procurement Policy: the Experience of the Power Plant Sector in the Republic of Korea*, UNCTAD/TT/60, Geneva, 12 July 1985.

Figure 6.2 Localisation of ROK nuclear technology—chronology of Korea's nuclear power plants

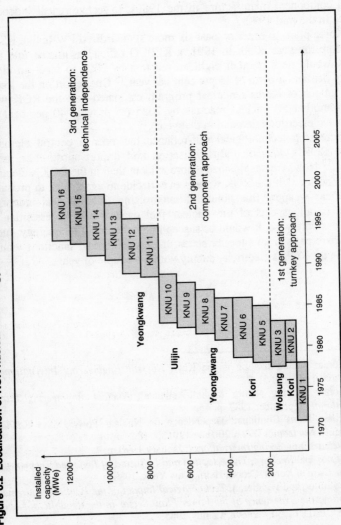

Source: 'Korea: moving nearer to self-reliance', *Nuclear Engineering International*, September 1987, p. 44.

Plutonium production rate

Table 6.2a shows the plutonium production rate of different reactor types. In 1991, the ROK's 7.3 GWe of nuclear generating plant will produce about 1.3 tonnes of fissile Pu-239 per year (at a 70 per cent capacity factor for typical ROK PWRs and PHWRs). By the year 2000, the ROK's 10 GWe of assured nuclear generation plant will produce approximately 1.98 tonnes of fissile Pu-239 per year (see Figure 6.3).

Table 6.2a Plutonium production in various types of reactors

Type of reactor	Irradiation level of heavy metal (mwd/kg)	Average enrichment (% U-235)	Initial fuel inventory (kg/MW(e))		Pu-239 production (g/MW(e)yr)
			Core (natural U)	Blanket (depleted U)	
BWR	17	2	434	-	250
PWR	22.6	2.3	365	-	255
AGR	-	1.6	620	-	100
HWR(CANDU)	6	0.711	143	-	490
HTGR(USA)	54.5	~93	326	-	-
SGHWR	15.5	1.8	520	-	150
FBR(UK)	~70	-	9.5(depleted U)	16.9(depleted U)	2850(core Pu)[b]
			2.8(Pu)[a]		409(blanket Pu)[b]

Notes: [a] Plutonium composition is 57 per cent Pu-239, 24 per cent Pu-240, 14 per cent Pu-241 and 5 per cent Pu-242.
[b] Total of 2980 kg/yr containing 58 per cent Pu-239, 28 per cent Pu-240, 9 per cent Pu-241 and 5 per cent Pu-242.

Source: B. Jasani, 'Introduction', in *Nuclear energy and Nuclear Weapon Proliferation*, eds F. Barnaby et al., Taylor and Francis, London, 1979, pp. 2–3.

The ROK has already accumulated about 10 tonnes of Pu-239 in spent reactor fuel. By the year 2000, this stock should increase to about 24 tonnes, assuming that no recycling of Pu-239 takes place by then (see Figure 6.4).

What are the nuclear weapons implications of these huge stocks of spent reactor fuel? A critical mass of Pu-239 requires from 15 to 23 kg/critical mass (at 100 and 70 per cent Pu purity, without a beryllium neutron reflector); and 4.4 to 9.6 kg/critical mass (at 100 and 50 per cent Pu purity, but with a reflector) (Table 6.2b shows the critical masses of various fissile materials). In 1990, the ROK was amassing

Figure 6.3 ROK plutonium 239 production per year, 1978–2000

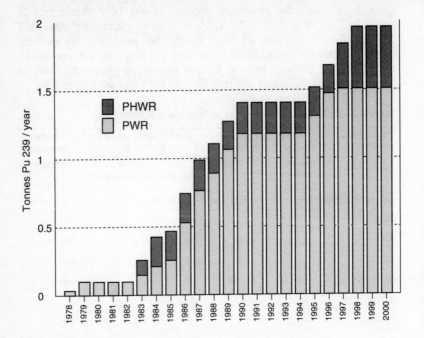

Figure 6.4 ROK plutonium 239 stocks in spent fuel, 1978–2000

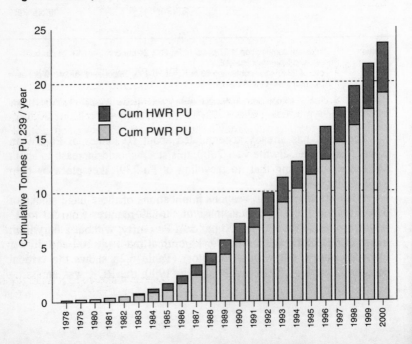

THE REPUBLIC OF KOREA AND THE NUCLEAR ISSUE 61

plutonium at a rate equivalent to 60 to 92 critical masses per year (without a reflector), and 145 to 315 critical masses (with a reflector). By the year 2000, it would generate plutonium sufficient to make 86 to 132 critical masses per year without a reflector, and 206–450 with one.[19]

Table 6.2b Critical masses of various materials

Enrichment (% of U-235 or Pu-239)	Uranium-235		Plutonium		Uranium-233	
	Without reflector	With Be reflector	Without reflector	With Be reflector	Without reflector	With Be reflector
0	-	-	-	-	-	-
10	-	~1300	-	-	-	-
20	-	~250	-	-	-	-
30	-	-	-	-	-	-
40	-	75	-	-	-	-
50	145	50	-	9.6	-	-
60	105	37	-	7.8	-	-
70	82	-	23	6.7	-	-
80	66	21	-	5.6	-	-
90	54	-	-	5.0	-	-
100	50	15	15	4.4	17	4 to 5

Source: B. Jasani, 'Introduction', in *Nuclear energy and Nuclear Weapon Proliferation*, eds F. Barnaby et al., Taylor and Francis, London, 1979, pp. 2–3.

In short, the ROK will accumulate a lot of plutonium. Assuming that the North has only 0.3 MWe of combined research reactor output by 2000 (that is, no power reactors on line, as is almost certain), then the North will be producing about 70kg of Pu per year—about one 30th of the ROK's rate, but still enough for between three to sixteen critical masses per year, depending on Pu purity and whether or not a neutron reflector is used.

Uranium enrichment

The ROK has no independent uranium enrichment capability nor technology. Until 1990, it relied completely on US and French supply of enrichment services (55 and 45 per cent respectively), although the

---

[19] This estimate does not include plutonium generated in research reactors. A second HWR is assumed to come on line in mid-1998.

ROK began to seek to diversify its sources of supply in 1989, with China and the Soviet Union in mind as suppliers.[20]

One unconfirmed report claims that a ROK team of industrial and atomic power personnel visited Soviet nuclear research facilities and factories in the summer of 1990, including the Tubuna nuclear research facility 100km west of Moscow (where many North Korean nuclear researchers are said to have been trained). The itinerary included Soviet uranium enrichment and reprocessing plants where the visitors were able to 'view each and every aspect of the process'.[21] The report asserts that the team, and in particular, KAERI staff, explored the possibility of joint ROK–Soviet research on laser-induced separation of uranium isotopes.[22]

In November 1990, the first 40 tonnes of Soviet enriched uranium arrived in the ROK on an Aeroflot plane. This was part of a ten-year contract for 1000 tonnes of fuel between KEPCO and Techsmab Export.[23]

KAERI has invested substantial resources in long range development of laser spectroscopic technology that would be necessary for an enrichment program. The ROK Ministry of Trade and Industry intends to develop domestic ultra-high speed centrifugal separation technology—a technology that would be useful for an enrichment program.

Uranium fuel fabrication

In December 1985, the Korean Nuclear Fuel Company Ltd contracted with Kwaftwerk Union to supply the know-how needed to construct and operate a 200 tonnes/year PWR fuel fabrication plant at Taejon. Construction of the plant began in 1986, and it began to operate in September 1989.[24] The first Korean-fabricated fuel rods were loaded into the Kori 2 PWR in February 1990.[25] An unconfirmed report[26] asserts that KAERI developed nuclear fuel for HWRs in 1986, and has provided all the nuclear fuel for the Wolsong HWR since 1987.[27]

---

20 *Yonhap Radio*, Seoul, 7 February 1990; in JPRS-TND-90-005, 2 March 1990, p. 5.
21 Yu Yong-won, 'Korea Must Obtain'.
22 ibid.
23 '40 Tons of Uranium from USSR Arrives', *Yonhap Radio*, Seoul, 29 November 1990; in JPRS-TND-91-001, 4 January 1991, p. 6.
24 'Nuclear Fuel Processing Plant Dedicated at Taedok', *Korea Times*, 29 September 1989, p. 8.
25 *Yonhap Radio*, February 15, 1990; in FBIS-EAS-90-034, 20 February 1994, p. 44.
26 Yu Yong-won, 'Korea Must Obtain'.
27 The source of this report states that this activity uses French-funded fuel processing test facilities. Almost certainly, he is referring to the PIE facility that is used to analyse the isotopic composition of spent fuel from the Wolsong PHWR (the PIE is described in a later section of this chapter) but

Spent fuel storage

The ROK still relies on its increasingly crowded storage racks at each reactor's spent fuel pool to store its spent fuel. In 1990, the ROK contracted with the French company Societe Generale pour les Techniques Nouvelles (SGN) for design of an interim, 3000 tonne, spent fuel storage facility to become operational by 1995.[28] The reactors on-line through 1995 will accumulate about 2700 tonnes of spent fuel (assuming roughly 40 tonnes of spent fuel per GWe-year of operation)—that is, virtually the whole capacity of the planned storage facility. In January 1992, Hyundai Heavy Industries Co. Ltd, entered into a licensing agreement with a US firm, Pacific Nuclear, which allows Hyundai to fabricate and sell Pacific Nuclear's spent fuel storage technology in Korea.[29] After massive protests were made against an interim storage site at Anmyondo island off the West Coast in November 1990, the ROK is still to select a final site.

In March 1991, ROK and Soviet officials began a consultation on nuclear power in Seoul to discuss, among other topics, joint nuclear research projects—including the ROK's participation in the International Center for Chernobyl.[30] A few days later, the Korea Trade Leader Co. and an unnamed, recently privatised Soviet research institute announced that Soviet nuclear and industrial subterranean waste storage technology may be imported into the ROK.[31]

Reprocessing

As Anne MacLachlan of *Nuclear Fuel* noted in 1990, it is evident that the South Koreans have not abandoned the idea of reprocessing their spent fuel.[32] In October 1989, South Korea began informal discussions on a trilateral arrangement involving the ROK, the United States, and Canada whereby co-processing[33] would be established in South

---

which is not a fuel fabrication plant. I am not aware of any fuel fabrication capability in operation before that contracted for construction in 1985, other than small pilot plants for fuel pellet fabrication and testing constructed in the late 1970s and operated in the early 1980s by the Korea Nuclear Fuel Development Institute (established in 1976).

28 A. MacLachlan, 'SGN Wins South Korean Design Contract for Spent Fuel Storage Capacity', *Nucleonics Week*, 5 March 1990, p. 9.

29 'Pacific Nuclear Licenses NUHOMS Spent Fuel Storage', *Executive News Service*, 14 January 1992.

30 'Talks with USSR on Peaceful Use of Nuclear Power', *Yonhap Radio*, Seoul, 25 March 1991; in JPRS-TND-91-006, 23 April 1991, p. 5.

31 'Accord on Soviet Nuclear Waste Disposal', *Yonhap Radio*, Seoul, 28 March, 1991; in JPRS-TND-91-006, 23 April, 1991, p. 6.

32 MacLachlan, 'SGN Wins South Korean Design', p. 9.

33 Co-processing is a form of reprocessing of spent fuel which produces a mixture of plutonium and unfissioned uranium rather than separated streams of

Korea.[34] There is other evidence of the ROK's interest in fuel processing. In October 1989, an IAEA seminar in Vienna was told by the ROK Atomic Energy Commission (AEC) Commissioner that the ROK would like to reprocess PWR spent fuel. A 1989 Ajou University report on the ROK's long-run nuclear power strategy, recommended that the ROK eventually build plutonium-fuelled fast-breeder reactors (FBRs) in addition to PWRs and PHWRs.[35] In August 1990, the Ministry of Science and Technology in Seoul published an official long-range nuclear strategy drafted by KAERI. The document reportedly states that the ROK is to develop independently a 150 MW FBR by 2010, and actively to develop plutonium recycling to be commercialised between 2007 and 2016.[36]

There can be no doubt that South Korea remains committed to a plutonium economy, in spite of its unilateral and joint declaration with the North to abstain from reprocessing or enrichment activities on the peninsula.[37] Indeed, on 27 November 1991, the ROK signed a nuclear cooperation agreement with the British government to allow the UK nuclear industry, and in particular, British Nuclear Fuels Ltd, to supply fuel cycle services to South Korea's nuclear industry.[38] While committed to not reprocessing in South Korea,[39] the ROK may follow Japan's precedent and reprocess off-shore.[40] This strategy would require many large shipments of nuclear material.

---

plutonium and uranium; the product is then fed into nuclear reactors as mixed-oxide fuel known as MOX.

34 A. MacLachlan and M. Hibbs, 'North Korea Begins Negotiations with IAEA; South Korea Interested in Co-processing', *Nuclear Fuel*, 2 October 1989, p. 1.

35 *Nuclear Engineering International*, January 1990, p. 7.

36 Yu Yong-won, 'Korea Must Obtain'.

37 'Roh Declares Nuclear-Free South Korea', *Korea Herald*, 9 November 1991, p. 1; Shim Jae Hoon, 'Unity of Purpose, Nuclear Deal Paves the Way to Peace', *Far Eastern Economic Review*, 9 January 1991, p. 10.

38 UK Department of Energy, 'John Wakeham Signs Nuclear Cooperation Agreement with South Korea', News Release, 27 November 1991.

39 The UK–ROK agreement does not refer specifically to British supply of spent fuel reprocessing service to the ROK. It mentions only the transfer of nuclear material, equipment and technology for the 'management, storage and final disposal of irradiated fuel and radioactive waste', and elsewhere to commercial provision of unspecified 'nuclear and other material, equipment facilities and services'. South Korean officials have stated unofficially that the UK agreement is *not* intended to allow the ROK to obtain off-shore reprocessing. As announced, however, the UK–ROK agreement contains nothing to preclude such an arrangement.

40 P. Leventhal, Nuclear Control Institute, testimony to US Congress, Subcommittee on East Asian and Pacific Affairs, Committee on Foreign Relations, Washington DC, 14 January 1992, stenographic transcript, p. 7.

Thus, fuel rods containing MOX would most probably be fabricated at a reprocessing plant outside the ROK in any future plutonium program. Diversion of fabricated fuel rods containing PuO_2-UO_2 fuel could occur in transit (to/from the reprocessing and fuel fabrication plants), or at the fuel storage site (for example, by switching a uranium fuel assembly for a MOX assembly). Large-scale diversion of fissile material by this route could not go undetected with adequate inspection and gamma-monitoring equipment.[41] Small-scale diversion is another matter. 'Small' is particularly problematic when only 4–10 kgs of plutonium are needed to make a critical mass.

The ROK's commitment to a plutonium economy is driven largely by emulation of, and competition with, Japan's extensive plutonium program. By 2010, Japan estimates that it will generate no less than 84 tonnes of plutonium, of which 53 tonnes would be recycled (as MOX) into light water reactors (LWR) over the next two decades and the rest would be used in FBRs.[42] The dubious economic rationale[43] and ambiguities that surround Japan's plans to accumulate such an enormous plutonium stockpile in the near future, alarms Koreans north and south of the Demilitarised Zone who are suspicious about Japan's long-term intentions. A South Korean editorial in January 1992 noted that many countries 'tend to remain wary of Japanese use of plutonium'.[44] The North Koreans were more forthright:

'Japan's attempt at nuclear arming', broadcast a DPRK foreign ministry spokesperson on Radio Pyongyang in January 1992, 'has become the most dangerous act for creating a new nuclear threat in Asia'.[45]

The fact that in 1987 China announced plans to build a 100 kg/day hot pilot reprocessing plant for commercial use to enter service in 1996, and an associated cold test facility in the vicinity of the Lan Zhou

---

[41] K. Hannerz and F. Segerberg, 'Proliferation Risks Associated with Different Backend Fuel Cycles for Light Water Reactors', in *Nuclear Energy and Nuclear Weapon Proliferation*, eds F. Barnaby et al., Taylor and Francis, London, 1979, p. 96.

[42] 'Plans to Introduce Plutonium Thermal Technology', *Kyodo News Service*, 22 June 1991; in FBIS-EAS-91-122, 25 June 1991, p. 14.

[43] Although the ROK argues that Pu recycling is economic, the evidence is otherwise, as witnessed by the general reluctance of OECD nuclear utilities to adopt the practice. The ROK itself argues that a large-scale program is required to make it economic. Thus, it argues that North Korea has no economic rationale for a reprocessing plant on any scale as it has no nuclear power program. However, the North has *plans* for a nuclear power program, which are consistent with an 'innocent' reprocessing research and development program to serve a long run plutonium economy.

[44] 'Japan's Plutonium Plan', *Korea Herald*, 17 January 1992, p. 8; in FBIS-EAS-92-013, 21 January 1992, p. 48.

[45] Pyongyang Korean Central Broadcasting Network, 20 January 1992; in FBIS-EAS-013, 21 January 1992, p. 24.

Nuclear Fuel Plant in Gangsu Province (north of Chengdu), can only reinforce South Korean determination to eventually follow suit. (By the year 2000, one Chinese official estimates that China will have accumulated 6.3 tonnes of commercial plutonium.)[46]

Research reactor

In February 1986, the Ministry of Science and Technology announced that KAERI would build a 30 MW (thermal) research reactor by 1990, supplementing three research reactors obtained from US suppliers.[47] KAERI contracted with Canada's AECL to supply the reactor, known in Seoul as the Korean Multipurpose Research Reactor or KMRR, in early 1988. The MAPLE (Multi-Purpose Applied Physics Lattice Experiment) plant combines the heavy water, vessel-type NRX reactor design with AECL's pool-type 'Slowpoke'. It is designed to give an intense neutron flux for both research and production of isotopes. The central core with 20 per cent enriched uranium fuel, is cooled and moderated by light water. An intermediate region is light water-cooled. Heavy water in the outer region shields against and reflects neutrons.[48]

The KMRR was due for completion at the end of 1992. One source states that since it can be remodelled quickly to produce plutonium, the KMRR has drawn particular attention from the United States.[49]

Post-irradiation Examination (PIE) facility

This facility was completed in November 1985 with French assistance. It is located in the KAERI complex. Since 1987, the PIE has been used to analyse the burn-up rate, isotopic mix, etc., of small amounts of spent fuel that are transported to the site. The physics, chemistry, and handling techniques are directly applicable to reprocessing and are reportedly monitored closely by the United States.[50]

Other weapons-relevant capabilities

Obtaining adequate fissile material for a nuclear weapons program is only part of what must be acquired before a critical mass can be assembled, a nuclear device tested, or a nuclear weapon deployed and delivered. A state (or non-state actor) must acquire an array of design and computational, command and control, communications and intelli-

---

46 A. MacLachlan, 'Chinese Outline Plans for LWR Fuel Reprocessing Plants', *Nuclear Fuel*, 21 September 1987, pp. 4–5.

47 Shin Ho-chul, 'South Korea will Construct a 30-MW Research Reactor by 1990', *Nucleonics Week*, 6 February 1986, pp. 11–12.

48 R. Silver, 'KAERI to Build Research Reactor Combining Two Canadian Designs', *Nucleonics Week*, 4 February 1988, pp. 5–6.

49 Yu Yong-won, 'Korea Must Obtain'.

50 ibid.

gence, organisational, and delivery systems[51] before it can be said to be nuclear-capable or nuclear-armed.[52]

There can be little doubt that the ROK has the underlying industrial and technical capabilities needed to produce a bomb.[53] It also has no shortage of delivery options for a crude nuclear device which could be used south of the DMZ against an offensive attack from the North. It would be possible, for example, to truck a crude enriched U235 device that might weigh 500 or more kilograms to prepositioned sites in times of crisis. Such a device might also be delivered by air to deliver a retaliatory strike or offensive, first-use strike against the DPRK.

A crude enriched U235 device also could be delivered by one of the Nike Hercules missiles left by departing US forces in 1978. This missile could carry a 1 kt W31 warhead of some 500 kgs against a ground target 140 km away.[54] The South Korean military subsequently

---

[51] This list purposely excludes nuclear testing sites, equipment and activity from the list of necessary systems needed for a state to be nuclear-armed or -capable. Nuclear testing is only needed to emphasise credibility or resolve and to communicate explicit nuclear threats. Given the limited military utility of nuclear weapons in Korea, it seems unlikely that either Korea would have to test any hypothetical device or weapon in order to achieve the desired perceptions of capability in the minds of its adversary. The testing issue might be more relevant to a North or South Korean nuclear weapon program intended to send threats or to be used against external powers. However, the issue deserves further reflection as a nuclear test (or high explosive detonator test short of a full-scale nuclear test) might be an effective psychological weapon. Some partisan sources have claimed that the North has already begun such a limited 'proxy' test program at Pakchon near Yongbyon. I cannot confirm (or deny) the accuracy of such reports except to note that the 1990 French SPOT satellite photos reveal a new excavation with a few buildings and converging power lines and roads high in the mountains a few kilometres east of Pakchon.

[52] G. Rochlin, 'The Development and Deployment of Nuclear Weapons Systems in a Proliferating World', in *International Political Effects of the Spread of Nuclear Weapons*, ed. J. King, US Central Intelligence Agency, US Government Printing Office, Washington DC, 1979, pp. 1–26; for claims that the DPRK is testing nuclear detonator high explosives, see 'Nuclear Related Test Explosion Reported in the North', *Korea Times*, Seoul, 27 June 1991, p. 3; in FBIS-EAS-91-124, 27 June 1991, p. 39; and Tokyo NHK General Television Network, 'Defector Reveals Underground Nuclear Facility', 13 September 1991; in JPRS-TND-91-015, 27 September 1991, p. 7.

[53] See Hayes, *Pacific Powderkeg*, ch. 7, pp. 105–22, for a complete description of the ROK military's support role in US nuclear delivery operations in Korea.

[54] T. Cochran, et al., *Nuclear Weapons Databook. US Nuclear Forces and Capabilities*, Ballinger, Cambridge, 1984, pp. 45, 287.

modified and improved the NH missile.[55] The range of the modified version is said to have increased from the original 150 odd km to about 250 km (see Figure 6.1).

South Korea's rocket aspirations extend into space as well as the military sphere. In 1989, the ROK government announced that it would fund scientific research into system and structural rocket design; solid and liquid propellants; and ignition, guidance and control technologies. The program is officially intended to give the ROK the capability to eventually launch its own satellites. But given the considerable overlap between space-launch and missile technology, this program could provide the ROK with the capability to launch intermediate range, and even intercontinental range ballistic missiles.

The ROK's intentions

If the preceding appraisal is correct, then the ROK already has a near-term (less than five years) nuclear option in terms of its ability to manufacture and deploy nuclear weapons in the Korean peninsula.[56] In the medium term (by 2000), the ROK will become a 'paranuclear' state, i.e., one capable in a matter of months of developing and deploying nuclear arms and delivering them over short-range, intermediate or possibly even intercontinental distances. This latent capability arises from both the ROK's general technological and industrial capabilities, and its cumulative nuclear technological assets. The fact that a state has the technological capability to make nuclear weapons does not, of course, mean that it has the intention of doing so. Indeed between 1945 and 1982, only about 20 per cent of the 76 countries that were able to 'go nuclear' did so.[57]

The ROK's proliferation motivational profile

The proliferation propensity of South Korea may be examined in terms of what Stephen Meyer terms its motivational profile. This profile is a specific combination of the conditions that may motivate or dissuade a country from deciding whether or not to arm itself with nuclear

---

55   Kim Ki-sok, 'The Development Process of National Defence Science and Technology and Directions of Future Development', January 1989, pp. 36–51; in FBIS-EAS-89-056, 24 March 1989, p. 25; Ha Young-sun, 'South Korea', in *Arms Production in Developing Countries*, ed. J. Katz, Lexington Books, Lexington, Massachusetts, 1984, p. 228.

56   And has had a *latent* nuclear weapon manufacturing capability since 1972, according to Stephen Meyer's rigorous analysis. S. Meyer, *The Dynamics*, p. 41.

57   ibid., pp. 82, 86.

weapons. Meyer's estimate of ROK and DPRK proliferation propensity in the early 1980s is shown in Figure 6.5.

Table 6.3 lists nine such motivating conditions, and seven dissuading conditions. Each cell in the matrix couples a motivating condition for the ROK to proliferate with a possible constraining condition that might dissuade it from doing so.

Some cells are clearly null.[58] The cells should provide an indication of how an 'active' dissuasive condition might constrain the incentive to proliferate. Thus, cell 1.1-AA suggests that US extended nuclear and/or conventional deterrence may be sufficient to offset the incentive for the ROK to proliferate in response to a direct nuclear threat (say from China or Russia/CIS).[59]

Table 6.3 should be interpreted with caution in five respects. These are: (1) the graduations in weapons capability; (2) the geographical scope of the 'regional' concerns of the ROK; (3) the peculiar and unique significance of the domestic/foreign politics of Korean unification for the short- and medium-term proliferation propensity of the Korean peninsula; (4) the impact of the passage of time on each variable; and (5) the meaning of the term 'Korea' in the longer run.

1. Proliferation

'Proliferation' is not as simple a term as Table 6.3 suggests. The ROK could have a near-, medium-, or long-term nuclear option; it could become nuclear-weapon capable insofar as it develops a nuclear device, but does not test or deploy it; and it could, for example, become nuclear-capable with respect to the DPRK, but not because of its weapon numbers, mobility, hardness, and delivery range with respect to China.

2. Which region?

What constitutes 'region' for the ROK varies given the differing geographical scope of particular political and economic interests versus the military milieu. Broadly, 'region' is taken here to mean China/Mongolia, Russia/CIS, the United States, Japan and North and South

---

58   Cell 1.2-E, for example, asks if the reunification of the peninsula would constrain the new unified state from deciding to proliferate in response to superpower nuclear arms racing or control developments—a meaningless question. The proliferation propensity of Korea would be little affected by either its size or neutrality considered in relation to US–Russian/CIS nuclear arms control—or at least no more so than pre-unification South Korea.

59   Table 6.3 does not map any combined synergisms between sets of positive and negative incentives. Nor does Table 6.3 weight motivating and dissuasive conditions for relative impact on proliferation decisions. Finally, for a dissuasive condition to exist, a relevant motivating condition must be present.

Figure 6.5   Korean proliferation propensity, early 1980s (over two pages)

The Joint Distribution of the Population at Risk
Lag Time = Short (1)

	Salience		
	High(1)	Moderate(2)	Weak(3)
Nuclear Propensity High (1)	Israel*	South Africa*	
Moderate (2)			Israel
Weak (3)	Japan FRG	Argentina	Belgium Italy Netherlands Canada Spain

* May already have made proliferation decisions

Salience: measure of the impact that going nuclear would have on politico-military balances and/or proliferation

Propensity: measure of the relative strength of incentives and disincentives to go nuclear

Lag Time: measure of the time (t) available for antiproliferation intervention, from Short (t < 1 y) to Moderate (1 < t < 4y) to Long (4 < t < 6y)

Source: S. Meyer, 'A Statistical-Risk Model for Forecasting Nuclear Proliferation', in *Strategies for Managing Nuclear Proliferation*, D. Brito et al., Lexington Books, Lexington, Massachusetts, 1983, pp. 232–4.

The Joint Distribution of the Population at Risk
Lag Time = Moderate (2)

Nuclear Propensity	Salience		
	High(1)	Moderate(2)	Weak(3)
High (1)	Pakistan*		
Moderate (2)		Taiwan South Korea	
Weak (3)		GDR Brazil Yugoslavia	Switzerland Norway Sweden Austria Czechoslovakia

* May already have made proliferation decisions

The Joint Distribution of the Population at Risk
Lag Time = Long (3)

Nuclear Propensity	Salience		
	High(1)	Moderate(2)	Weak(3)
High (1)	Iran* Libya* Iraq*	Algeria*	
Moderate (2)	Egypt	Nigeria*	
Weak (3)	North Korea* Cuba*	Turkey Greece Mexico* Chile*	Australia Rumania Finland

* Boundary lag time

Table 6.3 ROK proliferation decision motivational profile—dissuasive condition in ROK

Motive condition in ROK	Nuclear ally AA/B	Treaty commitment BA/B/C	Unauthorised loss of control C	Preemptive strike by great power D	Peaceful reputation E	Reunification of Korea FA/B	ROK technological gap G
1. Nuclear threat							
1.1 Direct	AA	BA/B/C		D		FA	G
2.2 SP NAR/NAC	AB	BA/B/C					G
2. Latent nuclear threat							
2.1 Direct (DPRK)	AA	BA/B/C			E	FA/B	G
2.2 Regional (J)	AA	BA/B/C			E	FA/B	G
2.3 NPT/NFZ unravel	AB	BA/B/C			E	F/B	G
3. Conventional threat							
3.1 DPRK	AA/B		C	D	E	FA	G
3.2 Regional powers	AA/B		C	D	E	FA/B	G
4. Regional great power status/pretensions[a]							
4.1 in 3 dimensions[b]	AB	BA/B/C		D	E		G
4.2 deter G/SP regional intervention	AB	BA/B/C	C	D	E	FB	G
4.3 modern image	AB	BA/B/C		D	E	FA	G
4.4 regional fora	AB	BA/B/C			E	FB	G
6. Domestic turmoil	AB	BA/B/C	C		E	FA	G
7. Military defeat[c]	AA/B	BA/B/C	C				G
8. Reduce defence budget	AA/B	BA/B/C	C	D	E	FA	G
9. Nuclear ally							
9.1 ROK/US power ratio	AB	BA/B/C	C		E		G
9.2 loss of faith in US	AA/B	BA/B/C		D?	E	F	G

Key

AA=US extended nuclear and conventional deterrence
AB=US alliance dominance and ability to coerce ROK decisions
BA=ROK NPT commitment
BB=ROK Korean NFZ commitment
BC=Hypothetical Northeast Asian NFZ ROK commitment
FA=ROK reunification domestic politics
FB=Impact of reunified Korea
G/SP=Great/superpower
J=Japan

Notes: a We assume that the ROK has no global great power aspirations and is not a 'pariah' state because of its diplomatic relations and membership of the UN and of regional fora.

b The ROK could aspire to be one of the great regional powers in the political, economic or military dimensions. It is impossible for the ROK to surpass the other regional powers in the first two dimensions in this study's time frame relative to the United States, Japan, Russia/CIS, and China, even if Korea reunified. But the ROK or a reunified Korea could achieve nuclear–military great power status at the regional level in the long-term (2000 +). Here, the 'region' is defined as China/Mongolia, Russia/CIS, Japan, the United States, and the two Koreas.

c After hypothetical new ROK/DPRK war that ends in stalemate.

Source: S. Meyers, *The Dynamics of Nuclear Proliferation*, University of Chicago Press, Chicago, 1984, p. 97.

Korea. But some possible motive conditions—such as a Taiwanese decision to proliferate (indicated in row 2.2) dictate a somewhat broader concept of region.

3. Reunification

Meyer's decision-making model of the dynamics of nuclear proliferation has the advantage that it is not trapped in the realist model of international relations which treats states as if they are billiard balls bouncing off each other in accordance with their relative 'weight' (as measured by capability). It makes no assumptions about the unitary nature of state decision-making; it also admits the unusual circumstances of a bifurcated nation.

This latter point is particularly important in the case of Korea, where one nation is divided into two antagonistic states. The North–South split and its consequences dominate political life on both sides of the Demilitarised Zone. Knowledge of national culture, state system, nationalist ideology, and the historical evolution of North–South relations and domestic political legitimacy of both governments is far more important to an understanding of the interactions between the two Koreas than power capabilities *per se*. So long as the North–South relationship remains the primary focus of the two Koreas' external policies, the 'geopolitical' context will be a contributing, but only secondary determinant of their stances. The domestic political implications of the proliferation question for the prospects for reunification (column F) overlay and filter the impact of virtually every other variable in the matrix.

The argument which follows assumes that the ROK ruling elite is susceptible to popular opinion and sensitive to dissent about its policies. Both the reunification and nuclear issue are of enormous symbolic potency in South Korean politics.[60] Since 1987, the Left and Center opposition in the ROK has set a political agenda on reunification to which the Right has had to respond[61] and which made anti-reunification positions untenable for the Right. The Right under Roh Tae-woo claimed the mantle of Korean nationalism based in part on its claim to be able to negotiate a settlement with the North—a move which outflanked the Left.[62] The ROK Left is a largely endogenous and

---

60 M. Clifford, 'A Nuclear Falling Out', *Far Eastern Economic Review*, 18 May 1989, p. 55.

61 On power and agenda-setting, see S. Lukes, *Power, A Radical View*, Macmillan, London, 1977, pp. 41–43.

62 This view of the Left is based on my discussions with key opposition figures in Seoul in October 1991 and their response to the DPRK's nuclear gambits. (The united peace/green antinuclear movement in the South has not taken an actively critical stance of the North's activities for fear of being used by the Right in North-bashing.)

authentic popular response to the repressive and corrupt authoritarianism of the Right in South Korea.[63] Ironically, therefore, the ROK Right created a political force that in turn impelled it towards the 'nordpolitik' initiative, but which left it free to travel down that path largely unconstrained by democratic opposition.

4. Time horizon

The full complexity of the Korean situation is only revealed when the impact of different time horizons is considered. The impact of a given variable may change considerably when the horizon is extended from the short-term (1992–1995), to medium-term (1995–2000). For example, the effect of US extended deterrence on ROK proliferation propensity (dissuasive condition AA) will be compelling between now and 1995, but may decline rapidly thereafter.

5. Korea

Variables may shift over time not merely quantitatively (having a small, moderate or major impact on the propensity to proliferate) but also qualitatively. The significance of 'reunification', for example, could change dramatically in the long-term (2000 +). The two Koreas could reunify successfully without ROK–DRPK-driven nuclear proliferation (row 3.1), but then face a direct (China and Russia/CIS, row 1.1), or a latent nuclear threat (Japan, row 2.2). In the long run, reunification might lessen a united Korea's incentive to proliferate, simply due to its greater regional weight and lesser vulnerability to external power pressures.[64]

This latter constraint is very different, however, from that imposed on the ROK in the short- to medium-term by the volatile and potent reunification issue. A proliferation decision by the ROK government could be seen by ROK electors as creating an enormous obstacle to reunification. Such a step would be highly damaging to any ROK political party and would undermine its ability to exercise legitimate rule.

---

[63] Christian Institute for the Study of Justice and Development, *Lost Victory, An Overview of the Korean People's Struggle for Democracy in 1987*, Minjungsa Press, Seoul, 1988; T. Robinson, 'South Korean Political Development in the 1980s', (mimeo) unpublished contract research paper to US State Department, Washington DC, 1987; and Daljoong Chang, *Economic Control and Political Authoritarianism*, Songang University Press, Seoul, 1985.

[64] Equally, this development could increase some motivational conditions in rows 4.1–4.

ROK proliferation propensity

I will conclude this chapter by analysing the ROK proliferation propensity that arises from consideration of Table 6.3. Due to space limitations, I will not explain fully the logic underlying each and every one of the 84 cells in Table 6.3 that register as a hypothetical coupling of motive-dissuasive conditions. Rather, I will concentrate on rows 1.1, 2.1, 4.1, 9.1, and 9.1 on the motive side;[65] and columns AA/B, BA/B/C, FA/B, and G on the dissuasive side.[66]

1. Direct nuclear threat—1.1

Putative nuclear deterrence which the US extends to the ROK against external nuclear threats is the major dissuasive condition that constrains a ROK decision to proliferate.[67] However, the importance of this fact has declined given the collapse of the USSR and the rapprochement between China and South Korea. These trends have reduced the likelihood of the ROK being confronted with *any* external nuclear threats.

The ROK could also obtain additional protection against nuclear threat or attack from its commitment to the NPT. If protocols for great power no first-use commitments were attached to a Korean non-nuclear zone and signed by the relevant parties, then the ROK would gain further security guarantees against external nuclear threats. A hypothetical regional nuclear-free zone in Northeast Asia could reduce the ROK's geopolitical insecurity still further. In the short-term, therefore, I conclude that direct nuclear threat is not a factor motivating Seoul to proliferate.

In the longer run (2000 +), an ROK or reunified Korean decision to produce its own nuclear weapon in response to Chinese and Russian

---

65 That is (and in the same order), direct nuclear threats; latent nuclear threats from the DPRK and the region; ROK regional power status/pretentions; ROK increase in bargaining power in the US–ROK alliance; and ROK loss of faith in US commitment to ROK security.

66 That is (and in the same order), on US extended nuclear and conventional deterrence; US alliance dominance and ability to coerce the ROK; current and hypothetical ROK treaty commitments; reunification; and ROK technological gaps.

67 For this condition to pertain, someone must actively threaten the ROK for the United States to actively deter them with its own coercive capabilities. As Patrick Morgan and Richard Ned Lebow have shown, it is usually difficult to demonstrate that this state of affairs exists. This issue is avoided here by assuming that the ROK perceives such a threat to exist, whatever the true state of affairs. If the alleged aggressor had not actual intention of threatening the ROK, then the United States would be reassuring the ROK, but not deterring the 'aggressor' by extending nuclear deterrence to the ROK (although the 'aggressor' might be provoked or otherwise disturbed by this activity).

nuclear threat could invite these powers to strike ROK nuclear facilities before a bomb were completed. This possibility extends to the post-ROK production phase. An ROK nuclear weapons arsenal could be targeted in a future great power nuclear exchange if the ROK were seen by one or both of the great powers to be aligned with its adversary and against it (or if it still hosted US forces that might be involved in such a conflict).

By the year 2000, however, the ROK's technological dependence may have greatly diminished (see Figure 6.2). The NPT system may have unravelled. Both Koreas may have abrogated their non-nuclear commitments to each other. On the other hand, the population of a reunified Korea may feel more secure without nuclear weapons.

2. Latent DPRK nuclear threat—2.1

How will what is still a latent DPRK nuclear threat affect the ROK's propensity to proliferate? In the short- to medium-term there are a number of formidable dissuasive conditions. In the short-term, the US security commitment to the ROK is highly credible. The issue of burden-sharing and the ROK's assumption of increasing operational control in the combined force structure will likely dominate future US–ROK alliance politics,[68] but virtually the last place that a US ground troop withdrawal is likely to occur before the year 2000 is South Korea. In short, motive condition 9.2 (loss of faith in the US security commitment) is not likely to be activated.

This conclusion is based on three simple facts. First, the United States remains a global power and its interest in retaining a presence in the ROK include: (a) a concern with regional, extra-Korean interventionary contingencies in the Asia–Pacific;[69] and (b) global non-proliferation responsibilities that require the US to stay in Korea until the DPRK nuclear program is satisfactorily incorporated into the NPT regime.

Second, it is much cheaper for the United States to keep the second infantry division in Korea than to bring it home. Third, Korea is the

---

68 For example, T. With, 'Make Withdrawals Leverage for Peace', *Los Angeles Times*, 18 February 1990, p. M-7; M. Clifford, 'Ambivalent Allies, US Military Role on Peninsula Increasingly Uncertain', *Far Eastern Economic Review*, 3 January 1991, pp. 18–19.

69 Current US defence guidance calls for the Pentagon to be able to fight wars with Iraq and North Korea at the same time. B. Barber, 'Pentagon's War Never Ends', *The Age* (Melbourne), 13 March 1992, p. 11; T. Tyler 'Pentagon spells out US primacy', *The Age*, 9 March 1992, p. 6.

cheapest place to maintain such a force. The US force in the ROK will be streamlined; it will not, however, be removed in the short-run.[70]

The medium-term (1995–2000) is less clear. If the DPRK nuclear program has been checked by 1995, then the issue is moot. If not, then continuing US ground force deployment in Korea would rest on the economic logic of forward deployment, combined with a perceived need for a continuing US regional interventionary posture. It is conceivable, albeit unlikely, that by the year 2000 the United States would have retreated from these strategic goals and withdrawn its land forces from the region. Even then, however, it would almost certainly maintain air force and intelligence units in Korea. This continuing presence, combined with the other dissuasive conditions arising from the costs of the ROK abrogating its NPT commitment, from Seoul's desire to maintain a peaceful reputation, and, possibly, from domestic political considerations, would likely suffice to contain the push to proliferate which would be generated by a latent or even realised DPRK nuclear weapon threat.

The long-term (post-2000) is another matter altogether. A DPRK latent or actual nuclear threat combined with renewed regional great power contention (United States–China–Russia/CIS) would put great pressure on the proponents of non-proliferation in South Korea. However, the main motivation for a ROK proliferation decision by that time would most probably be the military and possibly nuclear posture of Japan, which in turn would be highly dependent on the state of the US–Japanese alliance. Korean views on Japan's nuclear program have already been cited. A recent article in Seoul indicated the degree of suspicion with which some Koreans regard Japan's intentions toward the region:

> Japan must be judged as our number one potential enemy at this point in time. In particular, when the ROK–US alliance disappears and equidistant diplomacy with each of the four peripheral superpowers is pursued, the threat from Japan is assessed as being the highest. The fact that Japan currently possesses the nuclear option is the primary impetus for us to have the nuclear option as well. Japan is able to produce nuclear weapons whenever it wishes since it has the technology for enrichment and reprocessing facilities. Japan is also actively pursing next-generation technology development such as high-speed [sic, fast] breeder reactors, nuclear fission, and laser enrichment. There are also some who fear what will happen when Japan combines these capabilities with its world-level aerospace and electronics industries...[T]here is a danger of Japan becoming a nuclear superpower as well...[71]

---

70   US Department of Defense, *A Strategic Framework for the Asian–Pacific Rim, Looking Toward the 21st Century*, US Government Printing Office, Washington DC, 1991, pp. 15–17.

71   Yu Yong-won, 'Korea Must Obtain'.

There is, however, no consensus in Seoul on this issue. Many South Koreans believe that the disadvantages of developing (let alone exercising) a nuclear option outweigh the benefits to the ROK because such a move would inflame Korea's neighbours.[72] By itself, the Japanese 'plutonium overhang' and other dual capabilities would not necessarily incite a ROK proliferation decision. But combined with a DPRK near-nuclear threat, or actual proliferation, the Japan factor could tilt the balance in Seoul in favour of proliferation after 2000.

This conclusion leads naturally to the next motive condition, the ROK's aspirations to become a regional great power.

3. Regional great power status—4.1

Table 6.4 shows three measures of regional great power potential: military expenditure and active duty military personnel in a combined index; plus GNP and regional trade. A state is defined here as a regional power only if it is found in the top four in each of the military and economic rankings shown. On this basis, the ROK is neither a military nor an economic regional power. Even given differential growth rates, these rankings are unlikely to change in the short- to medium-term (that is, before 2000).

This story hardly changes when the ROK/DPRK figures are combined as a reasonable surrogate measure of a reunified Korea's regional rank in a five-power regional system in the year 2000. Greater Korea is ranked fourth in military spending and third in personnel, and fifth and third in GNP and trade respectively. This result—likely to be robust over a decade—indicates that either the ROK alone, or a reunified Korea, might try to leap-frog into regional great power status by producing nuclear weapons.

Equally, these results suggest that no other regional power is likely to view a reunified and non-nuclear Korea as a serious military or economic threat. Even if a reunified Korea were to be aligned with any of the other regional powers, it would not change the relative rankings of any of these powers in military capability unless it were also to proliferate nuclear weapons.

Moreover, any ROK regional great power aspirations are likely to be constrained by the same dissuasive conditions as applied in the case of a direct or latent nuclear threat analysed earlier. The same considerations would apply to a reunified Korea by, say, the year 2000, with one exception. That is the role of domestic politics. The government of a reunified Korea might not face the same domestic opposition to proliferation that presently confronts the ROK government. Domestic opinion and nationalist sentiment may be more easily directed toward supporting nuclear proliferation in a reunified Korea than in a separate

---

[72] ibid.

South. A united Korea would also be marginally less susceptible to US pressure against proliferation than a stand-alone ROK government.

Conclusion

This analysis of ROK nuclear proliferation capability and propensity suggests that the ROK is highly unlikely to proliferate before the year 2000. It implies that two factors should be given particular prominence as priority short- to medium-term anti-proliferation policy goals if the residual pressures to proliferate are to be minimised.

First, the most important constraint against proliferation is the continuing ROK lack of reprocessing, uranium enrichment, and other dual-capable, nuclear weapons-related techniques and technologies (column G). This obstacle may not endure, but it may provide the time needed to activate other dissuasive conditions such as ROK treaty commitments and sanctions (uranium supply cut-off, for example).

Second, a regional nuclear-free zone (NFZ) could provide the regional security framework needed to constrain external powers from threatening the ROK (or a reunified Korea). I will conclude this chapter therefore with some comments on a possible Northeast Asian NFZ.

A regional nuclear-free zone: background

The peace movement in Northeast Asia, especially organisations affiliated with the Japanese Socialist Party, have long pushed the idea of a regional NFZ. At the official level, so too has the North Korean government. Until recently, the left wing origins of the NFZ proposal rendered it politically suspect among political elites, especially in the United States and Japan.[73] The Japanese and North Korean proposals also ignored the range of nuclear fuel cycle issues that are characteristic of community-based nuclear-free zone concepts.

For its part, until mid-1991, South Korea opposed US nuclear weapons withdrawal until a regional NFZ had been negotiated by the regional nuclear powers (China, USSR, US). In other words, Seoul used the regional NFZ proposal to block a Korean NFZ.[74]

---

[73] For the 'nuclear history' of the region, see Hayes, *Pacific Powderkeg*, chs. 1–5.

[74] For example, in June 1991, South Korean President Roh Tae-woo said that US nuclear strategy should be revised 'only if the Soviet Union, China and the United States agreed on a nuclear-free pact for all of Northeast Asia'. D. Sanger, 'Seoul Says North is Moving Forward', *New York Times*, 14 June 1991.

NFZs for the Pacific were anathema to the Reagan administration.[75] But in the aftermath of the Cold and Gulf wars, NFZs are back on the menu in Washington.[76] So too are '4+2' regional security conferences (involving the US/Russia/China/Japan and the two Koreas) proposed first by Gorbachev in 1986, then by South Korea's President Roh Tae-woo in 1989, and former US Secretary of State James Baker in 1991.[77] If the US perceives that its interests are served by a NFZ, then Washington may actively support such an initiative.

The current relevance of a nuclear-free zone

In early 1992, North and South Korea agreed to create a Korean 'non-nuclear zone'. However this zone is a long way from being realised. One particularly difficult issue preventing progress is that of inspections of suspect nuclear facilities.

As part of the North–South non-nuclear declaration, the two Koreas agreed to create an inspectorate to inspect suspect sites over and beyond the declared nuclear fuel cycle sites which are already subject to IAEA inspections. However, unless the four regional great powers (Japan, China, Russia and the US) lend it political support, and provide intelligence data, the proposed Korean inspectorate is likely to be stillborn. But a six power inspectorate (two Koreas plus the four great powers) currently has no institutional framework within which to operate.

The obvious solution is to blend the imperatives arising from the Korean stand-off with a regional zone that covers the Russian Far East, much of China, Japan, and, in the US, Guam/Aleutians/ Alaska.[78]

---

75 The US, however, has long supported NFZs for Africa, the Middle East and South Asia where they would have no implications for US nuclear deployments.

76 See, for example, the remarks by Thomas Robinson of the American Enterprise Institute in favour of a regional NFZ for Northeast Asia in 'Confidence-Building Measures Versus Conflict-Laden Scenarios in Post-Cold War Korea', paper to Institute of East Asian Studies Conference, Korean Options in a Changing International Order, Berkeley, California, 11 December 1991, p. 8.

77 *International Herald Tribune*, 4 November 4, 1991, p. 15; *Chungang Ilbo*, Seoul, 21 September 1989; in FBIS-EAS-89-184, 25 September 1989, p. 36. Interestingly, President Roh's six-nation conference proposal was made without prior consultation with the United States. Australia and Canada have also pushed for comprehensive security consultations for the Asia–Pacific and North Pacific regions respectively. For US and Japanese views on a six-nation conference on Korea, see J. Baker, 'America in Asia', *Foreign Affairs*, Winter 1991, pp. 1–18; and Yoichi Funabashi, 'Japan and the New World Order', *Foreign Affairs*, Winter 1991, pp. 58–74.

78 See P. Hayes, et al., *American Lake, Nuclear Peril in the Pacific*, Viking/ Penguin, New York, 1986, p. 392.

For reasons of their own, the North Koreans will shortly resurrect their demand for a regional nuclear-free zone. They will do so in full knowledge that this move is a signal that they intend to seek a nuclear-capable, although not nuclear-armed, status. In effect, they will be offering a 'compromise' to the opponents of proliferation, particularly in the US. It will consist of North Korea agreeing to forgo nuclear *armament* in return for obtaining a nuclear weapons *capability* in a regional context. A regional nuclear-free zone that constrains North Korean exercise of such a capability would also restrain the nuclear weapons and development of the other great powers, in particular, Japan, thus serving North Korean interests. It would also restrain US nuclear use and deployments in the region, which is a long-term North Korean goal.

The need for a NFZ study

Elements in the US national security apparatus are alert to North Korean demands on this score. They will move quickly to define the parameters of a regional NFZ in ways that suit the United States in particular and the great powers in general. They can be expected to try to exclude non-weapons nuclear issues (such as radioactive waste dumping); some dual-capable weapons activities (such as ballistic missile testing); to ensure maximum flexibility in nuclear and related operations and preparations; and seek a purely symbolic regional NFZ that will draw on the worst precedents of the Latin American and the South Pacific NFZs.

It is urgent therefore for peace researchers in the region to tackle this issue.[79] In addition to the nuclear issues in Korea, the regional NFZ offers a way to put pressure on China (which supports arms control and disarmament over everyone but itself), Japan (over its reprocessing program), the United States (for nuclear withdrawal from Guam, Japan and Okinawa, and the Aleutians), and Russia (likewise from the Far East and North Pacific).

The regional peace movement is taking up opposition to foreign military bases but this, in effect, concentrates only on the United States in the Asia–Pacific region. A regional NFZ offers a security system or regime that sets out the norms and rules of state behaviour, whereas simple US withdrawal would leave behind nothing but regional great powers with colliding aspirations. It is therefore important that social movements in regional states as well as policy-makers broaden their horizons to include a regional framework for common security.

---

[79] A full analysis of a regional NFZ for Northeast Asia would cover: historical background; pros and cons; geographical scope; weapons scope; nuclear scope; weapons trade-offs; strategic goals of regional powers; instruments; precedents; great power politics; practical politics; and complementary and contradictory forms of regionalism.

In conclusion, given the potential for nuclear proliferation in Korea, it is worth remembering the old intelligence aphorism: 'Capabilities change slowly, but intentions can change overnight'. A regional NFZ could increase the likelihood that Korean intentions remain non-nuclear on both sides of the DMZ.

7 The North Korean Nuclear Program as a Problem of State Survival

PAUL BRACKEN

The past several years have witnessed growing concern about the prospect that the Democratic People's Republic of Korea (DPRK) is developing a capability to produce nuclear weapons. The heinous nature of the North Korean regime, the impact on the region that a nuclear-armed DPRK could have, and the direct threat it would pose to United States' forces and those of its allies, have pushed the North Korean nuclear issue to the top of the international agenda. North Korea is today the most militarised, brutal, and undemocratic country in the world and poses a severe danger to Japan and South Korea, states which are among America's most important allies. Should Washington not respond appropriately to the DPRK nuclear threat, Tokyo and Seoul could well initiate their own nuclear programs as a countermeasure. If this were to occur, a broader regional nuclear spiral could ensue, threatening the regional stability which now exists in Northeast Asia.

At a time when the United States is pulling back from its Cold War leadership role, the prospect of a nuclear-armed North Korea is one of the very few threats sufficient to catalyse a decisive US reaction. But there is little need to convince anyone that the issue is a serious one. That is self evident. Nor is there much point in outlining a possible chain reaction of future proliferation events, highlighting the most dangerous paths. That is speculation. Not only are we today a long way from a regional nuclear arms race in Northeast Asia, but confidence in forecasting such a sequence of conditional events is low. The purpose of this chapter is rather to argue that the North Korean nuclear program is deeply inter-linked with the problem of state survival, and that everyone recognises this and is acting accordingly.

State survival is being pursued against a backdrop of non-proliferation and arms control manoeuvring. Our contention is that there are two 'games' being played on the Korean peninsula. The first game is non-zero sum in character. It amounts to bargaining around a military and nuclear negotiation where the gains of one side do not necessarily come at the expense of the other. The second, and more important game, is zero sum. It is a game of control, and only one state can gain control of the entire Korean peninsula. The composition of these two games can be described in the following way. In Korea, the non-zero sum game of non-proliferation and arms control is being used to conceal a more deadly second contest for control of the peninsula. It is possible in this characterisation for the long-term survival and sovereignty of both sides to be described as a win. That is, a two-state outcome may continue as a solution to the underlying contest. But it is the state survival competition, rather than one concerning non-proliferation and arms control, that shapes the dynamics of inter-state relations among all affected parties. Treating the North Korean nuclear program purely as a problem in non-proliferation makes little sense.

North Korea has good reason to build an atomic weapon. It is one of the very few ways in which that state might continue to exist. Nuclear weapons may serve to prop up both a sovereignty and security system that has fallen apart because of the collapse of global communism, skilled South Korean foreign policy, and North Korea's own economic bankruptcy. *A nuclear armed North Korea could buy time for the regime to adapt to new international circumstances.* The evidence that a weapon program is, in fact, underway, and the evidence that North Korea's negotiating posture on signing and implementing the Non-Proliferation Treaty (NPT) is basically one of stalling for time, reinforce this interpretation. The evidence is admittedly not complete. But neither are we in a court of American law. What has to be remembered above all else is that, just as North Korea seeks to remain an independent nation state, other states wish for its demise.

The interaction of these two forces—North Korea's striving to exist and the desire of other states—determines the behaviour of different actors towards the North Korean nuclear program. The point of this chapter is to describe how this dynamic and its associated interactions enfold. The following is the modal description of what is now taking place. First, some actors do not just want to eliminate the North Korean nuclear program; they want to eliminate the North Korean state. If the former proves useful in promoting the latter, then so much the better. Second, North Korea does not want 'stability' or 'removal of American forces' *per se*; these are sought not as ends in themselves but as means to ensuring state survival. Third, proliferation control strategies for North Korea should therefore be seen as a sub-game which is part of this larger metagame. Fourth, even if this modal description is incorrect in important respects, e.g., North Korea really *is* only developing a nuclear energy program, it still describes the cognitive maps held by senior officials in the nations involved. And it is this model of the situation on which action will be based. In an American jury, North Korea could in theory be proven 'not guilty'. But we are not in a jury trial, and North Korea has started a train of events which other nations will exploit to the limit.

This chapter is an academic one. It is not a policy document, and it is not constrained by diplomatic niceties. As an academic paper it will remain 'disinterested', attempting to lay out the main variables and their interaction without regard for the implications of where the argument is taking us. Because the paper will likely irritate readers because of its direct, some might say overly harsh treatment of sensitive matters, this disclaimer is necessary. But it is better to delve into these sensitive matters than to let them remain implicit or unstated, and hence unanalysed. The argument may affront the sense of decorum of some readers, but this issue is important enough to have a full deck of cards laid on the table.

Conceptualising North Korea's decisions

A first cut at conceptualising North Korean decision-making involves the four principal factors which shape the decision process: the military balance on the peninsula; the economic disparity between the two Koreas; the populations of the two; and the collapse of the communist bloc over the past several years as a force which at least loosely coupled states identifying themselves as bloc members. Figure 7.1 shows some of the salient features of this conceptualisation.

North Korea's long-declared ambition to reunify the Korean peninsula appears increasingly in doubt. The North's armed forces, while impressive in terms of numbers of weapons and manpower, have so many qualitative weaknesses that an attack on the South would amount to a cosmic gamble. These things, of course, are difficult to assess accurately, and it is always possible that different perceptions of the military balance reign in different capitals. But North Korea gives all appearances of having made a large military investment which provides more of an effective deterrent shell than of a force optimised for offensive operations against the South.

North Korean military forces are badly trained. Exercises have been extremely limited involving only small unit activities. Command and control is primitive, and is certainly not adequate to coordinate the kind of complex military campaign involving coordination of infantry, special forces, and mobile forces that has apparently been the strategic model of military development over the past decade. Intelligence on the South is also poor, although there is lots of it, based on the extensive man-reconnaissance penetrations which have taken place. But the capacity to pull all such intelligence together in near 'real time'—for artillery fire

Figure 7.1 A view of the basic problem in Korea

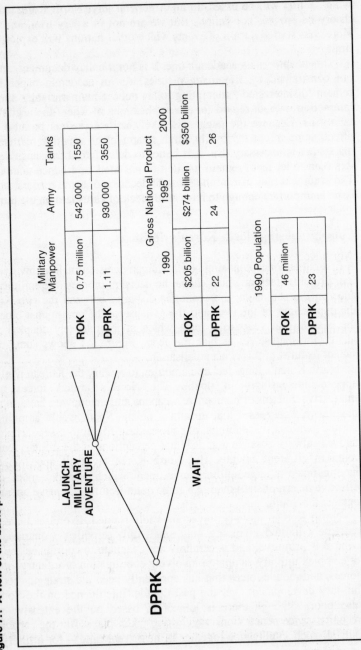

	Military Manpower	Army	Tanks
ROK	0.75 million	542 000	1550
DPRK	1.11	930 000	3550

Gross National Product

	1990	1995	2000
ROK	$205 billion	$274 billion	$350 billion
DPRK	22	24	26

1990 Population

ROK	46 million
DPRK	23

LAUNCH MILITARY ADVENTURE

WAIT

DPRK

direction and special warfare operations—is not even close to what is needed. Were a war to break out in the near future the mass of North Korean artillery would be fired and special forces despatched with little effect. North Korean armour would have great difficulty moving south over a sparse road network crowded with infantry and supplies. The transportation logistics and coordination of such a campaign would be extremely difficult for any army, but especially so for an army that has not invested in expansion of its vertical information processing circuits.

On the economic front, the disparity between North and South Korea is approaching a ratio of ten to one in terms of Gross National Product (GNP). No country in world history has ever conquered another when disadvantaged by a GNP ratio like this. The economic take-off of South Korea is well recognised, as is the stagnation of North Korea. Official US estimates of North Korean growth, around 4–4.5 per cent per annum in the 1980s were almost certainly misplaced. It is far more likely that there is a range of negative contractions, leading to food, energy, and raw material shortages that are beginning to have very serious political consequences for the regime.[1]

The population differences, 46 million South Koreans to 23 million North Koreans, reinforce the economic disparity between the two nations. The South's economy is drawing more and more workers into high productivity occupations. In the North, the labour force is channelled into politically correct, but economically maladapted projects, which lowers national productivity even below levels which could be achieved. As in virtually all communist economies, labour (and capital) are directed into the least efficient sectors of the economy. Moreover, from what we know of the Kim Il-Sung *juche* system, workers are switched from one sector to another according to the doctrine of mass mobilisation. No learning curve effects are built up in a labour force that is constantly churned from one project to another, and only the most limited development of human capital is possible.

Finally, political changes in the form of the collapse of communism in the USSR and Eastern Europe have removed the underpinnings of the North Korean security system, exposing the vulnerabilities described above. The military, economic, and population imbalances on the peninsula have been known for many years; what was new in the North was the apparent *de facto* abandonment by the regime of its long cherished goal of reunifying the two Koreas. But at least while there was some form of extended security system being provided by the Soviet Union and China, Pyongyang could be confident that the tables would not be turned: that Seoul would not have the option of leading the charge for reunification.

---

[1]   A recent eyewitness account is described in 'Hunger and Other North Korean Hardships Are Said to Deepen Discontent', *New York Times*, 18 February 1992, p. 1.

The collapse of communism has removed this protective factor, and North Korea has developed no counterbalancing strengths.

By 1991, North Korea was a regime without friends, money, oil, or enough military strength to defend its interests. In such a context the nuclear option looked credible as a temporising solution to the regime's vulnerability. North Korea's nuclear program did not come about as a specific redress to the crisis of the early 1990s. Its origins go back at least to 1980, when work began on a 30 MW gas–graphite research reactor at Yongbyon.[2] The large size of this reactor suggested it was built to produce plutonium. By the late 1980s the reactor had been completed, and a number of other indicators of a nuclear weapons program have subsequently been revealed. For example, explosive testing grounds for warhead experimentation were detected, as was construction of two additional reactors based on different designs, and a plutonium reprocessing facility.

We cannot penetrate the wall of secrecy about the early motivations for a nuclear weapons program in the North. What can be said is that the environment in which the early decisions were made had completely altered during the decade of the 1980s. When the early decisions were made Pyongyang's Soviet ally looked like a strong power, while China also maintained good relations with the North. Yet by the end of the decade the lagging economic performance of the North, which directly undermined its military position relative to the South, meant that North Korean security was badly undermined. Indeed, if this deteriorating position persisted, the existence of the Kim regime and the North Korean state would be at risk.

It is useful to outline precisely what the above implies. If the North could have built a war-winning posture with which to intimidate the South, or if it had been able to foment so much trouble that South Korea would have suffered severe internal strains, there would have been some chance of reunification on the North's terms. Economic problems had greatly reduced this prospect by the mid-1980s, but not to the point that North Korea was itself threatened. North Korea could use its still substantial million-man army to deter military attacks, threats, or intimidation from the South. Although the military balance was already shifting in favour of the South, it would still have been extremely risky for the South to attack the North, even if it had wished to do so.

But North Korea's admittedly substantial military capacity is of little utility against the kinds of security threats that have now materialised. First, the changes in what was the Soviet Union and China mean that the probability of outside military support for the North was virtually eliminated. This also meant that the risk of a Korean war spreading to engulf

---

2   See Monterey Institute of International Studies, 'North Korean Nuclear Developments', 3 December 1991; and Andrew Mack, 'North Korea and the Bomb', *Foreign Policy*, no. 83, Summer 1991.

other regional powers was minimised. South Korean risk-taking, US risk-taking, and Chinese and Soviet opportunism were all relieved of the Cold War mechanisms which had restrained them. Moscow after the 1991 coup attempt, for example, had no basis for protecting the North. Similarly, while China might have some ideological reason for supporting a socialist regime because there are so few left, Chinese politics is extremely complicated and other interests would predispose Beijing against protecting the North.

Second, the immediate threat to North Korea is not military attack, but strategic isolation leading to greater economic isolation, and opportunities for international intervention in Korean affairs. This is what is now happening, most notably with the pressure on the North to open suspect nuclear facilities to inspection by the IAEA. But such demands must surely be seen as only the first moves to open up the entire North Korean state. Any such opening is fraught with risk for the regime. Economic advisors, human rights groups, academics, etc., are all awaiting the opportunity to travel throughout North Korea and freely critique the many outrageous things which undoubtedly occur there.

The North Korean economy is so bankrupt that it has been increasingly easy for Seoul to position itself as an essential middleman between Pyongyang and the outside world. This contributes to the North's strategic isolation, for the South is unlikely to be a completely neutral gatekeeper. Moreover, this economic middleman or gatekeeper role is exactly what West Germany did to East Germany. After the 1971 Berlin accords, Bonn consistently aided the economic development of the East. But the consequence of this was a growing linkage and dependence, which in turn produced a vulnerability that Bonn skilfully used in 1989 to bring down the faltering East German regime.

Pyongyang has scrambled desperately to establish ties with other states in order to barter food and oil with them to counter its vulnerability to the South. But barter with North Korea is not a winning business proposition. A wink or nod from Seoul may be sufficient to foreclose North Korean overtures to Russia, the Philippines, Indonesia, and others, because trade with the South is so much more important to these states than small barter deals with North Korea. Quite simply, South Korea, possibly in conjunction with the United States, can squeeze the North Korean economy and use economic pressure for political ends. There is considerable evidence that this is exactly what is happening. Seoul has offered to aid North Korea, to swap rice for shoes, to buy North Korean gold stocks, and to invest in new industrial zones on the Tumen river. But to accept such offers will increase the North's dependence on the South. It is almost impossible to believe that Kim does not see where this path is likely to lead. The parallels with West Germany's dealing with the East after the Wall was torn down but before the countries were united, is a clear example of what is likely to happen if the North cannot reestablish its economy on its own terms. Yet the North Korean economy is far worse off than East Germany's.

Conventional military strength cannot stop any of the above from taking place. But a nuclear weapon may be a different matter. It could increase the prospects that other countries, such as Japan, would treat the North as a state which had to be dealt with seriously rather than as a pariah. Japanese investments and technical 'know how' could help modernise the economy; help from Japanese trading companies to manage the commodity and light manufacturing sectors could also make a big difference. At least this is how things may seem to the North's leaders.

Reconceptualising the North's decisions

It is easier to change strategies than it is to change institutions. Since the beginning of the 1990s North Korea has shifted strategic direction seeking to escape the dilemmas in which it is caught. But these strategy changes have not affected in any real way the organisation of the North Korean state. And it is this organisation—the institutions and norms of the North Korean state—that also shape its decisions. Figure 7.1 presented an *institution-free* description of the North's basic dilemma. Equally important is Figure 7.2, which is overlaid onto the decision problem in Figure 7.1. It reveals several important and significant constraints on the freedom of the North Koreans to use their nuclear weapon program to buy time until they can establish direct ties with other states and negotiate assistance in economic modernisation on politically acceptable terms.

North Korea has a highly departmentalised and compartmentalised state structure with Kim Il Sung and his son at the apex. They rule directly, sometimes through institutions like the Korean Workers Party (KWP), but sometimes through direct contact with officials many layers in the hierarchy below them. The state organisation is not designed to be efficient, but to enforce top down rule.

Examples of this tendency are manifest. A vast techno-structure of Party machinery intrudes directly into the state's coercive institutions. This techno-structure standardises the behaviour of the middle line, the officer corps and other officials with line responsibility. Every coercive and military organisation has a techno-structure to standardise behaviour in a big complex organisation. In the West, general staffs serve this function. But in North Korea, the Party, *not* the general staff, plays this role, and the Party does not promote technical or professional standards, but political ones. Enforcing political standards is more important than enforcing professional standards. This means that promotion, career paths, and competence are all judged by political criteria. Directing this vast coercive enterprise towards military objectives is exceedingly difficult.

Figure 7.2 North Korea's political hierarchy

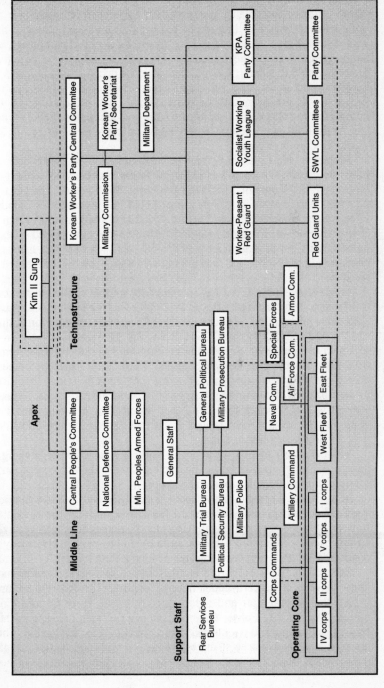

Another feature of the system in the North is the undersized military support staff—logisticians, transportation experts, food suppliers, and arms-makers. One very important, but usually unnoticed, point is that, while North Korea is thought to have enormous stocks of equipment, and ammunition, it lacks the critical institutional ingredients to pull these forces together to support the middle line in its decision-making, and the operating core of air, land and naval forces which do the actual fighting. Extant stocks are oversized for some critical items (like artillery), and undersized for others (like petroleum, oils and lubricants (POL)). There has never been any attempt to test logistical capabilities to see if they would function in a crisis.

Moreover, North Korea's road network north of the DMZ does not have the capacity to carry the logistical forces necessary to support the large operating corps of a million-man army. With such a spartan road network, extremely careful planning would be necessary to conduct effective war time operations. To gain such efficacy would in turn require extensive practice in moving supplies to where they are needed—i.e., to units moving out of staging areas and south. No such exercises have ever been seen in the North, and they are not something that can be learned on the spot.

In addition, North Korea has an extremely spartan command and control system. The function of the *control* part of such a system is to supply units with information, logistics, and reinforcements. North Korea, quite simply, has no such system. There is no way for an advancing infantry regiment to signal that it needs ammunition, or fuel, other than to send a rider on a bicycle back to headquarters. There is no capacity for headquarters to receive, absorb, and act on the thousands of reports that might be sent back by the enormous number of special forces troops. There is also no way for special forces to get to where they are supposed to be going, or to acquire new targets if current targets move—something which is likely in a war or crisis.

What does all of this mean for a North Korea which is seeking to pursue a foreign policy based on buying time? Several consequences follow from this organisational analysis.

First, North Korea is likely to be dangerously bad at crisis management. If a military crisis occurs on the DMZ, North Korean military forces may act in an unpredictable manner as a consequence of receiving wrong or late information. DPRK military forces cannot effectively be controlled from the top, once engaged beyond a certain level.

Second, the division of the North's forces into several autonomous units suggests a concern about internal control. The Red Guard units bypass the general staff and report directly to the Party Central Committee. The Special Forces units are only under nominal general staff control, and many of them instead report directly to the leadership. There are so many diverse special forces groups, all with constantly changing cover names, that the North Korean army has become a maze of complexity. When additional Party intelligence and special units are added to the picture the North Korean state emerges as a horrendously complex organisation with truly enormous information processing costs. But this seeming inefficiency also has the consequence of making an internally organised coup attempt against Kim Il Sung very costly. That is what it is designed to do. However, the experience of East Germany and Rumania, especially Rumania, which had similar but less extreme state structures, points to the fact that internal conspiracies *do* arise even in communist systems. They cannot be completely overcome through organisational design.

Third, although the economic structures of North Korea are not depicted in Figure 7.2 they are as complex, transaction cost-intensive, and inefficient as the coercive arms of the state. Enormous financial resources could be transferred to North Korea without them having any impact on economic efficiency. The money could be used to buy oil, or luxury goods for the Party elite, but it would do little to improve productivity because there are no markets to allocate goods, and the existing state institutions are grossly inefficient.

The problem for the North Korean leadership is that the delaying and diversification strategy cannot work with the existing state institutions, or can do so only with great risk. As the economy deteriorates the control system in the North will have to tighten up even more than it has already. Potential dissidents will have to be monitored more carefully. The general population will become more apprehensive. Resistance can be expected to increase as elites are no longer provided with luxury goods as they were in the past.

Far from opening up and becoming more efficient in order to pose a more deadly military threat to the South, or to better absorb foreign economic assistance, North Korea is likely to move in the opposite direction. The regime will have to become more defensive and paranoid and it will possibly be more dangerous as a consequence. This is what is meant by the statement that changing strategy is more easy than changing institutions. North Korea's situation today is roughly comparable with that of American automobile manufacturers threatened by Japanese competitors. In the early 1980s American firms knew they were in trouble. They changed strategies, but could not easily change their internal organisation. As conditions worsened, they began to push for government protection, even though they all knew that this was counterproductive. But given the difficulty of internal institutional change, and a dire immediate external threat, they felt that they had no choice but to buy time, even if the consequence of so doing would insulate them from the changes they needed to make over the long run.

Nuclear weapons and other actors

The final components to the arguments summarised by Figures 7.1 and 7.2 are the roles of nuclear weapons and of other states. Each state has a different set of interests. Many Japanese, for example, view the prospect of a united Korea with a certain reluctance—a factor which North Korea hopes to exploit. What counts, however, is the *balance* of costs and benefits which dealing with North Korea, especially a *nuclear-armed* North Korea, presents to other states.

Both Adolf Hitler and East Germany's Erich Honecker calculated that the allies arraigned against them would prefer dealing with independent German states. Both calculated incorrectly. To the wartime allies, defeating Hitler was worth the cost of allowing Soviet forces into the heart of Europe—and dividing Germany. In 1989, bringing down communist East Germany, or, more accurately, not acting to prop it up, was something that Washington, Bonn, London, and *even* Moscow and Paris thought worthwhile, notwithstanding the fact that the French were openly opposed to German reunification.

There was nothing that France, yet alone Britain or the United States, could do in 1989 to stop the unification process, regardless of their past interests. For Paris to have massively lent money to Honecker in the context of the politics of 1989 would have carried *realpolitik* unacceptably far. It simply could not happen with a character, and a regime, like Honecker's. Applied to North Korea the logic is equally clear. Neither China, nor Japan, can bail out Kim because his regime is the most brutal and repressive in the world—it makes East Germany's look like a democracy.

Aiding a *nuclear-armed* North Korea would be even less acceptable behaviour. My conclusion is that if China, Japan, the United States, and Russia agree on nothing else, it is that a nuclear-armed North Korea is simply unacceptable. They may not act openly to neutralise the DPRK's nuclear capability. But they will tacitly agree to anything which pressures the regime, including strategic isolation, and allowing South Korea to pursue a German-style reunification process against the North. They will play ball with Seoul, their real motives concealed by the language of non-proliferation and arms control, because not doing so presents a worse alternative: a potential nuclear state with values that are utterly repugnant to a wide range of countries that do not have much else in common.

8 Arms Control and Confidence-building on the Korean Peninsula

BYUNG-JOON AHN

With the end of the Cold War in Europe, the collapse of the Soviet Union, the end of the civil war in Cambodia and progress towards peace in the Middle East, the Korean peninsula is now one of the world's most dangerous crisis points. What former US Secretary of State James Baker called 'the last glacier of the Cold War in Asia' seems to be beginning to thaw, but his point that 'the very real danger of nuclear proliferation on the Korean peninsula is now the No. 1 threat to stability in the Asia–Pacific community' remains true.[1] On this strategically located peninsula the Cold War still continues between North and South Korea although two accords on reconciliation and non-aggression and on de-nuclearisation entered into force on 19 February 1992. Over 1.5 million armed men still confront each other along the demilitarised zone (DMZ).

If there is one place in Asia where a European-style arms control process might be appropriate, it is the Korean peninsula. But is arms control feasible in Korea, and if so, what is the context within which negotiation can succeed? What kind of security and arms control policy is South Korea seeking? What are the most important issues at stake and what are the prospects for success? These are the central questions that this chapter addresses.

Analysis of these questions is necessarily based on the reality of the North–South Korean confrontation and on some recent changes on the peninsula.

---

[1] James A. Baker III, 'America in Asia: Emerging Architecture for a Pacific Community', *Foreign Affairs*, vol. 70, no. 5, Winter 1991, p. 12.

The Korean context: the primacy of political reconciliation

An arms control process in Korea involves negotiation between two adversaries who have conflicting military doctrines and political ideologies. The need for political reconciliation arises because once the two Koreas are prepared to accommodate each other politically it will be relatively easy for them to control their military competition.

In order for a Korean arms control process to get under way, therefore, there should be some degree of political confidence-building before negotiations on military confidence-building measures and force reductions take place. To illustrate this central theme, we can enumerate four major points.

First, favourable political conditions must be present for North and South Korea to achieve substantive results in arms control negotiation. This is because, as long as the two sides remain engaged in the struggle for political legitimacy, it is difficult, if not impossible, for there to be common interests on security. The rapidly changing international environment has impelled North and South Korea to embark on negotiations, but North Korea's reluctance to make a genuine political reconciliation with the South is becoming the major obstacle to making substantive progress. Should the North change its old thinking and seek seriously to implement the Basic Agreement with the South which entered into force in February 1992, this will open the way to an era of peace and cooperation on the peninsula.

Second, preventing the proliferation of nuclear weapons is essential to building peace and confidence in Korea. But this requires an international process involving the International Atomic Energy Agency (IAEA) and other concerned parties such as Japan, the US, and possibly even the UN Security Council. It also requires a bilateral Korean process involving implementation of the North–South denuclearisation accord. The issue of proliferation affects peace and stability, not only on the Korean peninsula, but also throughout Northeast Asia and the world. In the short run, Japan's decision to make diplomatic normalisation with North Korea conditional on Pyongyang's acceptance of international inspections of its nuclear facilities and the implementation of the North–South denuclearisation accords is perhaps the most effective means of discouraging North Korea's nuclear ambitions. But, in the long run, the IAEA regime must be strengthened to permit challenge inspections on suspected nuclear facilities. Coercive sanctions against the North may be necessary before Pyongyang will accept such inspections.

Third, in order to correct military asymmetries in conventional forces, bilateral negotiations to institute 'transparency' confidence-building measures will be necessary. Such measures would create the confidence necessary for negotiations on cuts in armed forces and constraints on their deployments. Progress in this area will be slow because the North still sees arms control as a means for forcing the US to withdraw troops from the South, whereas the South sees arms control as a means for building peace, cooperation and reconciliation with the North.

Fourth, given the above, the most realistic prospect for arms control in Korea is a gradual process of political reconciliation, together with multi-lateral and bilateral measures for the non-proliferation of nuclear weapons and ballistic missiles, bilateral confidence-building and arms control measures, and international supports and guarantees.

A beginning to this process was made on 19 February 1992 when the prime ministers of North and South Korea put into force the 'Agreement on Reconciliation, Non-aggression, Exchange and Cooperation between North and South', and the 'Joint Declaration of the Denuclearisation of the Korean Peninsula'. Despite this breakthrough, however, reconciliation is still far away because the implementation of these historic documents is yet to be realised. Both sides are interpreting them according to their own criteria. It was possible for the North and the South to conclude these agreements mainly because the positions each had sought were included in them. But this fact is bound to cause conflicting interpretations of the agreements on each side from now on.

On balance, the South's criteria are pragmatic, while the North's are those of revolutionary ideologists. The North still puts an enormous emphasis on such symptoms of confrontation as the presence of US troops and the US–ROK 'Team Spirit' exercise. The South focuses on the lack of trust and cooperation.

Thus, North and South Korea are still reiterating their respective positions instead of probing each other's real interests. As was the case between East and West before the Cold War ended in Europe, this tends to lock the parties into a conflictual relationship.[2] And concession-making or compromise is difficult without significant change in the international or domestic political environments.

In fact, changes in the international environment have prompted North and South Korea to talk with each other, but the lack of change in North Korean domestic politics seems to be preventing the state of North–South Korean relations from moving from acceptance of the status quo to seeking political reconciliation.

The process of the six high-level talks went from September 1990 to February 1992 and revealed much about the nature of North–South relations. The first prime ministerial talks in Seoul in September 1990 were convened in the wake of collapsing communist systems in East Europe. At the talks the South made proposals for exchanges and cooperation and for political and military confidence-building measures. The North countered with demands for the release of those who were in prison in the South charged with unauthorised visits to North Korea, and for its own programs for easing political and military confrontation.

---

2   Linda P. Brady, ed., *The Politics of Negotiation*, The University of North Carolina Press, Chapel Hill and London, 1991, pp. 212–13.

At the second round of talks in Pyongyang in October 1990, the South advanced a draft agreement for improving North–South relations, along with proposals for promoting increased North–South communications, trade and travel. The North proposed a draft non-aggression declaration. At the third meeting in December in Seoul 1990, the South made a revised proposal on a draft agreement which incorporated some of the North's non-aggression declaration. The North then called for a new declaration on non-aggression, reconciliation and cooperation.

Pyongyang then suspended the talks citing as its reason the annual US–ROK 'Team Spirit' exercise. The fourth meeting resumed in Pyongyang ten months later in October 1991. It was on this occasion that the sides agreed to adopt a comprehensive document on 'reconciliation, non-aggression, exchange and cooperation'. After the Communist Party fell in the Soviet Union in August, after both North and South Korea were simultaneously admitted into the UN, and after Kim Il Sung carried out a state visit to China early in October, the leadership in the North apparently realised that without some progress in North–South Korean relations it would be almost impossible for them to normalise diplomatic relations with Tokyo, let alone with Washington.

Hence, the most important political issue that had to be resolved still remained whether North Korea was prepared to negotiate a peace agreement with South Korea to terminate the state of war that is implicit in the existing armistice. It was South Korea's position that North Korea should make a clear-cut commitment to do this, and drop its consistent demands for negotiating no more than a non-aggression declaration with South Korea, and a separate peace agreement with the US—the latter ostensibly to replace the armistice. South Korea saw their demands as intended to destroy its alliance relationship with the US and to undermine its legitimacy and for this reason rejected them.

Finally, North Korea abandoned its insistence on a non-aggression declaration prior to any other accords and concluded an agreement with the South at the fifth round of talks in December 1991, in the wake of the demise of the Soviet Union. According to the agreement, which went into force at the sixth round of talks in February 1992, the two sides recognised each other's political systems, and pledged not to interfere in each other's domestic affairs. Most importantly, Article 5 of the document says:

> The two sides shall endeavor together to transform the present state of armistice into a solid state of peace between the North and the South, and shall abide by the present Military Armistice Agreement until such a state of peace has been realized.

If these provisions are fully implemented, as the South expects them to be, they have considerable potential to serve as a peace agreement which will gradually substitute for the armistice. But when the North–South Political Subcommittee subsequently met to discuss the detailed means of implementation of the agreement on 9 March 1992, the North reverted to its previous line calling for the withdrawal of American troops, abrogation of the National Security Law in the South, and the release of prisoners in the South. This, once again, was a 'united front' strategy which aimed at creating divisions in South Korean society.

It should be clear that the North signed these agreements with the South in an attempt to protect itself against the sea changes sweeping across the world, and to preserve its own system by resurrecting its old line on unification. The South, by contrast, is committed to pursuing a consistent policy of seeking genuine denuclearisation and confidence-building measures with the North. It is also committed to maintaining bilateral deterrence and the mutual defence treaty with the US for security not just on the peninsula but throughout the region. Seoul will also continue to pursue its growing relationship of economic interdependence with Japan and other powers.[3]

It is important to note that the accords are like gentlemen's agreements in the sense that they can be implemented only when both sides have the intention and will to do so. Under the current circumstances, the North seems to be interested in using them primarily as a shield against external challenges and as a means of securing international recognition and economic cooperation from the South, whereas the South is more interested in enhancing political and military confidence, in improving mutual communications and in achieving visits between separated families with the North.

The accords have still to undergo a reality-testing process as North and South Korea probe each other's real interests through negotiations. The significance of the agreements is that they are opening an era of reconciliation and cooperation in the spirit of national self-determination.

Non-proliferation of nuclear and chemical weapons, and ballistic missiles as global and Korean processes

Controlling nuclear, chemical and biological weapons, and ballistic missiles on the peninsula must be achieved through a combination of global and Korean action. Actions at the global and regional level which complement each other will be most effective in making North Korea abandon weapons of mass destruction. These proliferation issues are not ones that North and South Korea can resolve bilaterally. Judging from the Iraqi experience, one effective way of controlling nuclear proliferation may be to strengthen the IAEA regime so that IAEA inspectors can carry out unconditional inspections of any suspect sites with the legal sanction of the UN Security Council. Some type of challenge inspection regime is essential if the Iraqi experience is not to be repeated.

---

[3]   Byung-joon Ahn, 'Korea's Security Interests and Role in the Pacific Rim', in *Pacific Rim Security Cooperation*, Institute of Foreign Affairs and National Security, Seoul, 1992, pp. 53–66.

North Korea's motives for developing nuclear weapons are twofold. First, to use the nuclear option as a diplomatic card to exact maximum concessions from Japan and the US. Second, as a counterweight to the growing capabilities of South Korea's conventional forces.[4] Pyongyang signed the Nuclear Non-Proliferation Treaty (NPT) in 1985, but has since delayed implementation of the mandated IAEA Safeguard Agreements.

A 30-megawatt nuclear reactor now in operation in Yongbyon could produce enough plutonium annually to produce one or two bombs.[5] The construction of a nuclear fuel reprocessing plant at Yongbyon has also been a source of major concern. Such a facility is necessary to extract the plutonium from the spent reactor fuel.[6] In addition, the North has a deception plan for hiding nuclear capabilities according to a testimony made by CIA Director, Robert M. Gates, in February 1992,[7] while according to a Russian report (*Argumenty i Fackty*), the former KGB discovered in 1990 that North Korea had made nuclear detonators at a research centre at Yongbyon.[8]

While suspicion remains regarding North Korea's nuclear ambitions, the US and South Korea have met almost all the North's demands regarding the nuclear issue. On 27 September 1991, President George Bush announced that the US would withdraw all tactical nuclear weapons (which would include those in South Korea) from overseas. On 8 November 1991, President Roh Tae-woo announced that South Korea would not 'manufacture, possess, store, deploy or use nuclear weapons'; in so doing, he denied South Korea the option to create uranium enrichment and/or reprocessing facilities. On 11 December, Seoul and Washington announced that North Korea could inspect US bases in South Korea to verify the absence of nuclear weapons. On 18 December, Roh made a public statement that there were no nuclear weapons anywhere in the South. President Bush confirmed this statement when he visited Seoul in January 1992. Washington has also made clear its commitment not to use nuclear weapons against a non-nuclear state that has signed the NPT, except in the case of an armed attack on the US or its allies by such a state associated with a nuclear weapon state. US Undersecretary of State Arnold Kanter met with Kim Yong-sun, Director of the International Department of the North Korean Labor Party on 22 January 1992 in New York to convey directly Washington's stance to Pyongyang.

Moreover, by signing the Denuclearisation Accord in December 1991, both Pyongyang and Seoul promised not to 'test, produce, receive, possess, store, deploy or use nuclear weapons', and not to 'possess

---

4　Andrew Mack, 'North Korea and the Bomb', *Foreign Policy*, no. 83, Summer 1991, pp. 90–1.

5　Also under construction is a much larger reactor which would be capable of producing far more plutonium.

6　The reprocessing plant building is now subject to IAEA scrutiny.

7　*Korea Herald*, 27 February 1992.

8　ibid., 17 March 1992.

facilities for nuclear reprocessing and uranium enrichment'. To enforce this agreement, they also promised to 'conduct inspections of the objects selected by the other side and agreed upon between the two sides, in accordance with procedures and methods to be determined by the North–South Joint Nuclear Control Commission'. The South called upon the North to accept a trial inspection of facilities in Yongbyon and Kunsan, or a mutual inspection of facilities demanded by either side within the shortest possible period. On 8 January 1992, Pyongyang indicated its willingness to accept an IAEA inspection. Seoul responded by announcing that it would suspend the 'Team Spirit' exercise for 1992.

Pyongyang was thus deprived of any rationale for continuing to refuse to sign a Safeguards Agreement with the IAEA and to agree to mutual inspections with Seoul. In his 1992 New Year Message, Kim Il Sung said that North Korea had neither the intention nor capabilities for developing nuclear weapons and that the North was willing to accept nuclear inspections if fair conditions were guaranteed.[9]

Nevertheless Pyongyang continued to stall on accepting international inspections of its nuclear facilities,[10] and there is still no agreement between North and South on mutual inspections. During seven sessions of negotiations on establishing the Joint Nuclear Control Commission in February–March 1992 the North refused to set a timetable for either a trial or mutual inspection with Seoul; instead, it sought to negotiate a separate agreement on implementing the denuclearisation accord and on securing an international guarantee from the US and other powers for it. Finally, on 14 March the two sides agreed that:

> ...the North and the South will make joint efforts to adopt the documents that are necessary in verifying the denuclearisation of the Korean peninsula within two months after the North–South Joint Nuclear Control Commission holds its inaugural meeting, with the understanding that inspections actually begin to take place within 20 days thereafter.[11]

There is no doubt that Pyongyang has resisted accepting an inspection regime which is broad in scope, thorough and intrusive. This may be because it is trying to gain time to create a nuclear weapons development capability, or to exact maximum concessions from Tokyo and Washington in diplomatic negotiations, or to remove illegal nuclear facilities or materials from the designated nuclear sites prior to the IAEA inspections as Ronald Lehman, Director of the US Arms Control and Disarmament Agency suggested recently.[12] The worst possible scenario is

---

9   *Rodong Shinmun*, 1 January 1992.
10 The UN carried out routine inspections throughout 1992 but, as noted in the introduction, by 1993 the inspection regime had stalled completely.
11 *Korea Herald*, 15 March 1992. In October 1993 there had still been no agreement reached on mutual inspections. (Ed.).
12 ibid., 13 March 1992.

that the North has decided to develop nuclear weapons as a means of ensuring the survival of the Northern state no matter what happens.

The best way to prevent North Korea from developing nuclear weapons is to synchronise action at both the global and regional level. Japan has already made it clear that it will not normalise relations with North Korea unless Pyongyang subjects itself to unconditional international inspections. Russian Foreign Minister, Andrey Kozyrev has indicated Moscow's objections to North Korean nuclear ambitions and pledged himself to work closely with Seoul toward the goal of nonproliferation on the peninsula.[13] Now that China and France have joined the NPT regime, all the permanent members of the UN Security Council are in a better position to institute a process which will bring about compulsory inspections of suspect nuclear facilities in the North. If Pyongyang wishes to avoid international sanctions, it must subject its nuclear facilities to inspection by Seoul as early as possible and dismantle any nuclear weapons facilities it may have.

Similar efforts must be made to control long-range ballistic missiles and chemical weapons. North Korea is believed to be exporting SCUD missiles with a range of over 600 kilometres to Syria and Iran. It has helped Libya, Syria and Egypt build plants to produce their own SCUD ballistic missiles. Former US Assistant Secretary of State, Richard Clarke, has revealed that in March 1992, North Korea was developing a new 1000 kilometre-range missile which can threaten South Korea and Japan.[14] North Korea should be persuaded to join the Missile Technology Control Regime along with China.

North Korea is also suspected of having accumulated a large number of chemical weapons. Since DPRK Prime Minister Yon Hyungmuk specifically referred to the necessity to ban chemical weapons in his speech to the UN on 2 October 1991, it should be possible for North Korea both to join the Chemical Weapons Convention and to accept an international inspection to verify its compliance with the regime.

Vigorous economic sanctions and other measures of coercive diplomacy must be applied to keep North Korea from developing weapons of mass destruction. When Pyongyang is prepared to accept inspection regimes to verify its compliance with the various non-proliferation agreements, South Korea, Japan, the US and other concerned countries may then provide the North with the economic and diplomatic assistance necessary for its survival. The North's attitude on the nuclear issue will be a litmus test for determining whether or not it is serious about implementing the Basic Agreement and undertaking serious conventional arms control negotiation with the South.

---

13 ibid., 19 March 1992.
14 ibid., 15 March 1992.

Conventional CBMs and arms control as a bilateral process

The creation of confidence-building measures (CBMs) and controls on conventional weapons on the peninsula requires a bilateral negotiation process between North and South Korea. The North's force posture *vis-à-vis* the South has traditionally been with large numbers of weapons and military personnel forward-deployed along the DMZ. The South has maintained a more defensive posture with smaller numbers of weapons and troops than its rival. As Table 8.1 shows, there exist many asymmetries between the two sides which can only be remedied by direct negotiation.

Table 8.1 Military forces of South and North Korea as of 1991

Forces	South	North
Army	540 000	868 000
Navy	60 000	45 000
	including marines	excluding marines
Air Force	55 000	82 000
	including anti-artillery units	
Total	655 000	995 000
Tanks	1 550	3 600
Armoured personnel carriers	1 600	2 500
Artillery	4 300	9 500
Surface combatants	170	436
Submarines	-	24
Support ships	50	250
Tactical fighters	520	850
Support aircraft	190	480
Helicopters	580	290

Source: The ROK Ministry of Defense, *Defense White Paper 1991–1992*, Seoul, 1992.

Both North and South Korea recognise the need for confidence-building and arms control agreements but their interpretations of what this means differ considerably.[15] The North has sought a non-aggression declaration with the South, while also seeking to sign a peace agreement

---

[15]   Byung-joon Ahn, 'Arms Control on the Korean Peninsula: Its Prospects and International Context', in *Security and Economics in the Asia–Pacific Region*, eds Gerrit W. Gong and Richard L. Grant, The Center for Strategic and International Studies, Washington, DC, 1991, pp. 96–108.

with the US. The South has sought to negotiate a Basic Agreement directly with the North and a number of practical transparency and constraint measures on military operations and forces.

CBMs vs a non-aggression declaration

As long as North Korea was seeking to sever the security ties between South Korea and the US, the South was bound to doubt the seriousness of the North's commitment to reducing tension on the peninsula. For this reason the South has consistently sought to institute a range of practical confidence-building measures which went well beyond the mere verbal declaration of a commitment to non-aggression which the North had consistently advocated.

The Basic Agreement between North and South embraces both positions. It contains such 'non-aggression' provisions as a mutual commitment to renounce the use of force and to resolve disputes through peaceful negotiation. At the same time, Article 12 provides for CBMs by stating that the North–South Joint Military Commission, to be established three months after 19 February 1992, will discuss and carry out steps to build military confidence, including the mutual notification and control of major movements of military units and major military exercises, the peaceful use of the DMZ, and the exchange of military personnel and information. There is also a commitment to the phased reductions in armaments, including the elimination of weapons of mass destruction, and to the verification of such reductions. These latter items were included largely as a consequence of pressure from the South.

When the first military subcommittee met at Panmunjom on 13 March 1992, the two diverging approaches surfaced again. The South proposed that the subcommittee first discuss the matter of establishing the joint military committee and military 'hotlines'; the North proposed negotiating a comprehensive agreement calling for the cessation of the South Korea–US military alliance and of air and sea surveillance of Korean territory by foreign forces.

The military commission confronts a daunting task in seeking to find a satisfactory way of bridging the South's interest in instituting effective CBMs, and the North's efforts to use the non-aggression rationale as a means of weakening the South Korean–US security relationship.

Transparency and constraints

CBMs and force reductions cannot be achieved without each side having accurate information about the force levels and military deployments of the other. This is the most important lesson to emerge from the European experience.[16] But while North Korea's arms control initiatives have

---

16 Jonathan Dean, 'Conventional Arms Reduction in Europe: Past, Present and Future', in *Arms Control on the Korean Peninsula, What Lessons Can We*

included proposals for force level constraints and reductions, so-called 'transparency' measures, the North has shown little enthusiasm for the verification of agreements—including on-site inspection.[17] In fact, the document presented by DPRK Prime Minister Yon in October 1991, revealed few concrete operational arms control steps.[18] Pyongyang's attitude to arms control since the Basic Agreement went into effect have not significantly changed.

It has been South Korea's contention that military transparency measures must precede actual military constraints and arms reduction in the Korean context. And unless there is agreement on a data base of the military forces on both sides, there can be no progress in negotiation on force level reductions. This is why Seoul has consistently sought exchanges of military personnel and data, establishment of 'hotlines', and implementation of on-site inspection as priority items to accomplish the confidence-building provided for in the Basic Agreement.

It is true, however, that the two sides do share several proposals in common. These include the creation of a 'hotline' between military commands, a joint commission to transform the DMZ into a genuinely demilitarised zone, and limits on exercises covering certain military units. Agreement on these measures could easily be reached by the Joint Military Commission.

Disengagement of forward deployment

In order to eliminate military activities that appear threatening to either side, disengagement of forces deployed forward along the DMZ is necessary. But disengagement negotiations must accord special consideration to the fact that Seoul is so close to the DMZ—no further than 30 miles—equivalent to the distance between Dulles Airport and Washington, DC. The North has been silent on this crucial issue.

Because over 60 per cent of the North's forces are deployed near, and in, the DMZ, the warning time for impending attack is less than 24 hours. Until the North's forces are thinned out and pulled back from the front line, it will be vital for the South to have access to accurate surveillance information about the North's deployments. The South currently has to rely on American capabilities for this intelligence. The thinning away of forces from both ends of the DMZ is also necessary to avoid the outbreak of inadvertent military incidents which could lead to full scale confrontation.

Learn From European Experiences?, Institute of Foreign Policy and National Security, Seoul, 1990, pp. 23–38.

17   Byung-joon Ahn, 'North Korea's Arms Control Proposals: Approaches and Problems', in _Arms Control on the Korean Peninsula, What Lessons Can We Learn From European Experiences?_, Institute of Foreign Policy and National Security, Seoul, 1990, pp. 129–40.

18   _Korea Herald_, 24 October 1991.

Reduction of offensive weapons and forces

In force level reductions, curtailing numbers of offensive weapons systems is more important than reducing the number of troops. Yet, it is the latter which the North has stressed again and again; the South by contrast, has urged the reduction of forward-deployed offensive weapons.

The purpose of force level reductions should be to create balance and stability in the North–South military relationship rather than to pursue rigid symmetry in quantitative terms.

Particularly threatening to the South are the North's forward-deployed units of mechanised artillery, and special commando forces. The North's strength in these areas is double that of the South as indicated in Table 8.1. In addition, the growing number of SCUD ballistic missiles poses an acute threat to such metropolitan areas as Seoul, Kwangju, Taegu and Pusan. On the other hand, the North may well fear the better quality of the South's jet fighters and destroyers.

Without reductions in these highly mobile and threatening weapons, mere reduction in the number of foot soldiers does not guarantee either balance or stability in force structure. The North's proposals for cutting troop levels from around one million to less than 100 000 within a period of three or four years is highly unrealistic.

If the North and the South proceed with these structural steps there may come a time when US forces become less important. Since 1987, Pyongyang has been advocating a phased withdrawal of US forces. In fact, Washington *has* been reducing its presence, linking the level of its reductions to the growing military capabilities of South Korea and to the progress of the North–South Korean dialogues. This process has been ongoing since the announcement of the East Asian Strategic Initiative in April 1990. Seven thousand troops were withdrawn at the end of 1992, leaving only thirty-seven thousand. A second phase of reductions of US troops was postponed at the November 1991 23rd Security Consultative Meeting between the then Defense Minister, Lee Jong-koo, and the then US Defense Secretary, Dick Cheney, in Seoul pending a satisfactory resolution of the dispute with North Korea on the nuclear issue.

Why Pyongyang should continue to call for American withdrawal is not clear. Since it now lacks a credible military alliance with either Russia or China, there should be less reason for Pyongyang to seek an abrupt withdrawal of American forces. These forces serve not only as a deterrent to a possible North Korean aggression, but also to deter South Korean retaliation to North Korean provocations. Only the US can be an 'honest broker' in the Korean peninsula as well as in the Northeast Asian region as a whole. As President Bush told the National Assembly in Seoul in January 1992, the American people share the goal of peaceful unification on terms acceptable to the Korean people.[19] Contrary to Pyongyang's claim, a US military presence is not an obstacle to unifica-

---

[19]   ibid., 7 January 1992.

tion but a stabilising force—a fact which Japan, China, and even Russia, appreciate these days.

Political–economic linkage in arms control

A prudent way of ensuring peace and development in Korea is to foster a coherent linkage between political reconciliation and arms control on the one hand, and economic cooperation on the other. Indeed, economic cooperation must be regarded as part of the confidence-building process. As a consequence of Pyongyang's garrison state mentality, it is spending about 20 per cent of its GNP on defence. This has exacerbated the economic crisis which now includes energy and food shortages. According to a recent report, 'the authorities have responded to the food short-age with a campaign urging people to eat just two meals a day'.[20]

The more the North is concerned about the state of its economy the greater its incentive to cut military spending. Thus offers of economic assistance from Japan, South Korea and the US can usefully be linked to progress in negotiations for CBMs and arms control.

North Korea has revealed an unusual degree of interest in the Tumen River development project over the past year. At a United Nations Development Program (UNDP) sponsored meeting on this project in Pyongyang in October 1991, for example, North Korean officials told their South Korean counterparts that South Korea could make direct investments in this project via the UNDP. Pyongyang has also announced that Najin and Sonbung, two northeastern ports, would be made 'special economic zones'. The volume of indirect trade between North and South Korea in 1991 will be over $180 million and will greatly favour the North. At the first North–South subcommittee meeting for exchange and cooperation, convened on 18 March 1992, the North displayed an unusual enthusiasm for establishing joint committees for economic and social exchange—in stark contrast to its negative stance at the political and military subcommittees.

To help North Korea choose the economic imperatives over the security imperatives, serious consideration must be given to making external economic assistance to the North contingent on progress in North–South negotiations on the key security issues. Japan is not likely to agree to provide compensation to North Korea for past Japanese actions unless the North gives credible assurances that it has abandoned its nuclear ambitions. China reportedly did not pledge any economic aid to Kim Il Sung when he visited Beijing in October 1991. Put simply, unless North Korea makes significant concessions in the negotiations on political and military CBMs and arms control, it will be difficult for South Korea to make concessions in the realm of economic exchange and cooperation. The flexible use of economic incentives—and disincentives—may help the reform-minded technocrats in the economic and foreign

---

20 *New York Times*, 18 February 1992.

ministries in Pyongyang gain the upper hand over the old thinkers in Kim Il Sung's party and military organisation.

Arms in themselves are not sources of insecurity. North and South Korea arm themselves because they feel insecure in a context of deep hostility and distrust. In the contemporary interdependent world, building a community of common economic interests is as important as, and sometimes more important than, promoting military confidence. More than in any other field South Korea has a vital role to play here. It is in Seoul's interest that economic imperatives prevail over the security imperatives in North Korea. That interest may best be advanced by the South working closely with other East Asian and Pacific countries, including such middle-ranking powers as Australia and Canada. China, in particular, as South Korea's fourth largest trading partner with $6 billion of trade in 1991, is in an excellent position to use its influence in urging North Korea to end its nuclear weapons program. Multinational coordination of political, economic and military pressure will be necessary should North Korea continue to refuse to dismantle its nuclear weapons facilities.

Prospects: political reconciliation, nuclear non-proliferation, bilateral negotiation, and international guarantees

The most realistic prospect for arms control in Korea is a gradual process of political reconciliation, nuclear non-proliferation, and bilateral negotiation on conventional forces reductions, all with international guarantees. We cannot expect that any rapid breakthrough will occur in this process unless the North Korean political system undergoes a systemic transformation as has happened in other socialist countries. Short of this, progress will be made in slow and incremental steps. But once favourable political conditions emerge, progress can be advanced by unilateral action from both sides, and by other concerned parties.

In conclusion, several points need making. First, political reconciliation is the key to arms control progress in Korea. Real progress will come when North and South Korea are building political confidence to the extent that they can launch institutional arrangements for reunification on a continuous basis. Then, and only then, will they be able to both uphold their respective positions and probe each other's interests in a spirit of 'common security' and economic cooperation.

But this state of North–South relations will not come, to repeat an earlier point, unless some compatibility of values between the two sides emerges. With the adoption of the Basic Agreement, the two sides have begun to explore some of the common interests necessary for peaceful coexistence and mutual benefits. But progress has been minimal thus far.

Second, nuclear non-proliferation is of concern not merely to the two Koreas but also to the surrounding powers and the international community. In the wake of the end of the Cold War and the Gulf War there is emerging a consensus in favour of preventing states like Iraq and North Korea from acquiring nuclear weapons and ballistic missiles. As a consequence, the task of nuclear non-proliferation has become a multilateral and indeed global endeavour. Achieving this goal will be facilitated if the permanent members of the UN Security Council agree to strengthen multilateral regimes designed to control weapons of mass destruction with enforceable sanctions, while at the same time using their influence to persuade both North and South Korea to intensify their own efforts to denuclearise the peninsula.

It is inconceivable that North Korea will be able to continue to develop nuclear weapons in the face of objections by such powers as Japan, China, Russia and the US.

Third, bilateral negotiations are necessary for North and South Korea to make progress in confidence-building measures and in the control of conventional forces. The European experience indicates that 'transparency' is a necessary first step in building confidence and encouraging arms control negotiations. The European experience is particularly relevant for Korea. The phased withdrawal of US troops is making such bilateral arms control negotiations inevitable.

Finally, such negotiations need international support and any resulting agreements should be guaranteed by the concerned powers and the UN. But with the exception of the nuclear issue, bilateral negotiations must yield results before any international guarantees can be implemented. As for the so-called 'two plus four' formula, only after the two Koreas reach agreement on confidence-building and arms control negotiations can the four powers, i.e., the US, China, Russia and Japan, provide their support and guarantees. Until then, they must do whatever they can to persuade North Korea to engage in productive confidence-building and arms control negotiations with South Korea.

North Korea contends that the UN Command must be disbanded. But this can be done only when North and South Korea agree to terminate the armistice and to institute a permanent peace system between themselves as they pledged to do in the Basic Agreement. Other powers can endorse whatever accords the Koreas reach and guarantee them internationally—either by themselves or via the UN.

9 The Political Economy of Security on the Korean Peninsula in the Regional Context

CHUNG-IN MOON

Over the past several years, East Asia's political landscape has undergone profound transformations. These include the demise of the Soviet Union and its replacement by the Commonwealth of Independent States (CIS); the increasingly problematical value of America's power and presence in the region; and the realignment of Japan's regional position as a consequence of a more assertive projection of Japanese influence. China's regional posture, meanwhile, has become increasingly passive and introverted. The bipolar logic that has governed the regional politics since the late 1940s is on the wane and threat perceptions among regional actors are being diluted. This new regional configuration makes it harder for Asia–Pacific states to contrive threats and other excuses for hostility, and although limited, coexistence and cooperation have emerged as the new *modus vivendi* of regional interactions. This changing regional context has bred fresh optimism about the future of inter-Korean relations and Korean security. The optimism is, however, derived from a rather simplified reasoning, namely that the termination of the Cold War could lead to the end of national division and the Korean conflict.[1]

---

[1] Ecological or balance of power determinism has been the dominant paradigm of security studies in South Korea. Given the origin of national division and the evolving pattern of Korean conflict, superpowers and regional actors have played important roles in shaping Korean security, but they did not alone cause the division of the peninsula. For an overview of this debate, see Chung-in Moon, 'Assessment of researches on the Korean Conflict: An Aggregate Analysis', in *New Developments of Theories of North–South Korean Unification*, ed. Sung Chull Yang, Kyungnam University Press, Seoul, 1988 (in Korean).

In the shadow of this optimism, uncertainties and anxieties are looming. The regional situation does not automatically guarantee peace, security and unification on the Korean peninsula. But it does impose a set of opportunities—and constraints—which ruling elites must perceive, process and translate into policy. Leadership perception, decision rules, and strategic choices are in turn shaped by the political calculus of regime survival. Regime interests serve as a critical intervening variable in the causal nexus between the regional security environment and policy outcomes. As regime interests change, the perceptions and assessments of the regional security environment, as well as the choice of national security policy, will also change. Democratic transition in the South, and the increasingly visible erosion of political legitimacy in the North (taking place amidst economic stagnation), make the dynamic of regime interests all the more important in understanding the security dimension on the Korean peninsula. The interaction of regime interests with national security interests can distort the regional order and precipitate new insecurities.

Against this backdrop, this chapter attempts to explore how the politics of regime survival in the two Koreas affects conceptions of national security and the formation of regional policies. It is organised into five sections. The first section examines the changing nature of security conceptions in both Koreas focusing especially on linkages between national security and regime interests. The second and third sections trace how changing security conceptions have influenced and altered regional policy. The fourth delineates three alternative scenarios which explore the interplay of the two Koreas' regional policies and the regional reactions to these policies and the impact of both on Korean security. Finally, the concluding section presents a brief discussion of the political economic implications of Korean security in a regional context.

Beneath national security: regime interests and the political economy of security

National security has been one of the most debated topics in the study of international politics since World War II. The 'realist' paradigm has prevailed in this debate. National security has been conceptualised primarily in terms of physical protection from external military threats and the preservation of the political and territorial integrity of the state concerned. In the 'realist' tradition, military force and conventional diplomacy are the primary instruments for ensuring national security. In the anarchic 'realist' model, military self-help and alliance politics are indispensable. In the real world, however, the concept of national security is rather elusive, and the military dimensions of security are not always the most salient. As Robert Osgood puts it, 'national security, like danger, is an uncertain quality; it is relative, not absolute; it is largely subjective and takes countless forms'.[2] Likewise, the core values which underpin national security concerns are not fixed but vary across nations and over time.

At times of acute economic depression or external economic turbulence, the security hierarchy ranking may shift with economic values becoming more salient than military–strategic ones. Severe ecological crises (e.g., arising from shortages of food, energy and water etc.), which threaten the survival of national populations may force political elites to redefine and redirect national security priorities. In countries where ethnic fragmentation and secessionist movements endanger the social and political fabric, communal harmony and integration may become the principal value of national security policy.[3]

The conception of national security is also context-bound. The military–strategic dimensions of security are important, but do not always dictate the content of national security policy. The economic, ecological and communal dimensions of security may be more salient.

What, then, accounts for variations in the security value hierarchy? Objective threat environments count, of course, but they are simply necessary conditions or input variables. The perceptions of political leaders which filter the external threats, decision structures and rules that formulate security policies are also important. But these perceptions and decision rules are not always guided by *national* interests. On the contrary, the *regime* interests of leaders more often serve as the guiding principle of national security conduct—particularly in those developing countries where arbitrary, authoritarian rule is pervasive. In these cases, military security is valued if and when it enhances or complements regime survival interests. In many cases the regime's emphasis on military security is intended not only to cope with external threats, but also to consolidate political power, to exclude opposition forces, and to justify authoritarian rule. To this end, rulers like Iraq's Sadam Hussein and Argentina's Galtieri have either contrived or provoked external threats. However, if the pursuit of military security threatens regime security, national leaders may emphasise the non-military dimensions of national security. National security and regime security are closely related.[4] North and South Korea do not seem to be exceptions to this general trend.

---

[2] Robert Osgood, *Ideals and Self-Interest in America's Foreign Relations*, University of Chicago Press, Chicago, 1953, p. 443.

[3] For an overview of divergent interpretations of national security in the Third World, see *National Security in the Third World*, eds Edward Azar and Chung-in Moon, Edward Elgar, Hants, England, 1988; 'Third World National Security: Toward New Conceptual Frameworks', *International Interactions*, vol. 11, no. 2, 1984, pp. 103–35.

[4] See Edward Azar and Chung-in Moon, 'Legitimacy, Integration and Policy Capacity: The "Software" Side of Third World National Security', in *National Security*, eds Azar and Moon, pp. 77–101; Mohamed Ayoob, 'The

South Korea has been facing an unambiguously hostile enemy, North Korea, since the Korean nation was divided in 1945. Threats from the North have been real, and military confrontation with the North has been acute and protracted. In coping with these threats South Korea has relied heavily on American military protection. The presence of American troops in, and a firm security commitment to, South Korea have served as an effective deterrent to North Korean military aggression. But despite signs of heightened military hostility from the North, the US security commitment gradually, but visibly, eroded in the early 1970s, while efforts to settle the Korean problem through peaceful means remained stagnant. President Park Chung-Hee responded to this changing security environment by taking two policy actions: first, the maximisation of South Korea's endogenous military capabilities and, second, the re-organisation of political and ideological systems to cope with North Korean threats.[5]

In order to maximise military capabilities, Park opted for force modernisation and the development of military–industrial capabilities sufficient to keep up in the arms race with the North. The shift in emphasis from security dependence on the US to military self-help required heavy investment in the defence sector. In order to finance force modernisation, defence spending, which averaged less than 30 per cent of government expenditure during the 1962–1975 period, was increased to 37 per cent in 1978, accounting for almost 6 per cent of gross national product. At the same time, a defence tax system was introduced. Meanwhile, the Park regime pursued an ambitious heavy industrial drive which incorporated backward and forward linkages with the defence industry. Between 1975 and 1979, during which period defence industrialisation was actively pursued, more than 75 per cent of available investment funds was allocated to the heavy industrial sectors which had linkages to the military industrial sector.[6] Realigning macroeconomic and industrial policies to enhance conventional military capability has, however, had serious negative economic consequences. In addition to the inflation which was blamed for the economic downturn in the late 1970s and early 1980s, this realignment of macroeconomic and industrial policy has deepened sec-

---

Security Problematic of the Third World', *World Politics*, no. 43, January 1991, pp. 257–83.

5 For an overview of South Korea's security situation during this period, see *The Politics of the Korean Peninsula*, eds Young C. Kim and Abraham M. Hallpern, Praeger, New York, 1977; Chae-jin Lee and Hideo Sato, *US Policy Towards Japan and Korea*, Praeger, New York, 1982. For Seoul's policy reactions, see Young-sun Ha, 'South Korea', in *Arms Production in Developing Countries*, ed. James E. Katz, Lexington Books, Lexington, MA, 1984.

6 Chung-in Moon, 'South Korea: Between Security and Vulnerability', in *The Implications of Third World Defense Industrialization*, ed. James E. Katz, Lexington Books, Lexington, MA, 1986, pp. 247–51.

toral imbalances and economic concentration, and made substitution effects between guns and butter more pronounced.[7]

Radical political restructuring was also undertaken in tandem with economic and military restructuring. In the name of national security, Park dissolved the Third Republic, and instituted the Yushin regime, the pinnacle of a hard and unashamed authoritarianism. Stressing the supremacy of national security and a doctrine of 'total defence' as an official guiding ideology for the Yushin regime, Park reorganised, mobilised and controlled social forces in order to enhance both national and regime security. Potential opposition forces such as organised labour were excluded and repressed, while business organisations were co-opted as agents of economic growth and defence industrialisation. The needs of national security thus justified political deformity and blocked progress towards democracy.[8] Little changed under the Chun regime. Common to both Park and Chun regimes was the fact that national security concerns were both authentic and were used for regime security ends. They were authentic in the sense that threats from the North were real, and national consensus on the nature of the threats existed. But both rulers also manipulated security concerns to enhance power consolidation and regime survival.

Since the late 1980s, however, the confluence of two trends has altered the consensus on national security in South Korea. First, the ebbing of the Cold War was as visible on the Korean peninsula as anywhere else, improving prospects for the peaceful resolution of the Korean conflict. Within the South, dissension over excessive arms expenditure began to grow and there were calls for more assertive policy initiatives on arms control, arms reduction, and peaceful national unification. Second, the democratic transition in the South in 1987 has created a new social and political milieu that allowed people to challenge the rigid national security doctrine that was previously dominant. The more open political systems permitted the emergence of a broad range of interest groups. These groups' demands included equality, welfare and justice. They exerted formidable political pressure on the regime through a variety of means, ranging from the ballot box to street protests. Today, national security can no longer serve as *deus ex machina*. People's expectations are high, and failure to address demands for increased welfare and equality could deal a significant blow to the regime's legitimacy and political stability.

---

[7] Chung-in Moon and Intaek Hyun, 'Muddling Through Security, Growth and Welfare: The Political Economy of Defense Spending in South Korea', in *Security, Growth and Welfare*, eds Steve Chan and Cal Clark, Unwin and Hyman, New York, forthcoming.

[8] On links between national security, the Yushin regime and political opposition, refer to Hak Kyu Sohn, *Authoritarianism and Opposition in South Korea*, Routledge, London, 1989.

President Roh responded speedily and flexibly to these new demands by realigning national security policies to suit the new domestic and international environments. On the domestic front, sweeping reforms were introduced. The anti-communist and national security laws were amended. Roh pledged to reduce defence spending and to cut government subsidies to the defence industrial sector, and to diminish the authoritarian legacies of the past which were closely associated with the rigid national security doctrine. Equality, welfare and justice were emphasised over growth and national security.

Along with domestic reforms, Roh undertook new foreign policy initiatives. In its 7 July 1988 declaration, the Roh regime implied that hostile relations with the North could be terminated, and promised to engage in a more constructive dialogue with Pyongyang. In a similar vein, Seoul's regional policy has been radically altered. Departing from the Cold War bloc logic, a more assertive 'Nordpolitik' policy was pursued in order to improve diplomatic and economic ties with the communist states. Military security no longer remains as an unassailable national priority. Economic security and domestic tranquillity have emerged as central elements in a new national security agenda. Both the latter affect the political legitimacy of the regime in the south and its prospects for survival during a period of precarious democratic transition.

North Korea is in a similar situation. Having suffered greatly in the Korean War, North Korean political leaders have been obsessed with military security. Defending the nations political and territorial integrity from the military threat posed by the US imperial power and its surrogate government in the South, and liberating the southern part of the fatherland from American imperial occupation, have constituted two cardinal objectives of the North's national security policy. These goals also have important domestic political implications because the political legitimacy of Kim Il Sung has emanated from his consistent pledge to defend and liberate the fatherland from American imperialism.

Confronting US military power required the North to engage in a massive military build-up. For this purpose, Kim Il Sung adopted and vigorously pursued the doctrine of the 'four military lines' in the 1960s: arming the entire people, fortifying the entire national territory, giving all military personnel elite status, and modernising the entire military sector.[9] To ensure speedy implementation of this security doctrine, North Korea has allocated almost 30 per cent of government expenditure to the

9   National Unification Board, *Outline of North Korea*, National Unification Board, Seoul, 1980, pp. 208–11 (in Korean). For a more recent comprehensive overview see Jae-kyu Park ed., *Military Policy of North Korea*, Kyung-nam University Press, Seoul, 1983; Taek-young Hahm, 'Juche Ideology and North Korea's Defense Policy', in *Juche Thoughts—the Political Ideology of North Korea*, Jae-in Yang et al., Jyungam University Press, Seoul, 1990, pp. 155–86 (in Korean.)

defence sector, equal to 20–25 per cent of the DPRK's Gross National Product (GNP), for the past three decades. As with South Korea, economic development strategy was designed to promote military self-help through defence industrialisation, favouring the heavy industrial sector over the light consumer industrial sectors. Preparing for military contingencies, North Korea also accumulated immense stocks of wartime material at the expense of the economic welfare of its citizens. North Korea has long been organised and mobilised in preparation for war and has become a regimented garrison state unprecedented in modern history. The sacrifice of citizens has been both justified and tolerated in the name of national security.

The North's preoccupation with military security and the arms race with the South have had severe negative consequences. Arms racing with South Korea drained fiscal resources, while the drive to build heavy industry distorted the economic structure and retarded industrial productivity. Most accounts suggest that the North Korean economy is on the brink of collapse today. After a period of rapid economic growth in the 1950s and 1960s, economic problems began to loom in the late 1970s. In 1978, North Korea's economic growth rate was still 5.8 per cent but it declined sharply during the 1980s. In 1990, the North Korean economy experienced negative economic growth (minus 3.7 per cent) for the first time. Shortages of consumer goods have worsened. The structural rigidities of the North Korean economy, which resulted both from a planned, self-reliant socialist economy and on heavy emphasis on the heavy industry with linkages to the defence industry, severely undermined the agricultural and light industrial sectors, impeding the stable supply of foodstuffs and consumer goods. In addition, chronic shortages of raw materials, capital and intermediate goods, and electricity, have precipitated a sharp drop in industrial productivity. Mounting foreign debts ($US7.86 billion as of 1990), which far exceed exports ($US2 billion as of 1990), have further aggravated economic hardship in North Korea.[10]

The North's obsession with maximising military power has resulted in economic exhaustion which has proven to be dysfunctional for national security interests, and has gradually eroded the legitimacy of the Kim Il Sung regime. Social instability emerging from growing economic hardship could pose a major barrier to the successful political succession of Kim Il Sung by his son, Kim Jong Il. Although it is said to be both clandestine and limited, popular questioning of the legitimacy of Kim Jong Il, if not Kim Il Sung, *is* taking place. The most serious difficulties for Kim Jong Il arise from failures in the economic arena. There is a widespread consensus among North Koreans that the current economic crisis is caused, at least in part, by Kim Jong Il's economic mismanagement—

---

[10] Research Institute for National Unification (RINU), *The Real Picture of the North Korean Regime and Prospects for Change: Report 91–13*, RINU, Seoul, 1991, pp. 187–245 (in Korean).

including the waste of resources on non-essential projects. Popular dissatisfaction appears to have been accelerating due to increasing exposure of some North Koreans to such external events as the collapse of the Eastern European socialist bloc and the economic success of South Korea.[11]

This does not, however, imply that North Korea will, in the near future, follow the paths of Honnecker's East Germany or Ceausescu's Rumania. Kim Il Sung is still alive and well, and he is neither Ceausescu nor Honnecker. North Korea is neither Rumania nor East Germany. *Juche* is still the dominant ideology, and mass indoctrination is much deeper in North Korea than in Eastern Europe. The North Korean state is much more systematised, disciplined and penetrative, while the unity of purpose among ruling elites is strong. Less than one per cent of the North Korean population has been exposed to the outside world. Given all this, the prospect of mass revolts from below may turn out to be mere wishful thinking. Nevertheless, continued failure to cope with the current economic failures could drastically alter existing domestic political equations by weakening the foundation of Kim's political legitimacy, as well as posing a major stumbling block to smooth political succession.[12]

North Korean rulers are now trapped in a Catch-22 dilemma. Attempting to keep up with the South in the conventional arms race could exhaust the national economy and endanger regime stability, but avoiding arms races through negotiations and curing economic stagnation by gradually opening up the economy could also jeopardise regime security because of potential backlash effects which opening up could generate. It is against this background that North Korea embraced both the nuclear option and embarked on its southward diplomacy. The nuclear option, if successful, could minimise the economic burden of an arms race with the South, while permitting the North to maintain military deterrence against the South. The pursuit of the southward policy is not simply designed to overcome diplomatic isolation, but is a calculated move designed to ease economic hardship via an incremental opening of new channels of economic cooperation with rich capitalist nations. Rulers in the North are walking on a tightrope as they seek to balance the perceived needs of national security and of regime survival.

---

[11] This pessimistic view is well presented in ibid., pp. 396–441.

[12] For a recent discussion of North Korean politics, see Sung Chull Yang, *Thesis on North Korean Politics*, Bakyoungsa, Seoul, 1990, chs. 6–8.

New frontiers and 'Nordpolitik': evolving patterns of South Korea's regional policy

In his inaugural address on 25 February 1988, President Roh Tae-woo outlined the direction of foreign policy under the Sixth Republic as follows:

> We are determined to press forward with our Northern policy designed to broaden the path for international cooperation with those influential countries with which we have no exchanges.[13]

The northern policy ('Nordpolitik') subsequently became a guiding principle for the Roh government's foreign policy. 'Nordpolitik' represented a radical departure from South Korea's traditional emphasis on relations with the US and Japan. The northern policy was designed to create a regional milieu conducive to the peaceful unification of Korea. To this end, the Roh government pursued an assertive diplomatic policy towards the Soviet Union, China and Eastern Europe. The diplomatic normalisation with these countries which Seoul sought, would weaken the military links with the North, and eventually force North Korea to come to the negotiation table.

This exercise in 'Nordpolitik' was not completely novel. There had been previous attempts to alter the regional security environment by improving diplomatic relations with socialist countries. On 23 July 1973, President Park Chung-Hee had indicated a willingness to enhance political ties with socialist bloc countries on the basis of the principle of reciprocity and equality. Park's move, which was triggered by the growing possibility of American disengagement from the South and by the emerging US–Soviet *détente*, was bold and imaginative. However, it was ultimately impeded by the logic of the Cold War which continued to prevail over the East Asian region. Neither Moscow nor Beijing were willing to accommodate Seoul's new initiative. The Chun Doo Hwan regime was more forthcoming in promoting the idea of northern policy than was President Park.[14] Lacking independent domestic sources of legitimacy due to his illicit seizure of political power, Chun exploited diplomacy as an alternative means of enhancing popular support for his regime. Chun's efforts to host the Asian and International Olympics and

---

13 *Korea Herald*, 26 February 1988.

14 The term 'Northern Diplomacy' was coined by Lee Bum-Suk, then Foreign Minister. See Sikryul Yu, 'Seoul Efforts to Create a Favourable Atmosphere for Unification—With a Focus on its Northern Diplomacy', *East Asia Review*, vol. 3, no. 1, Spring 1991, pp. 40–55; Chongwook Chung, 'The Rise and Development of Diplomacy Toward the Communist Bloc: Tasks and Strategy of the Northern Diplomacy', in *The Peace Structure of North and South Korea*, Youngrok Koo et al., Bubmunsa, Seoul, 1990, pp. 231–66 (in Korean).

to organise and host Pacific summit meetings should be understood in these terms. In other words the pursuit of regime interests motivated the northern policy. Chun did not, however, survive in office to enjoy its fruits. Instead it was Roh who exploited Chun's initiatives and who extracted the political dividends.

Several factors induced Roh to accelerate the northern policy, not least of which was the transformation in the global political climate. Gorbachev's *glasnost* and *perestroika*, the subsequent demise of socialist systems in Eastern Europe, and the newly emerging entente between Washington and Moscow all facilitated the policy shift. There were two additional factors. One was the changing domestic political environment. After many years of authoritarian rule which had been justified by appeals to national security, the Korean people had become wary of the old national security rhetoric. The democratic transition in 1987 fuelled popular demands for realigning national security policy and for peaceful unification with the North. Active pursuit of 'Nordpolitik' was a logical response to the changing domestic political climate.

Promoting cooperation through diplomatic normalisation with China and the Soviet Union was also intended to isolate North Korea and to pressure it to take a reconciliatory stance towards the South. Breaking the protracted stalemate with North Korea through 'Nordpolitik' promised a number of benefits—most obviously it could help the process of resolving the Korean conflict. It could also help ease the economic burden of the arms race, enabling scarce resources to be diverted to satisfying soaring welfare demands. Opening diplomatic relations with socialist countries also signalled a reduction in the anti-communist ideological rigidity which had long characterised South Korean national security policy. 'Nordpolitik' functions as a pre-emptive counter-offensive to the increasing visibility and influence of progressive forces which had followed political liberalisation.

Economic considerations were equally important. Since the 1970s, South Korea had emerged as a leader among the Newly Industrialising Countries (NICs). Economic success did, however, generate new problems. While the US and Japan have intensified their anti-protectionist pressures on South Korea, the second generation NICs have begun to threaten the South's position in world export markets. Caught between anti-protectionist pressures from the US and Japan and new NIC competitors, Seoul has been forced to search for new economic niches. Moscow's *glasnost* and Beijing's 'open door' policy offered a timely new economic opportunity—both in terms of markets and access to raw materials.

In pursuing 'Nordpolitik', South Korea pursued a multi-pronged strategy. First, it sought outright cooptation via a promise of official economic assistance to the USSR in the form of a grant of $3 billion in return for diplomatic normalisation. Such economic inducements did not work with China, however, because of Beijing's determinedly pro-North Korean policy.

Second, the South Korean government has utilised private sector corporations as agents for fostering economic ties. The size, diversity, technological competence and assertiveness of South Korea's big firms made them attractive to China and the Soviet Union, both of which had a desperate need for capital, technology and market outlets. This was especially true in China's case. Beijing had attempted to minimise official contacts with Seoul in fear of protests from Pyongyang. In the absence of official contacts, the private sector served as an indispensable link between the two governments. Finally, staging both the Asian and the Olympic Games in Seoul served as a forum for expanding mutual communication and understanding.

The northern policy proved very successful. South Korea established full diplomatic normalisation with the Soviet Union on 30 September 1990. Following two summit meetings between Roh Tae-woo and Gorbachev, Seoul and Moscow cultivated close political ties, close enough to worry both the US and Japan.[15] Since the collapse of the Soviet Union in August 1991, bilateral ties between Seoul and Moscow have become strained. But Seoul is seeking new venues of improving political and diplomatic relations with the CIS in general and Russia in particular. Rapprochement with China has been slower. Nonetheless, Seoul's diplomacy led to South Korea and China setting up trade representative offices in Seoul and Beijing in 1991. In 1992, the two countries formally recognised each other.

One outcome of this general improvement in Seoul's external relations was the joint admission of both Koreas to the United Nations. South Korea had long advocated the joint admission of two Koreas to the UN, but Pyongyang had rejected it, arguing that it was a conspiracy to perpetuate national division. North Korea counted on a Chinese veto, if not a Soviet veto, in the UN Security Council. The North Korean's calculation proved wrong. Reversing its previous stance, China persuaded the North to join the UN along with South Korea. Both Moscow's and Beijing's changed attitudes on this issue signalled the erosion of traditional alliance ties between Pyongyang and Moscow and Pyongyang and Beijing. The North's equidistant diplomacy which had successfully exploited Sino–Soviet rivalry in the past, failed to prevent joint admission. Furthermore, global, regional and domestic transformations meant that Beijing and Moscow reduced their influence over North

---

[15] At the third Gorbachev–Roh summit meeting held in Cheju, Korea, Seoul and Moscow agreed to sign a treaty of friendship and cooperation, a move which raised concern in the US and Japan. See Yu-nam Kim, 'Changes in Soviet–Korean Relations and their Impacts on the Balance of Power System in Northeast Asia', *The Journal of East Asian Affairs*, vol. 6, no. 1 Winter/Spring 1992, pp. 42–6.

Korea. The dissolution of East–West confrontation and the Beijing–Moscow rapprochement diminished the strategic value which Moscow and Beijing gained from their military alliances with the North. At the same time the ripple effects of domestic upheaval and economic crises undermined the willingness of both Russia and China to maintain their patron–client networks with the North. Weakening alliance relationships have in turn pushed North Korea to be more accommodating to Seoul's demands for the resumption of inter-Korean dialogues. All these developments indicate how 'Nordpolitik' has made a positive contribution to peace and security on the Korean peninsula.

Finally, South Korea has also made remarkable progress in the economic arena. Before the Northern policy was introduced, trade relations between Seoul and Moscow had been minimal. But as the political relationship improved, trade volume between the two increased, rising from $160 million in 1987, to $890 million in 1990. It is confidently forecast that bilateral trade will continue to increase.[16] Apart from commodity trade, leading South Korean business conglomerates such as Hyundai, Lucky-Gold Star, Daewoo and Samsung have aggressively undertaken direct investments in the CIS in the areas ranging from the manufacture of consumer electronics to natural resources development. Economic ties with China have also grown impressively. Even before the northern policy became effective, Seoul and Beijing had actively engaged in indirect trade via Hong Kong. In 1987, a year before the full implementation of the northern policy, bilateral trade was $1.68 billion. But after the introduction of the northern policy, the figure increased to $3.14 billion in 1989 and $3.82 billion in 1990, accounting for more than two-thirds of Seoul's trade with all the socialist countries. Direct investment is also on the rise. In 1989 Seoul permitted 51 South Korean firms to invest in China with the investments valued at $US69 million. At present, South Korean investment in China is heavily concentrated in three northeastern provinces, but is likely to be expanded to other provinces too.[17] Uncertainty still exists, but it seems almost certain that economic transactions and cooperation with China and the CIS will continue to expand and deepen in years to come.

All in all, the South's northern policy has brought about positive diplomatic, strategic and economic outcomes. But the most important gain lies in the domestic political realm. Given weak economic performance and the political disarray of President Roh's first two years in office, the northern policy was one of the few means by which Roh could enhance his popularity.

---

[16] ibid., p. 49.

[17] Jae-Young Lee, 'All about the Tumen River Basin Development Plan: the Core of the Northeast Asian Economic Sphere', *Mal Monthly Magazine*, December 1991, p. 82 (in Korean).

Risky Faustian bargain? North Korea's regional policy

Unlike the South, North Korea has not declared any explicit regional foreign policy doctrine.[18] However, despite official statements emphasising continuity with the past, North Korea has also shown signs of fundamental realignment in its regional policy. Underlying the realignment is Pyongyang's southern policy. The North joined the UN along with the South. Moreover, despite the anti-American and anti-Japanese rhetoric which still pervades the North Korean mass media and official statements, Pyongyang has increased its diplomatic overtures toward Tokyo and Washington DC. Its attitude to South Korea has also become more receptive and resilient. This was evident in the signing of the 'Agreement on Reconciliation, Nonaggression and Exchanges and Co-operation' on 13 December 1991 and the subsequent continuation of high level political talks. All of this represents a substantial redirection in North Korea's foreign policy line.

Why the shift? It may in part be construed as a desperate response by the North to deepening diplomatic isolation. Seoul's northern policy has reduced Pyongyang's diplomatic space, while internal collapses and changes in the former Soviet Union have virtually destroyed Pyongyang's most important alliance relationship. *Juche* ideology on its own, without the diplomatic and military patronage and support of Russia, is not enough. China still seems loyal to its old ally, yet the breadth and intensity of interaction between Beijing and Seoul—especially diplomatic recognition—have scared Pyongyang. The fact that North Korea felt it had no choice but to agree to joint admission of the two Koreas to the UN was not just a reversal of traditional DPRK policy, but an indication of the North's relatively weakened international position.

America's victory in the Gulf War also had a chilling impact on Pyongyang. The North can no longer treat the US as a paper tiger. In the post-Cold War world, the US can focus more attention on states like North Korea. Thus North Korea may perceive a clear security interest in seeking rapprochement with the US.[19]

Economic calculations were also a factor in the North's southward policy. North Korea's self-reliant development strategy has proved self-defeating. While chronic shortages of raw materials, energy, capital and

---

18 On southward orientation of North Korea's foreign policy, see Byung-joon Ahn, 'North Korea's Foreign Policy in the Post Cold-War Era', *East Asia Review*, vol. 3, no. 2, Summer 1991, pp. 27–40; Yongsoon Yim, 'North Korea's Efforts to Improve Relations with the US and Japan and their Effects', *East Asia Review*, vol. 3, no. 3, Autumn 1991, pp. 37–51. For a thorough analysis with detailed data of the North Korean policy shift, consult RINU, *The Real Picture of the North Korean Regime*, pp. 246–347.

19 Selected North Korean officials and diplomats revealed such a sentiment in informal talks with the author.

technology have crippled industrial productivity, the failure to supply consumer goods has demoralised the population, breeding the seeds of potential social instability. The North Korean economy has reached a dangerous threshold. Faltering economic performance and the limits of people's tolerance to hardship could have a devastating political outcome. Trade with, and economic assistance from, the Soviet Union and China helped prevent economic decline for many years. Indeed, despite the ideology of *Juche*, North Korea's economic dependence on the Soviet Union and China ran deep. Over one-third of North Korean trade in 1990 was with the Soviet Union ($2.56 billion); China was the second largest trading partner ($482 million).[20] These two states accounted for more than half North Korea's foreign trade. But the recent Russian and Chinese insistence that North Korea pay for its imports in hard currency has had a further devastating impact on the North's economy.

North Korea used to import 700 000–800 000 metric tons of oil from the Soviet Union per year, but in 1992, after Moscow insisted on payment for oil in hard currency, the North's level of oil imports dropped to one-tenth of their volume in 1991.[21] This was not all. On 28 April 1991, Moscow called for the immediate hard currency settlement of all North Korea's outstanding debts to Moscow, which amount to $4.6 billion (2.6 billion rubles).[22] Beijing also requested North Korea to settle all trade transactions in hard currency from 1992. Pyongyang has also realised that the new market-oriented policies being pursued in China and the CIS are inimical to its economic policy of self-reliance and state direction.

It is against this backdrop that North Korea's diplomatic overtures to Japan and the US should be understood. Japan was the most important target for two reasons. First, in addition to anticipated official development assistance, North Korea sought compensation for the hardships and privations imposed by Japan during the colonial period. Pyongyang is demanding almost $10 billion as compensation, while Japan has suggested a figure of $4.5 billion. Whatever compromise is reached between these demands, the hard currency which will eventually be released will be of major importance to the North.[23] Second, the North is interested in greater access to the huge reservoir of wealth in the hands of *Chosoren*, an umbrella organisation of pro-DPRK Korean residents in Japan. *Chosoren*'s official assets are estimated to be 20.3 trillion yen (roughly $150 billion). Total assets held by members of *Chosoren* are estimated to be 28.3 trillion yen ($210 billion). Once diplomatic

---

20 RINU, *The Real Picture of the North Korean Regime*, p. 280.
21 This information was revealed by Kim Jung-woo, Vice Minister of Foreign Trade, in his interview with Japanese journalists visiting Pyongyang. *Hankuk Ilbo*, 25 February 1992.
22 *Korea Herald*, 2 May 1991.
23 RINU, *The Real Picture of the North Korean Regime*, p. 316.

normalisation with Japan is realised, North Korea will have access to a total of $360 billion.[24]

Thus the North's new regional orientation does not derive solely from security and diplomatic interests. Economic factors appear to be even more salient. The economic motivation underpinning the new regional policy is in turn connected with the regime's concern about its own survival. Threats to the Kim regime are less external than internal. Economic hardship and popular demoralisation may create social and political instabilities which are more formidable threats to the regime than war with South Korea and the US. Recognising this, Pyongyang is seeking rapprochement with its sworn enemies. North Korea's political leaders may have reached the conclusion that incremental opening and economic revitalisation achieved through the southward policy is less risk-prone than continued economic closure and stagnation.

The North's southward policy has been pursued by very different instruments from those used by South Korea in its northern policy. Economic backwardness deprived the North of the economic leverage which the South has so extensively exploited in its 'Nordpolitik'. North Korea has, however, used a more shocking and unusual tool of diplomatic suasion: the nuclear card. Despite Pyongyang's persistent denial that it was seeking to acquire nuclear weapons, its reluctance to sign the International Atomic Energy Agency's (IAEA) safeguard agreement, its subsequent refusal to allow IAEA inspectors access to inspect nuclear sites, plus the revelations that it had produced plutonium at its Yongbyon nuclear facility despite previous denials, inevitably raised strong suspicions about its nuclear program.[25] But whether bluffing or not, the 'nuclear card' has turned out to be the most effective instrument of opening new channels of communications with Pyongyang's traditional enemies, upgrading levels of diplomatic contact, especially with the US[26] and ultimately drawing world-wide attention to a new and apparently conciliatory posture.

The North has also effectively exploited past disputes as bargaining chips. Since an initial contact was made on routine diplomatic matters in Beijing on 6 December 1988, North Korea and the US have had repeated bilateral meetings at the counsellor level. A major agenda item has been the return of remains of American soldiers killed during the Korean War. Both countries have agreed to regularise the talks on the return of remains.

---

[24]   ibid., p. 285.

[25]   Andrew Mack, 'North Korea and the Bomb', *Foreign Policy*, no. 83, Summer 1991, pp. 87–94.

[26]   Upgrading the level of US–North Korean contacts was revealed on the occasion of Kim Yong-sun's visit to the United Nations in January 1992. The Deputy Assistant Secretary of State met with Kim, who holds a ministerial post at the Labor Party.

Finally, North Korea has utilised non-governmental international contacts to increase its access to Japan and the US. In the case of Japan, the pro-North Korean *Chosoren* has played a significant role in helping to build bridges between Pyongyang and Tokyo. *Chosoren* is rich in human and organisational, as well as material, resources and has maintained close ties with the Japanese Socialist Party and some segments of the Liberal Democratic Party. Mobilising ethnic ties has proved an effective means of fostering bilateral relations between Japan and the DPRK. North Korea has also cultivated multiple channels of communication with other social groups in Japan. By contrast, the utilisation of transnational networks in the US has been less successful, despite a large pool of Koreans residing in the US. This is due partly to direct and indirect interventions by the US and South Korean governments, which have traditionally been hostile to such links, and partly to the material and organisational weakness of Korean organisations in the US. However, the North Koreans have made careful approaches to Korean–Americans who have separated families in the North. They have also made use of non-governmental organisations such as the Asia Society, the Carnegie Endowment, and various universities in diversifying channels of interaction with the US.[27]

What has the North achieved so far? Compared with the South, its success seems limited. But there have been some significant achievements. Formal and informal channels of communication have opened with the US and are being developed. The nuclear issue has attracted high profile attention in the US. Washington is deeply worried about nuclear proliferation, and the North believes that it may gain important concessions—including normalisation of diplomatic relations and economic assistance—by exploiting Washington's concerns.[28] Washington has already loosened its previous restrictions on North Korean visits to the US.[29] North Korea has made more progress in improving relations with Japan. Since the 28 September 1990 joint communique by the Liberal Democratic Party, the Japanese Socialist Party and the Labor Party of the DPRK,[30] Pyongyang and Tokyo have engaged in a series of rounds of negotiations on diplomatic normalisation. Despite obstacles such as the nuclear issue, disagreements over compensation and over the

---

27 It is not the North Korean government, but non-governmental actors in the US that have taken initiatives in bilateral exchanges.

28 As to this line of reasoning, see William Crowe Jr., and Alan Romberg, 'Rethinking Pacific Security', *Foreign Affairs*, Spring 1991, pp. 132–5.

29 However, the US government is still reluctant to permit full-scale political exchanges.

30 The communique reaffirms Japan's obligation to admit wrongdoings during the colonial period and to apologise and compensate for damages done to North Korea. The communique can be construed as the pretext for negotiations on diplomatic normalisation.

status of Japanese living in the North, plus the South Korean factor,[31] both countries are likely to continue to increase the level of contact.

Pyongyang's southward policy has also yielded positive payoffs in the military area. The North's 'nuclear card' was instrumental in the withdrawal of American tactical nuclear forces from the South and on winning Seoul's pledge to denuclearisation. Both were longstanding North Korean demands. The US and the South also responded to longstanding North Korean demands where they agreed to cancel the huge annual 'Team Spirit' exercise in 1992.[32] The southward policy has also contributed to reducing inter-Korean military tensions by increasing interest in and discussion of arms control and confidence-building measures.

Compared with gains in the diplomatic and military areas, economic returns from the North's policy are less obvious. Macro-political barriers, the rigid economic structure of the North, the lack of economic complementarity with other regional actors, and an uncertain business environment, have all impeded economic cooperation. Nonetheless, there are some signs of improving economic transactions. The US government has eased restrictions on the private sector's business transactions with North Korea, allowing American businessmen, mostly from the Korean community in the US, to explore the North's markets. Bilateral trade between the US and the North was $8.4 million in 1989—previously it had been near zero.[33] Since Japan has pursued a policy of the separation of political and economic issues, trade between Japan and the DPRK has existed since the 1970s. Although Pyongyang's default on its debt payments to Japan has slowed the pace of economic cooperation, the overall outlook seems promising. As noted earlier, diplomatic normalisation will bring hefty financial rewards to the North in the form of official development assistance and compensation. Detecting this, leading Japanese corporations like Mitsubishi, Itotsu, Mitsui and Marubeni have already begun venturing into the North. Some plan to open offices in Pyongyang. Also noteworthy is the United Nations Development Program's (UNDP) recent efforts to sponsor the development of special economic zones along the Tumen river in the far north of the DPRK. This project, which may be financed by Japan, the US and South Korea, will benefit North Korea to a great extent if it goes ahead. But the development of most significance for the North's economy has been the sharp expansion in

---

31 Immediately after his visit to North Korea, Kanemaru Shin paid a visit to Seoul and agreed with the South Korean government to observe five preconditions in conducting diplomatic normalisation talks with Pyongyang: (1) prior consultation with Seoul; (2) promotion of inter-Korean talks; (3) fostering the North's signing of the IAEA's safety agreement; (4) no compensation or official economic assistance before diplomatic normalisation; and (5) inducing the North's opening and international cooperation. *Hakuk Ilbo*, 9 October 1990.

32 It was reinstated in 1993 due to lack of progress on the nuclear issue. (Ed.)

33 RINU, *The Real Picture of the North Korean Regime*, p. 331.

indirect trade with the South. Inter-Korean trade increased from $24 million in 1990, to $120 million in the first eight months of 1991. It has since fluctuated according to the state of the political relationship between Seoul and Pyongyang. Economic cooperation will undoubtedly accelerate if the two Koreas can work out detailed terms of economic cooperation.[34]

The southward policy has delivered mixed blessings to North Korea. On the one hand, it may help North Korea cope with economic stagnation, escape diplomatic isolation, and with an improved security climate, reduce the North/South arms race. On the other hand, opening up the North may undermine the political foundation of the Kim Il Sung regime by allowing the penetration of liberal ideas and institutions, and information about the outside world. The southward policy could mean exchanging long-term regime security for the short-term alleviation of economic hardships and diplomatic isolation. The Kim regime recognises this risk and the policy of opening to the external world could well be revised. The political calculus of regime interest will dictate the ultimate direction of the North's southward policy.

Shifting alignments, regional context and Korean security: three scenarios

How may the foreign policies of the two Koreas described above evolve? What impact may they have on regional order and stability in East Asia? Three possible scenarios can be envisaged.

1. The convergence scenario

The convergence scenario sees cross-recognition between two Koreas and the US, Russia, China and Japan evolving smoothly into a unified Korea. This scenario assumes several conditions hold. First, East Asia should be freed from regional hegemonic contestation. American disengagement, the continued low level Russian presence, the presence of a non-militaristic Japan and relative Chinese isolationism would satisfy such regional order. Second, inter-Korean dialogues would be intensified in such a way as to expedite the process of national unification. Finally, domestic opposition to unification, and to severing alliance ties with external actors should be kept minimal in both Koreas.

Under this scenario, the convergence of the North's southern policy and the South's northern policy could lead to a unified Korea. The combined economic and military capabilities of North and South Korea could make a unified Korea a formidable middle power able to project power regionally. If such a united Korea could work with the major

---

34   *Business Week*, 15 October 1991.

powers to create a new regional order based on the collective coordination of economic and security policies, this would certainly contribute to enhancing regional peace as well as ensuring security on the Korean peninsula.[35] Without such cooperation there could be serious threats, both military and economic, to the security of the new unified nation. The greater the number of actors the more unstable the regional system. Without cooperation, deep-rooted historical distrust, emergent patterns of economic rivalry, and growing military capabilities, all of which are rather peculiar to East Asia, will make the region's security more precarious and place the Korean peninsula in a position of perpetual insecurity. The convergence scenario is Janus-faced.

What of feasibility? There are real grounds for pessimism. Currently, neither domestic nor external factors seem conducive to realising the convergence scenario, although in both Koreas ordinary citizens would welcome such development. Nationalism runs deep in the minds of Koreans, transcending ideological, regional and even class cleavages, but political elites will be less susceptible to the convergence option since national unification and regime survival may be antithetical. Of four likely models for national unification—the German, Vietnamese, the Commonwealth and the Confederation—the German model, in which the South absorbs the North, seems the most plausible. But failure to cope with the negative political, economic and social consequences likely to emerge from such a unification process could also jeopardise the regime in the South. Anticipation, on both sides, of the potential cost of reunification are most likely to prevent the convergence of the northern and southward policies into actual reunification.[36]

Nor does the external environment appear to favour unification either. The US will not easily give up its regional hegemony. For the US, the advent of a unified Korea without alliance ties to Washington is unthinkable and undesirable. The hegemonic mindset and the economic stakes are too big to ignore and discard. A 1992 US Department of Defense document stated:

> We must also remain sensitive to the potentially destabilising effects that
> enhanced roles on the part of our allies, particularly Japan but also
> possibly Korea, might produce...[the US] should seek to maintain an
> alliance relationship with a unified democratic Korea.[37]

The US, in other words, does not want Korea to slip from Washington's sphere of influence. Japan does not simply oppose, but is

---

[35] For alternative scenarios of East Asian regional orders, see Chung-in Moon, 'Managing Regional Challenges: Japan, the East Asian NICs and Patterns of Economic Rivalry', *Pacific Focus*, Fall 1991 pp. 23–48.

[36] Chung-in Moon, 'Calculus of National Unification: Divergent Interests', paper presented at a conference on The Future of the Korean Peninsula, Michigan State University, 30–31 January 1992.

[37] Cited in *New York Times*, 8 March 1992.

fearful of, a unified Korea. A delicate synergy of historical distrust of Korea, guilt about its militarist past and concern about possible future Korean relations, all feed Japan's distrust of Korea. In Korea, there remain deep concerns about Japanese ambition for regional hegemony. Kenichi Takemura, a well-known Japanese television commentator, stated in 1991 that:

> An all-out invasion of Japan by Korea is inevitable if Korea is unified... [when it comes] it will be blitz attack like the Iraqi invasion of Kuwait... therefore it is in Japan's best interest to help North Korea economically so the Korean peninsula remains divided as now.[38]

Neither China nor Russia will welcome the creation of a unified Korea because they do not want to have a potentially uncontrollable and relatively powerful middle power in their backyard. So, for both internal and external reasons, the convergence scenario is unlikely to be realised in the near future.

2. The divergence scenario

The second scenario involves a divergence of the northern and southward policies. The South seeks deeper relations with China and Russia, while North Korea gets closer to the US and Japan. This scenario is predicated on Seoul's defection from the US–Japan camp. Such a defection is possible under the following circumstances. First, the US abandons its hegemonic patronage over South Korea. This could result from increased economic pressure on Seoul, particularly on trade issues, leading to growing anti-US feelings in the ROK. Mutual US–ROK disaffection could in turn lead to the withdrawal of US military forces from South Korea. Second, the US and Japan may seek to create a bigemonic regional order which marries US military power to Japanese economic power, but which excludes South Korea.[39] Third, Japan may seek regional hegemony (e.g., a new East Asian Co-Prosperity Sphere) to fill the vacuum of a US regional military withdrawal. Finally, progressive forces in South Korea may gain political power, while pragmatists prevail in North Korean politics. Under these conditions South Korea might defect from the US–Japan axis and accelerate its northern policy by seeking to create a new regional bloc comprising South Korea, China and Russia. Seoul's defection could, in turn, foster rapprochement between North Korea and the US–Japan axis.

---

38 *Far Eastern Economic Review*, 31 January 1991, p. 31.
39 Bigemonic regional order refers to the formation of an economic, military bloc through Japan–US collective leadership in the region. It would take a form of tight regionalism comprising the dollar–yen bloc, a free-trading system, and other shared burdens of regional public goods. The order presupposes an extended Cold War structure. See Chung-in Moon, 'Managing Regional Challenges', p. 43.

Such a partnership could trigger fundamental realignments of the regional system. Three power poles could emerge: a Seoul–Beijing–Moscow axis; a Tokyo–Pyongyang axis; and the US in a rather ambiguous regional role. A tripolar region would be more stable than that of the convergence scenario discussed previously. The implications for security on the Korean peninsula are, however, less encouraging since the divergence scenario presupposes the perpetual division of Korea and the continuance of inter-Korean military confrontation and hostility. This would mean that the old alliance politics were reversed, with North Korea feeling much more secure, while the South became more insecure.

Viewed from the domestic political perspective, this scenario is not entirely implausible. Increasingly impatient with US and Japanese economic policies and less concerned with external threats, progressive forces in South Korea have attacked the government's attitude towards the US and Japan, while calling for closer economic, technological and even military cooperation with Russia and China. Surprisingly, the middle class seems to share this view.[40] The domestic political response to the trade frictions with the US and Japan has narrowed the ROK government's margin of political manoeuvrability. By contrast, North Korean political leadership has begun to pursue a more pragmatist line following the Chinese model and seeking rapid rapprochement with Tokyo and Washington.

But South Korea is too dependent on the US and Japan to cut economic links with them. Forging new economic bonds with China and Russia, at the expense of the US and Japan, would be counterproductive. The economic gains realised from increasing economic relationships with China and Russia could not offset the losses which would arise from abandoning American and Japanese markets. Furthermore, China and Russia will not wish to form a new alliance with South Korea if this means the risk of loss of access to American and Japanese markets and their economic assistance. Japan, however, might capitalise on this development by cultivating new economic and political ties with a newly pragmatic North Korea.[41]

3. Continuation of the status quo

For all of the above reasons, the most likely scenario for the Korean peninsula would be a continuation of the status quo, the South's northern policy and the North's southern policy continuing and converging slightly. The pursuit of the northern and southward policies is not likely

---

[40] Even conservative elements appear to support this position.

[41] In a recent interview, Shin Kanemaru, who was a 'king-maker' in Japanese politics and has been active in improving Tokyo–Pyongyang ties, revealed that he assumed the vice-chairman position of the ruling Liberal Democratic Party in order to realise Japan–North Korean diplomatic normalisation. *Hankuk Ilbo*, 8 March 1992.

to achieve national reunification. Deep and binding economic, political and military ties with the US will constrain South Korea. North Korea may accelerate its southward policy, resulting in rapid rapprochement with Japan. But several obstacles, such as the DPRK's offensive conventional force structure, its ambiguous nuclear intentions and its political deformity and record of human rights abuses, will delay any significant diplomatic improvements between Pyongyang and Washington, unless the ruling regime in North Korea risks its survival by complying with American conditions for diplomatic normalisation. Japan may be the only actor which would seek to strengthen its ties with North Korea. Such a move could restrain South Korea economically.[42]

In view of the above, the realignment of the two Koreas' regional policies will not significantly affect the existing regional order. American regional hegemony will remain the central element; China, and especially Russia, will be less assertive in their regional hegemonic projection. Japan, however, might emerge as a new aspirant. The new regional policies of the two Koreas cannot alter these facts. Only if a Japanese quest for regional hegemony becomes more visible might Seoul take an initiative to form a counter-Japanese alliance involving the US, China and Russia.

The status quo scenario also foresees growing constraints on North Korean aspirations for regional military expansion or adventurism. These constraints should contribute to alleviating military tensions on the Korean peninsula. A continuation of the status quo favours both the national and regime security of South Korea, but it could endanger North Korea's regime security, if not national security. If threats to regime survival take more concrete forms, North Korea may suspend its southern initiative, again placing the Korean peninsula on a perilous path.

Concluding remarks

What implications can we draw from the above? First, that the regional security environment does not necessarily dictate the security policy of the two Koreas. It is the dynamic interplay of security environment and regime interests that shapes national security policy in general, and regional policy in particular. Second, the regional policies of North and South Korea, and the reactions to them by regional actors, are no longer guided solely by geostrategic concerns. Economic factors such as national economic growth and welfare have emerged as key determinants of

---

42 A recent research finding argues that economic cooperation between Japan and North Korea can undermine that between North and South Korea due to the similar economic structure of Japan and South Korea. Japan's economic cooperation with the North will deter North Korea from seeking economic assistance from the South. *Hankuk Ilbo*, 1 February 1992.

regional dynamics and of Korean security. This is because economic values are so intricately intermeshed with issues of legitimacy and regime security. Moreover, the diluted structure of military threats in the region is likely to foster this shift towards geoeconomics in national security thinking and policy. Third, the evolving patterns of both Koreas' regional policies are likely to have only a limited impact on regional order and stability for reasons noted above. A continuation of the status quo is anticipated. This will favour the South's national and regime security, but undermine those of the North. Finally, any failure to sustain the status quo might lead to a more unstable regional order and to greater economic and military insecurity on the Korean peninsula.

10 The Two Koreas and Rapprochement: Foundations for Progress?

JAMES COTTON

In 1971 and again in 1984 the two Korean states initiated a series of contacts which were ostensibly aimed at achieving reconciliation and the first steps to an eventual unification. On both occasions documents were signed and pledges given; in both cases the talks foundered in an atmosphere of mutual acrimony.

The reasons for the failure of these early attempts at reconciliation are complex. The division of Korea since 1948 had created powerful interests, military and political, the *raison d'être* of which was the maintenance of antagonistic division. The most important factor was the inability of North Korea to accept South Korea without equivocation as a legitimate authority and dialogue partner. Although engaging in negotiations with Seoul, Pyongyang never ceased to represent the government of South Korea as a creature of the United States, and always attempted at some stage to involve other South Korean groups (typically those critical of the government) in the negotiations. For their part the authorities in Seoul emphasised the need to move first to a recognition of the status quo, a demand which was open to the interpretation that the South did not really wish to realise unification.

The third round of the North–South contacts, which began in earnest with the meeting in September 1990 between the Prime Ministers of the two states, initially repeated many of the steps taken in the previous rounds. Differing positions were stated but with little prospect of their reconciliation. The North wished the two sides to adopt a non-aggression declaration which would commit the South to severing its military alliance with the United States. By contrast, the South wished to implement a series of political and military confidence-building measures in

137

order to ensure that any comprehensive agreement between the two governments (such as that signed with much fanfare but no result in 1972) would be erected on a real foundation.

As the contacts developed—stalling in early 1991 but reviving later in the year—the issue of North Korea's nuclear ambitions became increasingly prominent. Contradictory statements from Pyongyang as to its nuclear intentions increased apprehension in Seoul and (with the example of Iraq in mind) elsewhere in the international community.

Pyongyang had avoided assenting to the International Atomic Energy Agency (IAEA) system of nuclear safeguards after having signed the Nuclear Non-Proliferation Treaty (NPT) in 1985.[1] It sought consistently to link its acceptance of these safeguards to a withdrawal of American nuclear weapons from South Korea.

The 1991 agreements

In December 1991, however, the two sides made public the text of an agreement covering both reconciliation and provisions for realising mutual non-aggression as well as various types of exchanges and contacts. The 25 articles of the agreement (subsequently ratified in each of the states) are comprehensive, but the ease and speed with which they were composed suggested that there had been some rethinking by the parties of the issues involved.

It is clear from the format and content of the agreement, and from a comparison of the final documents with the negotiating drafts circulated by the delegations at successive prime ministerial negotiations, that both sides had been prepared to modify their positions. North Korea demonstrated unusual flexibility. The agreement incorporates six articles concerned with measures to promote non-aggression, a long-standing North Korean aim. Yet none of these could be taken as specifically requiring South Korea to abandon the American alliance. A number of social and economic confidence-building measures which the South Koreans had insisted should be the foundation of any lasting accord were included in this agreement, but all the various measures are incorporated in a single declaration of grand principles.

From the perspective of the past history of North–South Korean exchanges, it is noteworthy that the concrete measures to be realised are defined in very general language. In the most difficult area of all, military confidence-building measures, the actual steps to be taken have been left to a Military Committee to decide. Both sides commit themselves to exchanges in diverse fields, freedom for their residents to visit the other

---

[1] As a new party to the NPT, the North should have signed an IAEA safeguards agreement within eighteen months of acceding to the treaty.

state, and the resumption of every kind of communications and economic intercourse. Again, however, no specific steps are stated.

The process moved a stage further when, at the end of December 1991, an agreement was announced which appeared to resolve the issue which had become the key to the Korean confrontation—that of nuclear weapons. In the December agreement both sides declared that they would not store or possess such weapons, nor the means to produce them. They also stated their commitment to establish an inspectorate to verify by mutual observation the absence of such weapons and facilities.

Again the concessions are noteworthy. North Korea had always linked the nuclear issue with the alliance between Seoul and Washington. Latterly the North Korean position had been that a withdrawal from Korean territory of American nuclear weapons would only be sufficient if accompanied by a declaration or 'guarantee' that the US would not use nuclear weapons against it. Such a guarantee has not, of course, been forthcoming. For their part the South Koreans have assented to a significant limitation upon their military relationship with the United States, since the agreement commits them to refusing to 'accept' nuclear weapons, phraseology which could be interpreted as implying a prohibition upon visitations by (potentially) nuclear-armed naval vessels, or the redeployment of nuclear weapons on South Korean soil.

It was widely reported that two unwritten mutual concessions helped provide the foundation for the agreement. North Korea undertook to sign and implement the IAEA safeguards agreement, while South Korea promised to cancel the annual 'Team Spirit' joint military exercises with the United States.[2]

Progress in this round of North–South contacts was initially remarkable, but has subsequently stalled. However, even to have come this far was unprecedented. So what had changed by comparison with the early 1970s and the mid-1980s?

South Korean policy

In South Korea, as a consequence of the increased susceptibility of the government to democratic pressure, public apprehension at the prospect of a nuclear-armed North Korea required new governmental efforts to seek rapprochement. This was necessary both to placate the citizenry and to avoid giving hawkish elements of the military any excuse for pre-emptive action (in the manner of Israel's raid upon Iraq's Osiraq reactor in 1981). Government estimates of the time it would take for North Korea to complete a nuclear weapon imposed a two year deadline upon the negotiations.

---

[2] *Far Eastern Economic Review*, 9 January 1992, p. 10.

After the heady successes of the South's 'Nordpolitik' and the openings to the Soviet Union and Eastern Europe, the manner of the collapse and death throes of East European socialism had led some of the more thoughtful members of the governing elite in Seoul to reassess their approach to Pyongyang. Instead of promoting the isolation and then collapse of the North Korean system as the prelude to unification on Seoul's terms, they began to see the need to cushion the North's system from crisis and thus, to an extent, prolong its life. The German reunification experience suggested that the costs of unification on the Korean peninsula were likely to be ruinous. Events in Rumania (where the Ceausescu cult was modelled directly upon the Kim Il Sung prototype) and elsewhere, also suggested that the rapid demise of socialism would breed dislocation and discontent which could trigger dangerous disorder. With a million armed troops and weapons widely dispersed in North Korea the potential for bloodshed and misery was considerable.

Finally, President Bush's September 1991 announcement that the United States would withdraw all its theatre nuclear weapons deployed overseas, although in part a response to developments in the Soviet Union, also met a long-standing North Korean demand. Although their presence was never officially confirmed, it was widely held that the United States had stationed nuclear weapons in Korea since the 1960s. In December 1991, President Roh was able to declare that the territory of South Korea was nuclear free.

North Korean policy

Evidence of a preoccupation with timetables and deadlines can also be seen in North Korea's policy choices.

The most significant impetus to change for Pyongyang has come from the regime's loss of external patronage. While revolutionary ties still figure in the relations between Kim Il Sung and Deng Xiaoping, China's interest in North Korea has waned. Beijing cannot provide the aid necessary to sustain the present North Korean model of socialism, and in any case is now developing a fruitful economic relationship with South Korea. Thus, in 1991, China indicated it would not block Seoul's application to join the United Nations, a move which forced Pyongyang to reverse one of the stated fundamentals of its policy and seek entry also. To the intense chagrin of Pyongyang, Beijing subsequently agreed to establish full diplomatic relations with Seoul.

The collapse of the USSR has had an impact upon the foundations of North Korea's world strategy which can only be described as cataclysmic. Moscow's recognition of South Korea, taken together with Soviet insistence that future trade with North Korea be conducted in hard currency, signalled the effective end of a close economic, political, and military alliance that had existed since 1948.

Until 1990, around 60 per cent of North Korea's trade was with the Soviet Union. The Soviets continued up to that year to provide significant aid, and were also the source of all the North's high technology weapons systems (apart from those acquired through the clandestine world arms market). As late as 1991, the North Korean leadership still appeared to hope that something could be retrieved from its relationship with Moscow. But the collapse of communism and the repudiation of socialism has forced Pyongyang to rethink both its political and economic strategy.

The imposed nature of North Korea's recent policy innovations should be particularly stressed. From recent (elliptical but still intelligible) statements on the state of the economy, it is clear that the country faces a severe energy shortage largely because Russian supplies of oil have all but dried up (the Soviet Union being formerly the chief source of this energy input). Perennial shortages of food and consumer commodities have grown worse, and without an infusion of capital and technological assistance a worsening economic crisis looms.

North Korea's need for capital and for trade diversification lies behind the attempt, initiated in 1990, to pursue contacts with Japan. However, during the 1991 negotiations, North Korea demanded reparations from Japan, not merely for the colonial period, but also for the years from 1965 during which Tokyo recognised Seoul but not Pyongyang. This was quite unacceptable to Tokyo. For their part Japan's negotiators did not wish to achieve too much progress in the absence of a Seoul–Pyongyang rapprochement and as long as the nuclear issue remained unresolved. North Korea's increasing willingness to treat with South Korea, albeit largely on its own terms, arises from Pyongyang's belief that improved North–South relations are the key to opening direct and official relations with Japan.

From the early 1970s, Kim Il Sung has been committed to handing power on to his eldest son, Kim Jong Il. Much of the inflexibility of North Korean policy in the last decade may be interpreted as a consequence of this commitment. The elder Kim (always a close student of events in China) has observed how badly the reputation and policy inheritance of Mao Zedong fared at the hands of his successors. The rationale for the family succession in North Korea was to ensure that, unlike China, for 'generation after generation' there would be no deviation from the correct revolutionary path.

Now even Kim Il Sung has been forced to acknowledge, albeit tacitly, that changes must be made. His reasoning is likely to be that, if changes have been forced, it is better to give them his personal imprimatur rather than leave them to Kim Jong Il to realise. This would open the latter to charges of 'revisionism', a failing associated with so many fallen leaders of the former socialist world.

The limits of policy reform

What are the prospects for social and economic opening, and hence social and economic reform in North Korea? Even within the limitations imposed by the continuation of the Kim dynasty, some at least of the features of the Chinese model of economic innovation coupled with political stasis could be adopted.

The limited measures to facilitate joint ventures and market openings which were adopted in 1984–85, but then largely shelved, could be revived. North Korea could open Special Economic Zones (regulations for which have already been announced) at selected sea ports and border locations to take advantage of its comparative advantage in labour costs, proximity to raw materials, and transport connections with the Russian Far East and Manchuria. The Tumen river project (involving collaboration between North Korea, China, and Russia) which has been the subject of a number of preliminary studies since 1991, and the attempt to interest the South Korean Daewoo *chaebol* in joint export production facilities at Nampo, are all indicators that some elements of the China model are being considered. North Korean ministries have already had years of experience supplying the Soviet/Russian Far East with labour, while segregating the individuals concerned from the local population. The segregation of workers would be much easier to manage on North Korean territory particularly if (as is the case with the Tumen river) the site concerned was remote from the major centres of population.

Reform of domestic economic policy would be difficult to manage, however, given the rigidities and extremes associated with North Korea's agricultural and industrial practices. But, some concessions could be made, including the use of private peasant plots to boost agricultural productivity sufficiently to extinguish North Korea's dependence on grain imports (which must be paid for in scarce hard currency). Greater enterprise initiative, an approach discussed for some years but yet to be effectively implemented, could introduce a degree of economic rationality in the industrial sphere. And the overall position of North Korea in the world trading order would be very much transformed if North Korea repaid its outstanding international loans from the 1970s; it would not be beyond the capacity of the economy to do so. With external capital available as a consequence of dealing with the debt problems, international investment in the DPRK economy would be possible. There is some indication that the 'reparations' being sought from Japan as part of a mutual recognition package are intended for such investment.

Of course, there are many features of the 'Chinese model' that could not, or would not, be applied in the North Korean case. North Korea's limited market size and relative remoteness could never attract outside capital as China has done. In addition, the newly-industrialised country (NIC) route to modernisation will not be as easy to pursue in the 1990s as it was in the 1970s and 1980s. Moreover, it is clear that both Chinese advice and independent North Korean assessment will incline the leadership in Pyongyang to avoid the political dimensions of the Chinese reforms. Against these factors it is already evident that, for political as much as for economic reasons, international agencies (such as the Asia Development Bank) would be prepared to assist North Korea if the circumstances were propitious. Future multilateral investment involving South Korean capital is also a possibility. The Hyundai group has signalled its willingness, even under present conditions, to collaborate in improving North Korea's tourist potential.

So far none of the policies discussed would be beyond the limits of the possible for the Kim dynasty, though agreeing to accept responsibility for international debts, for example, would lead to some loss of face. What is lacking in the North is the knowledge of external conditions necessary to choose the right policy elements. (Some cautious experimentation could make good some of this deficiency.) Dispensing with the two Kims, however, would open the way to a rapid adoption of such innovations—and many others.

The prospects for more comprehensive reform

It is possible that Kim Jong Il will be shunted aside after his father's demise, although, having been heir apparent for almost two decades, and in control of much government business since about 1980, he has had every opportunity to surround himself with loyalists. The removal of Kim Jong Il is undoubtedly a step contemplated by some members of the Kimist court. They will be well aware that the younger Kim is the one leader who cannot openly repudiate Kim Il Sung's policy except at the price of undermining his own legitimacy.

Should Kim Jong Il be displaced, the primary interests of the elite of this most highly bureaucratised and socially constrained of societies would be to retain its power and privilege while adopting economic policies which would give the system at least some chance of survival. Such a strategy would be assisted by the inheritance of the Kimist political culture, incubated by isolation and government propagated xenophobia. A purist Kimist strategy would not be a viable option, however, since it would risk provoking a backlash which would threaten the survival of the elite.

A new leadership would be bound to take a leaf from Deng Xiaoping's book, written in either a minimalist 'seek truth from facts'— or a maximalist—'four cardinal principles' style. Kim's more egregious claims for his own achievements would be deflated, and a more realistic version of the nature of the outside world (and South Korea) would become current. But the existence of a separate North Korean state with its own character and aspirations would be retained.

This scenario is not one which could be maintained indefinitely. Economic reforms would require some opening to the forces of the world economy which would, in turn, set in motion a process of social transformation. A North Korean population which had accurate first hand knowledge of South Korea would eventually succumb to the forces of nationalism which are amongst the most powerful factors at work in the Korean equation. In such circumstances unification, though not entirely on Seoul's terms, would be the ultimate outcome. But all of this would take time. Meanwhile the example of Vietnam shows just how far a relatively open economic system, much of it dependent upon the operations of free but mostly illicit market exchange, can subsist under a leadership still trapped in the verities of socialist theory. With Kim Jong Il in charge market forces would be slow to emerge but would do so nevertheless; with a Deng-style transition leadership the same forces would encounter fewer obstacles.

The nuclear problem

By the end of 1992, North–South Korean negotiations on the nuclear issue had reached an impasse. Although the Joint Nuclear Control Commission, formed as a result of the 1991 agreements, had met repeatedly, no formula could be mutually agreed which would permit each side to inspect the nuclear or nuclear-capable facilities of the other. Moreover, as a consequence of inspections arising from the nuclear safeguards agreement concluded between North Korea and the IAEA in January 1992, suspicions about the character of North Korea's nuclear program had, if anything, increased. The IAEA, after six inspection visits to North Korea, could not reconcile data obtained from analysis of nuclear material samples from the Yongbyon site with the explanations offered by North Korea's nuclear authorities.

The IAEA then requested a 'special inspection' of two suspect, undeclared sites at the Yongbyon nuclear complex. The North refused, claiming that the facilities in question were military and not nuclear. In fact the facilities are nuclear-waste storage sites. One had been buried and the other had been constructed to conceal a cavernous lower story connected by buried conduits to the spent fuel reprocessing plant. These details were known to American policy-makers for some time, but the CIA resisted the public revelation of the photographic evidence on the grounds that this would reveal too much about American intelligence gathering capabilities.

It was finally decided in Washington that if America was to require the United Nations and its agencies to take a more prominent role in the post-Cold War world, this information could not be withheld. Accordingly, at a closed meeting of the IAEA on 22 February 1993, the CIA released a sequence of photographs which clearly demonstrated the process of construction and concealment of the two suspect nuclear waste storage facilities at the Yongbyon complex. It was North Korea's consistent refusal to accept the inspections that the IAEA again requested, which precipitated the most serious challenge yet to the NPT regime.

Laboratory analysis had already indicated that North Korea had separated plutonium from irradiated nuclear cores on four occasions since 1989, rather than in the one 'experiment' in 1990 which North Korean officials admitted to. Samples from the two suspect sites would determine how much reprocessing had actually been undertaken at Yongbyon. It has been estimated that if North Korea had reprocessed all of the spent nuclear fuel that has become available since 1989, it could now possess sufficient plutonium for several nuclear devices.

Frustrated by the North's consistent stalling on the nuclear issue, South Korea and the United States warned that they were considering a resumption of the joint 'Team Spirit' military exercises in 1993. The huge annual exercise had been suspended in 1992 after the North agreed to submit to IAEA inspections.

At a news conference in Moscow on 29 January 1993, Son Song Pil, North Korea's ambassador to Russia, stated that if the joint US–South Korean 'Team Spirit' exercises went ahead, North Korea might boycott further IAEA inspections.

In fact North Korea has a clear obligation in international law arising from its membership of the NPT to submit to inspections of suspect facilities. This obligation exists independently of any differences Pyongyang has with the US—or any other state. However, the fact that the United States had made no secret of its desire to humiliate North Korea, and the fact that the IAEA had found it necessary to rely on intelligence data provided by the United States, lent some credence to North Korean claims that the pressure being placed on the North by the IAEA was in reality being orchestrated by the United States.

Following a meeting of the IAEA Board of Governors on 25 February, North Korea was given one month to accept the inspection of the disputed sites, after which time the issue would be referred to the Security Council. The North continued to refuse and the deadline was later extended to 31 March. The 'Team Spirit' exercises then commenced as Washington and Seoul had warned they would. North Korea responded by announcing that it would withdraw from the NPT, such withdrawal to be effective (following the three months notice specified in the NPT) on 12 June.

Finding North Korea to be in non-compliance with its international obligations, the IAEA Board referred the matter to the United Nations Security Council. On 11 May the Security Council adopted a resolution (China and Pakistan abstaining) which required North Korea to rescind its decision to withdraw from the NPT. The resolution warned that non-compliance could lead to 'further action' from the Security Council, the implication being that this could include economic and other sanctions against Pyongyang.

However, in a conciliatory move of a kind unlikely to have been seen during the Bush administration, the United States went some way to meeting North Korea's insistence that this was a matter which should be settled between Washington and Pyongyang. The US agreed to high level talks with North Korean representatives and, in the course of the subsequent dialogue, North Korea agreed to 'suspend' its withdrawal from the NPT. At the conclusion of a second round of talks, in exchange for the US undertaking to examine the feasibility of supplying North Korea with Light Water Reactor technology (which would replace the existing Gas–Graphite reactor with safer reactors whose spent fuel is far more difficult to transform into weapons-grade plutonium), North Korea undertook to resolve the impasse with the IAEA and resume dialogue with Seoul.

At the time of writing a series of negotiations to facilitate the inspection of the two disputed nuclear facilities had proved fruitless, with Pyongyang, on 27 September, apparently rejecting *any* further IAEA visits. This lack of progress caused the IAEA in October to declare North Korea in violation of its treaty obligations and to refer the matter to the Security Council.

Despite a flurry of proposals and counter-proposals, there have been no substantive negotiations between North and South Korea either. Pyongyang first insisted that contacts should proceed without an assurance that the nuclear issue would be discussed; later, the line was taken that the nuclear issue could only be addressed if South Korea renounced indefinitely plans to hold 'Team Spirit' and refrained from seeking international support for its position.

As neither of the two preconditions for further contacts had been met, the United States' position towards North Korea hardened. The American commander in Korea issued a blunt statement that any attempt by the North to use nuclear weapons would trigger a conflict on the peninsula which would lead to the utter annihilation of all North Korean forces and war potential. This statement was made in association with claims that North Korea had significantly strengthened its forces at the demilitarised zone (DMZ), and had also increased three-fold the number of military flight exercises as compared with 1992.

The renewal of the NPT is due in 1995. If the North Korean question is mishandled, and in particular if international sanctions are applied and fail to have the desired effect, this may encourage other would-be nuclear proliferators. The entire non-proliferation regime, and along with it hopes for the creation of further controls on nuclear proliferation, will have been undermined.

11 Writing the Final Chapter: Inter-Korean Rivalry in the 1990s

KYONGSOO LHO

With the advent of the 1990s, the long and embittered rivalry between the Republic of Korea (South Korea) and the Democratic People's Republic of Korea (North Korea) has entered into a critical phase—one which holds both unprecedented dangers for renewed conflict on the Korean peninsula as well as new opportunities for peace. Whereas meaningful improvement in inter-Korean relations was virtually impossible to contemplate during the Cold War years, in the 1990s new political openings make the peaceful resolution of the North–South Korean stalemate a realistic possibility. Indeed it is a necessity, if newly emergent regional trends toward pragmatism, interdependence and cooperation are to be consolidated into a durable new regional order.

Yet the new fluidity in Northeast Asia's contemporary strategic setting is clearly more welcome to some than others. For South Korea and the United States, the new regional environment offers previously unavailable strategic opportunities to advance their respective and mutual policy objectives. For China and Japan, the prospects are probably less clear-cut, but not, on the whole, disadvantageous to their respective positions. North Korea's circumstances, however, could hardly be more different; for Pyongyang, the ending of the Cold War, as a consequence of the collapse of the Soviet Union and Eastern Europe, can only represent a profound reversal of strategic fortunes.

In one important respect, however, the two Koreas are very much back where they started nearly 50 years ago. Much as was the case then, the changing external strategic environment in Northeast Asia today forces both Koreas to make difficult choices over how to define their political futures. If the two continue to define their futures as separate,

147

the possibility for renewed conflict on the Korean peninsula will remain and even grow in the months and years ahead. On the other hand, if Pyongyang and Seoul can begin to come to terms with the core issues that originally set them apart, the prospects for eventual accommodation and peace in Korea will be greatly improved. Unwarranted hubris, on both sides, foreclosed substantive dialogue in the past. Now Pyongyang and Seoul must not lose—either wittingly or unwittingly—this extraordinary opportunity, since reconciliation and accommodation may finally be possible.

Peacefully resolving the Korean question, however, will require more than just cooperation between the two Koreas. It will also demand the exercise of wisdom and restraint on the part of the major powers with interests in Korea and Northeast Asia. Germany's unification could not have been achieved, in the manner that it was, without the political and strategic wisdom of the United States, the Soviet Union, and Germany's immediate geographical neighbours (most especially France and Great Britain). So too stable political transition in Korea will depend on constructive steps taken by China, Japan, the United States and Russia.

A transformed North–South dynamic

The internal and external strategic circumstances facing the two Koreas have been transformed over the past decade. This is reflected in the fact that North–South dialogues have not stopped, despite the existence of serious disagreements (not least the controversy over North Korea's suspected nuclear weapons program). Previously, even inconsequential differences over discussion agendas or minor procedural matters would have constituted grounds for either side to walk away from the talks. The short-lived dialogues of the early 1970s and mid-1980s ended in this fashion due to North Korea's refusal to continue discussions with Seoul.

Whatever the reasons given, serious negotiations aimed at rapprochement between Pyongyang and Seoul were probably impossible anyway during this period. The heated emotions lingering from the Korean War had not subsided and the first North–South talks began in 1971, at a time when the war in Vietnam was going very badly for the United States and South Korea (which had the second largest contingent of fighting forces there). During this era there was a high level of uncertainty and fear of communist success in both Seoul and Washington. Under these circumstances, it was likely that the security establishment in Seoul would look with grave suspicion at whatever seemingly conciliatory measures might have emanated from Pyongyang. In fact, North Korea's continued refusal to acknowledge South Korea's political legitimacy, and Pyongyang's crude attempts to bypass the Seoul government as dialogue partner, not only heightened suspicion in the South, but worked to Pyongyang's tactical disadvantage. By the end of 1973, when North Korea announced that it would not return to the negotiation table, Seoul had grown tired of Pyongyang's machinations. The North had probably also realised that its tactics would not lead to any meaningful results.

The second round of North–South talks, which began in 1984, also took place against an unfavourable backdrop. The strategic relationship between Washington and Moscow was increasingly hostile. Neither the North nor the South was prepared to make meaningful concessions to the other, and neither possessed the means to persuade the other to enter into a cooperative relationship. Once again the talks foundered amidst charges of manipulation and deception. By the end of 1985, the talks ceased.

But despite these unfruitful exchanges in the 1970s and 1980s, the strategic underpinnings of North–South rivalry was being transformed. In the early 1960s, many doubted that South Korea could effectively match North Korea's industrial lead. The North enjoyed the advantage of having inherited the lion's share of the peninsula's industrial base after the Korean War. But, after three decades of double-digit economic growth, South Korea was transformed from a poor, agrarian economy dependent on external economic aid to a prosperous, industrialised middle-income country. By the mid-1980s, South Korea had a rapidly maturing, fully industrialised economy capable of producing not only heavy industrial and chemical products, but also sophisticated dual-use electronic equipment (with obvious military applications). Demands for a more equitable income distribution and for increased social welfare spending still remain challenges for South Korean economic policymakers, but the possibilities for Pyongyang to exploit public discontent in the South continues to diminish as a result of rapid overall economic growth.

Another important development in the South during the 1980s was, of course, the changes in political leadership. The Chun Doo Hwan regime, which emerged after the turmoil of 1979–80 following President Park Chung Hee's assassination, did not differ significantly from the Park regime in ideological orientation, but the succession in Seoul did carry some important messages for Pyongyang. First, the simple fact that political change, however volatile, actually could take place in the South. Second, that the southern system managed, however chaotically, to survive leadership change without debilitating consequences—especially to its economy. Third, the fact that with each change in political leadership in the South, Pyongyang's leaders faced a younger, better-educated and more energetic group of leaders in Seoul, whereas their own political system remained dominated by a core group of greying revolutionary leaders that had held power in the North since its founding in 1948.

In addition to these changes in the internal dimensions of the North–South dynamic, the external strategic environment which had operated at best as an uncertain and, at worst, a negative factor for the South up to the 1970s, began to work in favour of Seoul in the 1980s. With the decline in the influence of the Non-aligned Movement (NAM), Seoul was able to make dramatic diplomatic inroads into formerly socialist Third World countries assisted by a growing foreign aid budget and the presence of major South Korean transnational business firms in many of these countries. For Pyongyang, on the other hand, and as one would expect given the zero-sum diplomatic game between the two Koreas, the same period represented a time of serious diplomatic set-backs. In recent years, the pace of Pyongyang's diplomatic retreat from the Third World has become even more marked.[1]

The extent of South Korea's diplomatic success became even more visible during the 1986 Asian Games in Seoul which were attended not only by delegations from some of the more radical NAM-aligned Asian states, but also by a delegation from the People's Republic of China. The 1988 summer Olympic Games, attended by the Soviet Union and Eastern European countries, provided an even more visible boost for Seoul's diplomacy and international standing. South Korea's diplomatic fortunes, of course, improved far more dramatically toward the end of the 1980s as reforms unfolding in the Soviet Union and Eastern Europe opened up opportunities which would have been unthinkable in the past. By the close of the decade, Seoul faced few of the uncertainties and limitations in the external arena that had so long conditioned its outlook and behaviour.

But the changes that were so positive for the South were of great concern to the North. In the economic sphere North Korea's already low growth rates had slowed during the 1980s and were seriously behind the South. The North's current seven-year economic plan (already pushed back once) due to be completed in 1993, is most unlikely to meet its intended goals.[2] Given the serious shortages in capital, information and technology, the creaking infrastructure, not to mention the host of inefficiencies and waste characteristic of all command systems, the North Korean economy will not be able to get out of its structurally induced downward spiral in the absence of major reforms and external inputs.[3] Neither North Korea's half-hearted joint-venture schemes, nor its vaunted 'speed campaigns' (which were effective in raising production

---

[1] 'North Korea Closes a Dozen Resident Embassies in Africa', *The Korea Post*, April 1991, pp. 52–3.

[2] Park Choon-sam, 'The Self-Reliance Efforts of the North Korean Economy', *Vantage Point*, vol. XIV, nos. 10 & 11, October and November 1991.

[3] Reliable data on North Korea's economy is difficult to obtain in the best of circumstances. However, some idea of its current difficulties can be gleaned from Lee Hy-Sang, 'Bukhan-ui Kyongje Kaebang Noryok-gwa Jeonmang' (North Korea's Economic Opening: Efforts and Prospects), unpublished paper delivered at an international conference on Prospects for North–South Korean Economic Cooperation, Seoul, August 1989. For statistics, see, *1990 Nyondo Bukhan Kyongje Jonghap Pyongga (Overall Estimates of the North Korean Economy in 1990)*, Ministry of National Unification, Seoul, August 1991, especially pp. 26ff.

when the output levels were low during the 1950s and early 1960s), can be counted on to rescue the economy in the 1990s.[4]

North Korea's economic plight has obvious consequences for its military capability and, ultimately, its long-standing goal of uniting the Korean peninsula by revolutionary means. North Korea's actual military capability today is probably behind that of South Korea, though it retains some important *numerical* advantages in manpower, armour and artillery. The relatively low levels of combat readiness of these weapons systems, and the poor maintenance of most equipment and materiel in general—a condition forced on the North Korean military by budget constraints—undermine the real capabilities of Pyongyang's military machine. Moreover, North Korea's primitive intelligence gathering and processing functions could not cope with the flood of information that will need to be dealt with in wartime. The overgrown North Korean military machine has only a rudimentary 'brain' in its obsolete and antiquated command and control system. In this critical area, the North is no match for the state-of-the art C^3I capability in the hands of the South Korean and American forces in Korea.[5] Finally it seems that morale, especially in the rank and file, has declined considerably, not a particularly good sign for an officer corps whose own confidence may be shaken as well.

Thus having lost to the South the diplomatic and economic advantages that it had once enjoyed, and now struggling to retain control over a precarious internal economic situation, North Korea today faces the prospect of losing its military predominance as well. But if present trends continue, there is no way in which the North can hope to redress the growing gap. In terms of military spending alone, Seoul's defence budget, at about 5 per cent of Gross National Product (GNP) for the past decade, has in absolute terms been substantially larger than that of the North, in spite of Pyongyang devoting an estimated 20–25 per cent of its own GNP to the military sector. Given the South's much larger economic base (roughly ten times that of the North and growing), the defence burden will continue to lessen for the South and worsen even further for the North.

Making matters worse at this juncture is the fact that the North confronts, for the first time in its political development, the prospect of an uncertain power transfer. Some observers have noted that the process of

---

4   Mark Clifford and Sophie Quinn-Judge, 'Caught in a Vice', *Far Eastern Economic Review*, 29 November 1990, pp. 30–1. A cogent and more detailed analysis of the socio-political factors underlying North Korea's economic malaise is provided by Rhee Sang Woo, 'North Korea in 1990: Lonesome Struggle to Keep Chuch'e' (Juche), *Asian Survey*, vol. XXI, no. 1, January 1991, pp. 71–8.

5   For a discussion on the North–South military balance, see, Kyongsoo Lho, 'The Military Balance in the Korean Peninsula', *Asian Affairs*, vol. XIX, Part 1, February 1988, pp. 36–44.

transferring power from the 'Great Leader' Kim Il Sung (GL) to his son, the 'Dear Leader' Kim Jong Il (DL) has been underway since at least the mid-1980s, with the implied notion that the actual transfer may be no more than official recognition of the DL's already unchallenged authority and control in North Korea. North Korean representatives at academic discussions held overseas during the past few years, constantly stress this point to sceptical listeners. However, while not disputing that the DL's personal authority may rest on a support structure separate from that of his father—one likely composed of the DL's cronies from Kim Il Sung University and by personal dependency networks linked to the DL's political survival—it is difficult to attach much credence to the claim that the DL enjoys widespread popularity beyond such groups. More likely, the DL's essential authority and power depends on his father and his father's old-guard colleagues, including the DL's uncle O Jin U.[6]

Doubts about Kim Jong Il's leadership capacity (and therefore also about the DL's political survival after the GL's death) persist in part because, *inter alia*, in the highly credential-oriented society that is North Korea, the DL has few if any qualifications, aside from bloodlines, that would buttress his claim to succession. He has, for example, no record of military experience (always a solid revolutionary credential), no real expertise in any profession other than a reputed appreciation of film and arts, nor even much foreign experience. The DL's half-brother (and potential rival), Kim Pyong Il, sent into overseas 'exile' in Pyongyang's diplomatic service, can at least claim to have the last.

As it prepares for political transition in North Korea, Seoul cannot realistically expect—at least not over the short term—meaningful co-operation from inside the North. There is no civil society, no organised religion (other than perhaps 'Kim Il Sungism'), no unions, no political opposition in North Korea capable of placing effective demands on, much less challenging, the Party and its state organs.[7] In any case, most of the group whose values and beliefs would have been opposed to the Kim regime left the North and came South, either before or during the Korean War. The North Korean technocracy and the intelligentsia, the very groups outside observers look to as potential reformers, do not appear to have the means, or the will, to turn their influence into useable political power for achieving reform. As long as it remains under the grip of unreconstructed communist rule, North Korea probably cannot be expected to initiate major reforms by itself any more than communist rulers in yesterday's Eastern Europe and Soviet Union were able to

---

6 'Kim Jong Il's Personality Cult: Yesterday and Today', *Naewoe Press*, 8 February 1991.

7 On this point, see James Cotton, *'Civil Society' and Nationalism in North Korea: Foundation for Political Change?*, Working Paper 1991/7, Department of International Relations, Research School of Pacific Studies, Australian National University, Canberra, October 1991.

prescribe cures for their own ills. Ultimately and sadly, this bodes ill for evolutionary change in North Korea, and it is difficult to refute the growing view that catastrophic political turmoil will have to take place before serious reforms can be introduced. It may indeed be that both Kims, *pere et fils*, must fall in order for meaningful reform to succeed in North Korea.

North Korea's priorities and South Korean opportunities

North Korea's main policy objectives in the 1990s centre around one simple goal: survival. The regime no longer has the domestic resources, nor the external assistance necessary to sustain a campaign to topple South Korea, much less maintain pretensions of revolutionary leadership in the Third World. Neither Kim Il Sung's brand of revolutionary ideology, nor the North Korean model of socialist economic development, commands much attention in the developing world any more. The days when radical socialist states of the Third World looked to North Korea for inspiration are long gone; Pyongyang today cannot even afford to maintain its overseas missions.[8] In fact, it is highly doubtful that the regime can continue to maintain even its current level of economic activity, and still be able to afford its huge military budget. The state of the economy goes from bad to much worse. Reports have indicated that most North Korean plants are running at best at around 30–40 per cent of capacity due to energy shortages. Shortages of foodstuffs and other consumer goods are reported to be even more severe, with the exception of Pyongyang and its environs where special rations are provided. There have been reports of food riots in provincial areas that were put down only by the mobilisation of troops.[9]

Deepening domestic economic problems will inevitably impact on the political leadership's ability to hold onto power. Together with the loss of Moscow's patronage and uncertainty surrounding ties to Beijing (especially after the present Chinese leaders pass from the scene), awareness has grown in Pyongyang that regime survival now critically depends on stabilising its competition with Seoul, and reaching out for support from Japan and the United States. Pyongyang, in addition, appears to finally have accepted the reality that material improvements with Tokyo and Washington will not be possible without first improving ties to Seoul. Therefore, for Pyongyang, the December 1991 North–South Agreement on Reconciliation, Non-aggression, Cooperation and Exchange is a key step in its strategy to escape its current dilemmas. Although the language

---

[8] 'North Korea Closes a Dozen Resident Embassies', p. 52.
[9] *Asian Wall Street Journal*, 27 December 1991. Also, 'Shortages of Food, Clothing and Housing Still Remain Urgent Problems in North Korea', *North Korea News*, 13 January 1992.

of the agreement remains general, and specific areas for detailed discussion have been left to the three working committees (political, economic, and defence/arms control), this agreement can be considered an important step toward tension reduction in Korea. Follow-on developments such as the two sides' declaration of their non-nuclear principles, and South Korea's announcement in January 1992 that it would cancel the 'Team Spirit' joint military exercise with the United States, indicate how much more flexible the South has become in dealing with the North, and reflects Seoul's newfound willingness to give North Korea the strategic breathing space it needs.

But until the North provides credible guarantees that it is not making nuclear weapons, it will not gain the political and economic goals it has been seeking in its talks with the US and Japan. Pyongyang does not appear to fully appreciate that Washington's chief concern is not just to prevent a DPRK bomb, but to prevent other potential proliferating states, in Asia and elsewhere, from sparking off regional nuclear arms races.[10] Washington, even if it were sensitive to North Korea's feelings of strategic vulnerability, could not condone Pyongyang's nuclear option without severely jeopardising its global efforts to contain proliferation of weapons of mass destruction and the means to deliver them. North Korea's exports of SCUD-C missiles to the Middle East, which runs counter to the United States' efforts to prevent the spread of missile technology through the Missile Technology Control Regime (MTCR), is another serious bone of contention with the United States.[11]

North Korea's nuclear gambit has so far neither strengthened its security nor enhanced its international standing. Even as a strategic bargaining chip, it has failed miserably. Although it has led to the withdrawal of US nuclear weapons from the South, this has made no difference in terms of US security guarantees to South Korea. Japan has hardened its position toward Pyongyang. The nuclear question has, moreover, led to extraordinary and almost certainly unanticipated international pressure being brought to bear on North Korea, the degree of which it probably did not fully anticipate. If Pyongyang continues to delay opening its nuclear facilities, or seeks to hide parts of its suspected facilities from outside inspections, it could well invite more forceful actions including economic sanctions and, possibly, even military action.[12]

---

[10] Leonard S. Spector and Jacqueline R. Smith, 'North Korea: The Next Nuclear Nightmare?', *Arms Control Today*, March 1991, p. 8.

[11] The United States recently threatened to board North Korean vessels suspected of transporting Scuds to Iraq. See, Patrick Tyler, 'U.S. Considers Boarding Ships That Hold North Korea Scuds', *International Herald Tribune*, 7 March 1992.

[12] In a much-noted instance of sabre rattling by Seoul in 1991, the South Korean Defense Minister, Lee Jong Ku, spoke in terms of an 'Entebbe-style'

But it is clear that Pyongyang sees the possession of nuclear weapons as first, a cost-effective 'equaliser' to Seoul's growing military power, and second, as a shield against mounting external pressures to change and open up to the outside world. While it is clear why the nuclear option might appeal to a North Korea under extreme duress, Pyongyang should understand that the nuclear option has severe liabilities. In the end, the rationale for North Korea having nuclear weapons, even from Pyongyang's perspective, has to be suspect. At best, Pyongyang's drive to acquire nuclear weapons is based on a mistaken understanding of what truly threatens regime survival. North Korea is no longer (if it ever was) under any threat of a unilateral military attack by either South Korea, the United States or the two together. Neither can the North use its nuclear capability to threaten or blackmail the South, which, even after the removal of US nuclear weapons from its territory, remains firmly under the United States nuclear umbrella. In addition, it is highly unlikely that China or Russia would condone the use of nuclear weapons by North Korea given the geographic proximity of each to the Korean peninsula. Militarily as well as politically, it is not a weapon that could be used in the inter-Korean contest. As a deterrent against external threat, it is a waste of resources because neither the United States nor South Korea intends to strike militarily against the North (the only exception might be strikes against the Yongbyon nuclear complex if the North persisted with its nuclear program).

For Pyongyang, the real threat to regime survival, as should be clear by now, is the potential of internal collapse. The way to prevent that is not by possession of additional military capability, including nuclear weapons capability, but by gradual political and economic reforms. In the immediate future, when the need for internal political stability will be most acute, Pyongyang could begin by allowing a limited opening to the outside aimed at attracting investments into North Korea and by permitting a variation of the early Chinese agriculture reforms of the late 1970s. Limited opening of markets for foreign goods could go a long way in alleviating the severe shortages of consumer goods. A good proportion of such goods could be supplied on concessionary terms by South Korea and could be negotiated in the North–South economic committee meetings. The effect would be to shore up the unstable situation in Pyongyang. Over the longer term, if the North Korean economy begins to find its feet again, Seoul could facilitate sizeable capital flows into the North, either through its own resources or by supporting Pyongyang's loan requests in the international capital markets. With renewed productivity in the

---

pre-emptive strike (presumably a mistaken reference to the Israeli raid on Iraq's suspect Osiraq nuclear facilities in the 1980s) on North Korea if it did not desist from its covert nuclear program. Following strong domestic criticism of these incautious remarks, Lee was made to resign from his portfolio.

North, Pyongyang could begin repayment of its defaulted loans from the 1970s, and thus regain its international credit-worthiness over time.

It ought to be clear to Kim Jong Il, if not his father, that a reformist approach would best assure the regime's prospects for political survival. Reforms, in addition, need not fundamentally detract from the younger Kim's political legitimacy, which many often presume will have to be derived from a continuation of his father's revolutionary legacy. For instance, at an appropriate moment a pragmatic Kim Jong Il could state that, while the revolutionary methods of his father suited *his* times, different policies that are aimed at economic modernisation and intended to consolidate and accelerate socialism's achievements, are necessary for the future. This is essentially how the Chinese leadership rationalised and explained the Party's decision to embrace economic reforms. In the end, of course, sustained economic growth along market lines is not possible without some accompanying internal political liberalisation. As the Chinese leadership found out at Tienanmen in 1989, such changes can have major costs for Party control. On the other hand, as the Chinese leadership also surely realises (as must Pyongyang), it was the Party's willingness to accept some reforms, however slowly and fitfully these reforms were implemented, which saved the Beijing regime from the cataclysmic extinction suffered by the communists in Eastern Europe and the former Soviet Union. Whether the Kims have absorbed this lesson remains to be seen.

For South Korea, the choices are no less clear. It has three broad policy options. First, it can continue applying incessant external and internal pressure on North Korea in order to wear down and ultimately bring about a collapse of the present order in Pyongyang. Second, it can reassure the North at a time of great insecurity, provide aid when asked and deemed justified, and patiently wait out the period while North Korea transforms itself. Third, it can offer a mixed menu of pressure and inducement. During the first heady days of collapsing communist regimes in Eastern Europe, and as realisation hit Seoul as to how internally corroded and weak these systems were, there was for a time a strong argument made that a similar process of collapse could be effected in North Korea if only sufficient outside pressure was applied.

This hard-line view, however, changed to a softer one as policy-makers in Seoul watched with horror and concern the internal chaos and violence in Rumania and Yugoslavia that followed the collapse of communist rule. The change from the hard to the soft line gained added support in the aftermath of East Germany's sudden collapse and Germany's reunification under West German terms. Though East Germany's absorption into the West was greeted with initial enthusiasm, a more sober view soon emerged as the South Koreans became aware of the immense costs that an all too rapid reunion with the North would entail. Learning from the German experience, Seoul decided that attempting to induce instability in the North was not a wise policy. Instead, against the advice of foreign as well as domestic critics, Seoul chose to take a 'softer' line in dealing with Pyongyang even at the cost of prolonging survival of the Kim regime.[13]

The nuclear issue has diverted both attention and momentum from this new policy orientation, yet its outlines remain intact and will probably resume once the North accepts full-scope IAEA nuclear safeguards and inspections.

It seems likely that Seoul will persist in its relatively soft-line policy, ie., that it will not seek to undermine the stability of the northern regime. There is a tacit understanding in Seoul that the power transfer in Pyongyang should not be interfered with. Seoul realises that the process of unification will entail enormous challenges even if it comes gradually and in a non-chaotic manner, and that any ill-conceived attempts to accelerate the process could very easily disrupt the political, economic, and social conditions in the South as well as in the North. Seoul perceives good reason for building cooperation and understanding with the North, and working to assure gradual, rather than radical and destabilising, reforms there. South Korea's strategy provides Pyongyang with valuable time in which to reconsider its defunct southern strategy. It gives the North the chance to convert the deadly stand-off in Korea into a more peaceful and mutually beneficial non-zero sum game.

Forging interdependence, preparing for unification

While Seoul's cautious approach is useful over the short term in that it avoids exacerbating the North's insecurities, it is questionable whether it can be sustained over the longer term. Today, both Seoul and Pyongyang have a common interest in seeking to make the gradual, evolutionary approach to cooperation and eventual unification work. As economic cooperation and interdependence grow between the two Koreas, and especially as North Korean citizens discover the realities of the outside world (read, South Korea), they will recognise how deprived they have been, and how much they have been lied to. In such a context, it is difficult to imagine that North Korean citizens would continue to accept Pyongyang's suffocating controls. Even though no organised opposition exists at the present time, it would not be long before one emerged under these circumstances. The majority of the North Korean population are young, and will not have much real attachment, emotional or political, to the perpetuation of the existing system once it is known to be dysfunctional. The communist leadership might be able to suppress challenges to its rule for some time but, in the final analysis, could not hold onto power without massive and violent repression.

---

[13] Claudia Rosett, 'Aid to North Korea Will Only Extend the Communist Ice Age', *Asian Wall Street Journal*, 23 September 1991.

In other words, the new flexibility in Seoul's approach to Pyongyang ultimately cannot stave off North Korea's eventual collapse. For South Korean leaders, and South Koreans more generally, the challenge is clear. However much Seoul may wish to delay the process of unification until such time as it feels ready, the reality of the situation is that these choices are not South Korea's to make. It is probable that, in the period ahead, the timing and pace of unification will be set by internal changes in North Korea far more than by the policies of South Korea. Thus, in addition to seeking to pursue its dialogue with the North, South Korea should be thinking hard about how to deal with the aftermath of a sudden political collapse in the North. The monetary, economic and social implications of political collapse in the North are extraordinarily serious and must be accorded the highest priority by the new South Korean government.

12 The Gradualist Pipe-Dream: Prospects and Pathways for Korean Reunification

AIDAN FOSTER-CARTER

'If productivity is not developed rapidly to lay the material and technological foundation commensurate with the socialist system...socialism, like a building with an unsolid foundation, can[not] maintain its existence long...' (Kim Jong Il, January 1992)

Introduction

This chapter is about what is going to happen in Korea. It will attempt to review various scenarios for change on the peninsula over the next few years, and to evaluate which are the most and which the least plausible.

As its title suggests, the chapter also argues a particular case. My own close watching of North Korea during the past decade has led to the conclusion that some kind of system-collapse cannot be long delayed; and hence that the form which Korean reunification will take will essentially be, as in Germany, the absorption of the failed system into and by the successful one.

When I presented this argument (in terms drawn from Habermas's theory of crisis) at a conference on North Korea held in Seoul in the autumn of 1991, however, it seemed to be very much a minority view—at least among the South Korean participants. Their opinion, to the contrary, tended to be that a process of gradual change was now beginning, whereby Seoul and Pyongyang would increasingly normalise and expand their *de facto* political, economic and other relations, rather as the two Germanies did in the 1970s and 1980s.

Quite whither such a road would be expected to lead, in the longer run, was and is unclear to me. The main thrust of the argument, however, is directed toward the short- and medium-term. The prediction, and the hope, are for a belated outbreak of peace and normalisation on the

159

peninsula. The vision is of two states and two systems, both continuing to exist and learning to get along better and cooperate more for their mutual benefit.

Would that it could be so. I share the hope, but cannot assent to the prediction. Although in the light of these arguments I have thoroughly re-examined my own, I still conclude that gradualism is wishful thinking for Korea in the early 1990s. The wish in itself is wholly understandable. I think it has two aspects, looking Janus-like toward both past and future (wistfully, in both cases).

Partly, it is a nostalgia for what might have been. Although counter-factuals are tricky, it is my view that the two Koreas could indeed in principle have got along better over the past two decades. Although it was outside forces which first divided Korea, subsequently it has been the two Korean governments which have stubbornly maintained the absolute-ness of the partition. The history of the North since the 1970s could have been different. Perhaps would have been, in a nation with a less harsh and unyielding political culture. But it is too late for that now.

The second reason for the gradualist hope is more practical. Watching the German experience since 1989 has brought home to South Koreans the possible political and security risks, but above all the vast and unavoidable economic costs, of any reunification which arises from the collapse of the North and its absorption by the South. This in turn has led, understandably enough, to a fervent hope that reunification will not happen that way. The ironic consequence is that now, after almost half a century of bitter hostility, there are many in Seoul who, despite them-selves, have begun to wish Kim Il Sung good health and a long life in order to stave off what is seen as an apocalypse. The wish is father to the thought.

As will be argued below, however, it strains credibility to imagine a gradualist scenario being sustained. The gradualist view has four linked weaknesses:

1. It is too optimistic regarding the *will* for change in the North Korean leadership.

2. Even if that were to alter, gradualists exaggerate the *capacity* of the North Korean system to survive whether or not Pyongyang embarks on any serious process of reform.

3. It fails to address key issues of *legitimation* and *power*.

4. It assigns an unwarrantedly passive role to the *people* of North Korea assuming (in true Korean style) that whatever the governments cook up between them and decree will automatically come to pass.

All this will be considered more fully below. The aim will be to unpack and evaluate both the 'gradualist' and 'collapsist' scenarios, by rendering explicit and then examining their key assumptions and modes of reasoning. These assumptions, as will be seen, themselves operate at various levels: ranging from specific predictions or bets on what will happen, to more general and often unstated presumptions about how people may be expected to react in particular circumstances. Bringing all this into the light seems the best way to proceed.

An excursus on method

As a sociologist working on North Korea (a combination which sometimes occasions surprise), I have come to find the tools, debates and concepts of my discipline invaluable. Over and above the substantive concerns of comparative development sociology which first drew me to study Korea in the 1960s, more fundamental issues of method have also proved highly relevant.

Though a committed unbeliever in the conventional disciplinary boundaries which divide the social sciences, I think it has been sociology's particular fate to become the methodological conscience for social science as a whole. In the present case, faced with the twin difficulties of predicting the future of Korea in general, and penetrating the obscurity of North Korea in particular, there are a number of both classical and contemporary sociological debates and concerns which may be of service. These include:

1. The methodenstreit

The nineteenth century German debates on the proper methods for historiography and social science are resonant for our purpose in at least two ways. First, one major dispute in these debates concerned the relations between general and particular. Should social science, like natural science, aim to be nomothetic: that is, to arrive at generalisations (maybe even laws)? Or are the human sciences instead idiographic, focusing on what is particular and indeed unique about each society or even each event?

For most social scientists, this is less an either/or than a matter of balance. As regards North Korea, we 'collapsists' rely on nomothetic arguments of various kinds:

i) This regime is a member of a class of other similar regimes, mostly now defunct.

ii) Such regimes have congenital system-faults, especially within their economic structures (well analysed in the work of Janos Kornai), which cause them to malfunction and eventually to break down.

iii) All such regimes except two (North Korea and Cuba) have either drastically reformed their economies (like China and Vietnam), or collapsed.

iv) Ergo, North Korea will not be different.

Conversely, 'gradualists' must perforce embrace the idiographic side of the argument: that there is something *sui generis* about North Korea, such that it can survive where others have perished. Although not often spelled out, 'gradualist' assumptions here seem to include:

i) The suggestion that, unlike in other erstwile communist countries, the North Korean regime's hold over its citizens is unbreakable.

ii) The idea that Asia is different from Europe.

iii) The hope that North Korea will embrace economic reform, and survive that way (in effect by transforming the basis of the regime's legitimisation, as in China).

Only the first of these three arguments is fully idiographic. The other two are semi-nomothetic (or middle range), in that they seek to 'save' North Korea methodologically by placing it in a different category (be that the fact of Asia, or the hope of reform). While we shall return to the details later, the point for now is that 'gradualists' must in some degree be committed to, and be able to defend, the view that North Korea is different. Conversely, 'collapsists' are reasoning from a body of both empirical evidence (the fall of communism) and associated theory (e.g., Kornai), and arguing that North Korea is no exception.

Second, a slightly different *methodensteit* debate can also be helpful. Those who doubted the applicability of natural science methods to the study of society suggested that they be replaced, or at least supplemented, by something very different. It might be Dilthey's empathy (*einfuhlung*), or Weber's better known emphasis on meaning and understanding (*verstehen*), or the broad hermeneutic view of the human sciences as a kind of dialogue between different world-views or traditions.

Without getting too deeply into all this, let me just record that I find this kind of approach fruitful too. Trying to get inside Kim Il Sung's head (or heart, or gut) must be part of the Western social scientist's task. What would be his rationality? What are the limits of his world-view? What will he and his regime do, and what not? (Importantly, if eclectically, I see such considerations as complementing the afore-mentioned more mainstream nomothetic approach, not as a substitute for it.)

2. *Classical sociology*

In varying ways and degrees, the trio currently seen as sociology's founders all provide insights and pointers, both methodological and substantive:

Weber

Weber is especially valuable. As well as *verstehen*, we can take from him:

i) Methodologically, his emphasis on the role of sheer contingency—that which is intrinsically unpredictable—in human affairs. Korea's partition in 1945 is one example from the past; the timing (though not the fact) of Kim Il Sung's death is one for the future.

ii) In general, the insistence on the need to go beyond 'plausible stories' (which are usually several) to achieve maximum rigour.

iii) Substantively, an absolutely central area (arguably the crucial one) for predicting the Korean future is Weber's core concern with *legitimation*: particularly his insistence that the fact of obedience by peoples to their rulers always requires explanation, and should not be taken for granted. Both 'gradualists' and 'collapsists' alike make assumptions about this in the North Korean case, as we shall see below.

Marx

Marx too may have a role. As against the by now utterly unbridled voluntarism of *juche*, with its ludicrous assertion that those armed with correct ideology and loyalty can accomplish anything, it is highly pertinent to insist that productive forces do after all make a difference. North Korea's are in very bad shape, and this fact may yet determine its prospects for survival.

Durkheim

Durkheim's contribution is as exploder of *yuilsasang*: the North Korean insistence that all hearts do (should, must) beat as one. But this is to posit modernisation without modernity. As Durkheim argued, the complexity of modern society requires new forms of solidarity, based on acceptance of difference and a celebration of complementarity. By contrast, North Korea's neo-traditionalist paternalism purports to reject difference, individualism, and pluralism. To draw on another classical sociologist, Toennies, North Korea attempts to weld institutions based on *gesellschaft* (modern and formal) using an ideology of *gemeinschaft* (blood, warmth, community). The contradictions are acute.

3. Philosophy of (social) science

The paucity of data on all aspects of North Korea poses particular challenges to social science. To run any argument whatever involves an irreducible degree of assumption-making, just to fill in the gaps.

While of course empirical data are always to be preferred (and there are perhaps more than one might suppose; some useful sources, such as Kim Il Sung's *Works*, have been surprisingly little mined), any scholar must have strategies for the unknown. I am conscious, in the argument that follows, of using several techniques from the general philosophy of social science armoury:

i) Deduction *a priori*. For instance, if the target on land reclamation has not altered much in twenty years, we may reasonably suppose a lack of progress.

ii) Comparison. For example, insofar as Mao's China once really seemed to be what it presented itself to be—a new civilisation which had seized the masses' hearts and minds—but later turned out not to be so, then what price North Korea being at bottom any different?

Two general comments are also necessary. First, in all of this (as in all cross-cultural social science) there are two ethnocentrisms to steer between: the Scylla which proclaims that people everywhere are much the same, versus the Charybdis that insists on emphasising differences. As will be clear by now I am more likely to run aground on the former then the latter. Secondly, only time will tell (but it will tell, indubitably) which out of the gradualism or the collapse scenarios is correct. That is what gives the Korean situation its fascination for social science, as well as its awesome importance for the real history of the very near future.

The immediate issues: nuclear inspection and economic reform

Resurfacing from these philosophical arcana into the here and now of the real world, at the time of writing North Korea confronts two linked challenges. The first one, of course, is nuclear inspection. So important is this to all concerned (especially South Korea, the USA, and Japan) that it has become a touchstone of Pyongyang's good faith, as well as a *sine qua non* for progress in other spheres (of which the most important is economic aid).

At present, despite having formally signed not one but two agreements on nuclear inspection (with the IAEA, belatedly, and also with South Korea), North Korea is continuing to stall on the nitty-gritty of actually being inspected. This, if it goes on, will have one definite and one possible consequence, both adverse for Pyongyang.

Neither South Korea nor Japan will permit substantial economic aid to North Korea. Seoul may still be tempted, in order to avoid the danger of a cornered Pyongyang either lashing out or collapsing. After all, the whole strategy of (so to speak) putting a handful of food through the bars of the cage is inherently risky: you hope the tiger will chew the food, but it might prefer your arm. Nonetheless, in the final analysis the nuclear nightmare is even scarier than the collapse nightmare.

There is also the possibility that continued prevarication by Pyongyang could lead to a pre-emptive military strike against the suspect facility at Yongbyon, by US and/or South Korean forces. While others here are more expert than I, the consequences of that option seem literally incalculable, in terms of fall-out both literal and metaphorical. It could bring war; it is hard to see how it could bring peace. Going down that road would mean that Seoul and Washington had abandoned any trust in Pyongyang as a dialogue partner; and could well precipitate the collapse of Kim Il Sung's regime, with or without more general hostilities.

Assuming that North Korea goes on prevaricating, but is not bombed, then the *détente* processes between Pyongyang and both Seoul and Tokyo will be put on ice. (The latter is already frozen, in effect, having registered no progress since it began with much fanfare in the Autumn of 1990.) History would repeat itself. After all, the apparent breakthroughs of both 1972 and 1985 were each followed by years of retreat. North Korea, it might be assumed, will just revert to muddling along in *juche* mode, as per usual.

But it cannot, in my view. *Juche*—or at least its economic corollary, *chalip*—was always a myth, and in the 1990s it is a threadbare one. In the past, Pyongyang had both reserves of its own and other options.

In 1992, by contrast, Kim Il Sung (or Kim Jong Il) have very low options. While the parlous state of the North Korean economy is well known, the sheer depth of the crisis and closeness of the abyss tend to be under-estimated. (Curiously, we thus honour the Kims too much, by implicitly accepting their boasts of their system's indestructibility.)

The economic crisis can be illustrated on several dimensions:

i) The already decelerating growth rates of the 1980s have turned, at least since 1989, into actual contraction.

ii) On top of that came the body-blow of the effective ending of all Soviet aid in 1991 (even before the collapse of the Soviet Union).

iii) There were already reports of food shortages and riots last year, and the situation will likely worsen.

This cannot continue indefinitely. If nothing is done, the economy may seize up or implode completely (as opposed to merely marking time). In particular, pressure on already spartan living standards—officially admitted as a problem—must at some point (starvation?) produce a popular backlash, and/or an intra-elite coup in favour of thoroughgoing economic reform.

In this context, it is important to insist on just how unreconstructed the North Korean economy and attitudes both remain. Ever since Pyongyang's singularly unsuccessful joint venture law of 1984, there has been a steady stream of upbeat journalism by the usual suspects alleging that North Korea was on the brink of serious economic reform. A timely antidote to such optimism came in a major article which appeared over Kim Jong Il's name in February 1992. Setting his face firmly against any and all liberalisation, Kim specifically lauded the superiority of socialist economic planning over capitalism.

The short-run prospect: grudging compliance

Nonetheless, economic reform *à la chinoise* is the path down which North Korea will probably head—if only, like all the changes of the past year or so, because it has its back to the wall and there is nowhere else to go.

To summarise the argument thus far: much more prevarication on nuclear inspection will risk at best a denial of aid and at worst sanctions on military strikes against Yongbyon. Even the former would in turn risk economic and hence perhaps political collapse. Then the sensible course is for Pyongyang to allow nuclear inspection so that *détente* and in particular economic aid can proceed.

Although North Korea on past form can scarcely by accused of always following the sensible course, as others might perceive it, these days it has little option. Thus, at the very least, the North may go through the motions of both nuclear inspection and economic reform, if only in the same grudging spirit as Pyongyang's other recent concessions (such as separate UN entry, inter-Korean trade, and negotiations with Seoul). No previous concessions, it is important to stress, have been embraced warmly or spontaneously. On the contrary, all have been forced upon North Korea by adverse circumstances (both within and without) and the absence of any realistic alternative.

Consider then a fairly short-run scenario in which Pyongyang consents to real nuclear inspection and economic reform. What would this mean, both as regards North Korea's intentions and the likely results? (By no means should these two be equated: Merton's 'unintended consequences' is another valuable tool in sociology's conceptual armoury.)

1. As regards nuclear inspection, the modalities are that:

   i) There never was a bomb program (Yongbyon as a Potemkin village). This seems unlikely, although it has been seriously suggested.

   ii) There was a nuclear program, but it stops after a genuine inspection is implemented. On the strength of North Korea's past track record, simply giving up would seem out of character. So doing would entail the surrender of Pyongyang's sole remaining potential strategic card: indeed, the whole rationale for developing a bomb in the first place. Henceforth, real power in the relationship would pass unequivocally and irreversibly to South Korea.

   iii) North Korea's nuclear program continues underground, figuratively and indeed literally; i.e., an Iraqi-style strategy of concealment. This seems the likeliest option. The question is: could they get away with it. If they did, it would be a Pyrrhic victory; inasmuch as the eventual announcement of possession of a device (assuming no plan to really use it, in which case Armageddon beckons) would immediately end *détente* and any economic co-operation with Seoul or Tokyo, thereby thrusting Pyongyang back upon its own resources and hence risking the collapse scenario once again. Just possibly, North Korea may be reckoning in such a situation to seize Japanese and South Korean plants already introduced, in an act of piracy similar to its notorious failure to pay for Western technology in the mid-1970s: a theft, be it noted, which Pyongyang has never properly acknowledged, let along apologised or paid for. But it is unlikely to come to that. The prospect is rather of chronic mutual mistrust and fairly bad-tempered relations all round; which in turn would stymie the smooth development of economic relations, to which we now turn

2. Even if *détente* proceeds, and an ostensibly non-nuclear North Korea stands poised for South Korean and Japanese investment, the consequences are far from clear. According to the 'gradualist' scenario, increased economic relations are already under way. Inter-Korean trade in 1991 was not far short of $200 million; Pyongyang has declared its first Special Economic Zone (SEZ), and invited South Korean investment in the Tumen delta project, Daewoo's chairman Kim has visited; and so forth.

Sceptics may be more cautious. The trade, which has waxed and waned with the state of political relationships, has earned valuable foreign exchange for Pyongyang. But it is only a drop in the ocean of Seoul's overall trade volume, and it can easily be switched off if the North incurs the South's displeasure.

All the rest is just talk, so far. The Najin–Sonbong SEZ is as far from Pyongyang as possible; while all the hype around the Tumen overlooks competing visions of it by the different countries involved, not to mention the $30 billion question of who will put up that sort of money.

Two central questions remain. Will any amount of foreign investment save North Korea (indeed, especially as regards Japan, will such investment even be forthcoming at all), without thoroughgoing economic reform? And what would be the broader effects of such reform on the Kim Il Sung/Kim Jong Il regime and its legitimacy?

If Kim Jong Il is to be taken at his word (and who would dare do less), there is as yet no intention in Pyongyang of even admitting the need for economic reform, let alone grasping the nettle. For as long as that is so, then investment schemes like that of Daewoo will be too little—and maybe too late—to save the North Korean economy. The Chinese and Vietnamese experience is instructive here: *doi moi* is indivisible. It entails not only an openness (a real openness) to outside participation, but also the replacement, or supplementation, of state planning by market relations over broad swathes of the domestic economy: especially agriculture and internal trade, neither of which Pyongyang has ever shown the slightest sign of privatising. Economic collapse thus remains a real possibility in North Korea.

The medium-term: reform and its contradictions

To recapitulate, our argument is that an uninspected North Korea might get bombed, and an unreformed North Korea would collapse. For those reasons, and only for those reasons, Pyongyang is likely to go through the motions of both nuclear inspection and economic reform.

On this basis, the gradualist scenario envisages an outbreak of peace on this peninsula. Although I have yet to see this spelled out (or indeed thought through), the implicit mode seems to be what until 1989 we might have termed 'Germanisation': that is, two states still separate and indeed opposed, but nonetheless cooperating where there is mutual gain, allowing contacts between divided families, and so on. Or perhaps a more apt model would be the relations now obtaining between China and Taiwan, where even official non-recognition has not prevented substantial economic co-operation and visits (albeit overwhelmingly in one direction: it is Taiwanese who travel to and invest in China).

Yet these two parallels, it seems to me, illustrate well the perils and contradictions of any such course for North Korea. With hindsight, East Germany was stable only in the Cold War context which created it. Once that began to unravel, all the years of watching West German television began to take effect; and what had seemed a solid, and in its way successful, regime and state simply crumbled into dust. Faced with the alternative (even if idealised) of a palpably richer and freer way of being German, yesterday's seemingly loyal and well-drilled East Germans opted overwhelmingly for capitalism. Crucially, this swiftly unfolding process not only undermined the communist regime, but in so doing also destroyed any rationale for the continued existence of a separate East German state, to the chagrin of those who hoped for some third force or middle way. (*Minjung-mongers* in Seoul's dissident circles should ponder deeply on this.)

How or why might things be different in Korea? Gradualists would have to assert any or all of the following:

1. South Korea will not seem as attractive to North Koreans, as West Germany did to East Germans.

2. The North Korean regime, presumably with Seoul's connivance, will find a way to effect economic reform without seriously puncturing its information quarantine (i.e., 1. will not arise).

3. Despite 1. and/or 2., the Kim regime will keep its grip through blind faith or blind fear.

4. Alternatively, the prosperity and easing up produced by economic reform in the North will cause people to give thanks to Kim Il Sung and/or Kim Jong Il.

None of these statements seems to me plausible. Taking each in turn:

1. This could unpack into two propositions: either that living standards north and south of the DMZ are not so different; or that non-economic factors (pride, the *juche* spirit) would work to counteract the lure of Seoul. The former is plainly untrue in the 1990s. It requires no idealisation of ordinary people's lives in South Korea to state the difference. North Koreans work hard, for little reward or leisure. Recent wage increases (how will they be paid for?) seem unlikely to compensate for an overall standard of living which, in contrast to earlier decades, is now declining. South Koreans work hard too, but see the fruits of their efforts in steadily rising living standards; and their leisure time is their own. While in one or two sectors (housing, nursery provision) the North may offer more, the overall balance sheet is not in doubt.

   The second version ('poorer but proud') corresponds to an emerging Pyongyang propaganda line. Even Kim Il Sung has admitted to a lack of affluence (not his personally, of course; and I mean that not as a cheap jibe, but as an observation about relative living standards within North Korea which every citizen can and surely does make). Yet it strains credulity to suppose that the North Korean populace, once exposed to full knowledge of a southern per capita income more than five times greater than their own, would cheerfully buy the 'poor but proud' argument. Why should they? What does everyday life in the North Korea in the 1990s (as opposed to the heroic 1960s, say) offer to make its citizens spurn the affluence of the South?

2. The 'gradualist' argument might be sustained if North Korea could keep its information quarantine in place, and still reform. Very probably, that is what it will try to do. All SEZs or investment sites so far announced or mooted (the Najin–Sonbong SEZ, or Daewoo in Nampo) are either remote from the centre, or intended to be quarantined so as not to corrupt the citizenry.

   Yet there are many reasons to doubt whether this cake can be had and eaten. In the first place, the information blackout is already being pierced. Students returning from abroad, workers in foreign embassies in Pyongyang, and above all ethnic Koreans living in China or Japan who visit their relatives, cannot fail to convey in some degree the message that things are better in the South. That message also carries an undeniable corollary: your own government has not only failed you (all that sweat and sacrifice, for what?), but has also lied to you. More broadly, North Koreans know even from their own media that socialism has collapsed in many countries; that the Great Leader's great friend Ceausescu was killed; and that the USSR has ceased to exist. It must make them think.

To these breaches of quarantine must be added, in the last three years, the tangible evidence of imported South Korean goods. Although the scale is as yet small, and efforts are doubtless made to disguise their origin, nonetheless inevitably some people will know—and draw their own conclusions. *A fortiori*, once Daewoo or whoever are set up in Nampo or wherever, everyone who works for them will also have food for thought.

Beyond that there lies a Catch 22. On the one hand, mere tinkering at the margins—a bit of trade here, the odd factory there—will not suffice to save the North's economy from the abyss. On the other hand, as already noted, serious economic reform on Chinese or Vietnamese lines would entail such a degree of both internal and external opening of economy and society that today's trickle of information and trade would become a flood.

The only possible way out of the bind is via a path which may yet be attempted, whereby South Korea (once reassured on the nuclear issue) in effect drip-feeds the North—buying more of its products, sending more rice, perhaps even budgetary support—in order to keep the Kim regime going 'as is'. While the attraction for both Seoul and Pyongyang of such a course is clear, as stated at the outset of this chapter, it too has problems. For one thing, it is precisely not a strategy of reform. Rather, to pursue the medical metaphor, this would represent not a cure, but simply a life-support machine; and this for a patient who is arguably already semi-comatose, and who may die anyway.

In that sense, the drip-feed scenario is less a strategy than a tactic. Even if it 'works', it will at best postpone the day of reckoning. It also carries moral and political difficulties. Should, could, and would the South Korean government agree to a partial package such as aid to Pyongyang, but no cross-DMZ visits? Or is the northern *gulag* (with an estimated population of around 100 000) off-limits for discussion? All in all, though seemingly tempting in the short run, this option is a chimera.

3. The third gradualist variation would have to claim that a reforming North Korea could still retain its legitimacy, whether through faith or fear (or perhaps some mixture of the two), even after and despite exposure to the outside world in general and South Korea in particular. The modalities here can be put in terms of a contrast between two memorable dystopias of modern literature. Is North Korea like Aldous Huxley's *Brave New World*, where everyone has been conditioned to believe that their lives really are wonderful? Or is it more

akin to George Orwell's *1984*, where there is no illusion, people know perfectly well that the system stinks and their lives are hell, but fear keeps them in line?

Even today, the balance for North Korea seems more towards Orwell. (One could also cite *Animal Farm*: in Pyongyang, some animals are definitely more equal than others.) But in any case either model would be severely challenged by reform and opening. The Huxley version would simply be undercut; given that North Koreans are not in fact programmed androids (despite their government's strenuous efforts), learning of another and better reality would inevitably change their world view. The Pyongyang media's ceaseless warnings against 'pagan infiltration' suggest that the North Korean regime also shares this view of the premises of its own legitimation, ironically enough. (After decades of indoctrination, one might have expected *yuilsasang* or 'ideological monochromaticity' to be deemed a bit more secure in its foundations than this.)

One conceivable counter-argument comes from the social psychology of religion. Festinger (in *When Prophecy Fails*) used the concept of 'cognitive dissonance' to show how the faith of the members of a religious sect in their prophet survived, even when the world failed to end on the day the prophet had predicted. Certainly there are circumstances where people's beliefs or faith can withstand any amount of seeming disconfirmation. Somehow I doubt whether the North Korean case will prove to be one.

What then of Orwell and fear? Happily, there is evidence that North Korea is already reaching the limits of forcible compliance. It comes in the defecting diplomat Ko Yong Hwan's revelation in 1991 that senior economic officials:

> ...are said to denounce and besmirch the party policies concerning economic domains whenever they get together. The Public Security Ministry was said to be pining to put these complaining party officials, all of them, behind bars, but there were simply too many to imprison.

That problem would of course only be exacerbated by economic reform. The whole logic of *doi moi*—one might say, its intrinsic socio-logic or even psycho-logic—pushes individuals to think and act more autonomously (true *juche*, in a sense). A reforming communist state cannot be maintained simply as a gigantic goal, or reform will fail.

To say this, however, is not to succumb to the Eurocentric liberal fallacy that *perestroika* inevitably and fatally breeds *glasnost*. China and Vietnam, whatever the long-run contradictions of the mixed path they are now following, have shown that communist politics and market economies can be welded in a way that has at least some viability. In this version, the socialist stick is (if not abolished) at least supplemented by a capitalist carrot. This is precisely the hope of Korean gradualists.

4. Can North Korea then save itself, by economic reform along Chinese or Vietnamese lines? To repeat: unlike some, I do not believe such a model to be unviable in principle. Beijing and Hanoi—or rather Guangzhou and Saigon, whereby hangs a tale—indicate otherwise. It can work, economically. Politically, it involves a kind of relegitimisation: a change, or at least a broadening, in the basis of the regime's legitimacy, whereby it promises and delivers a degree of prosperity and autonomy.

For this to work in North Korea, one would have to assume not only that the regime would embrace this path (that is, execute a U-turn away from and against everything they have ever preached—and, crucially, are still preaching today); but also that people would thank them for it. I find this unimaginable, on several grounds.

First, North Korea, unlike China or Vietnam, is still ruled by its founding leader. It is easier for successor regimes to make U-turns, and admit mistakes. Second and relatedly, Kim Il Sung has foolishly and uniquely adopted a stance of papal infallibility. Since the party line is that the party line has never been and can never be wrong (even slightly), any U-turn (even if unacknowledged, as would certainly be the case) cannot but undermine legitimacy.

Third, real reform would unleash real social, economic, and political processes challenging the whole basis of the Kims' rule. By analogy, it would be as if Mao Zedong rather than Deng Xiaoping had launched the 'four modernisations', while not repudiating the Cultural Revolution or the Great Leap Forward. To do so would inevitably be to open up space for criticism and potential ouster, whether from rivals in the political elite or ordinary people (let alone such groups as students and intellectuals).

And fourth, of course, there is South Korea. (The previous three points, importantly, pertain solely to the internal solecism entailed in picturing the Kims suddenly turning into harbingers of real economic reform.) All in all, my contention is that North Koreans would be less inclined to bless their Great and Dear Leaders for belated conversion to good sense, than to curse them for all the years of privation and misery; or simply to shove them aside in favour of the genuine article in Seoul.

China and Taiwan are clearly relevant here. Granted, their burgeoning contacts, and the awareness of Taiwanese prosperity that this inevitably creates on the mainland, do not seem *ipso facto* to undermine the perceived legitimacy—or at least the tolerability—of

CCP rule. I think the three points just cited are pertinent, plus above all the huge difference in scale. If the communist bit of China had only half Taiwan's population and was similar in area (i.e., the same relative proportions as in Korea), then I do indeed believe that the sorts of ties now being forged in Fujian would undermine Beijing's legitimacy. For inexorably the question would arise: why not just join them? And, once raised, that question could neither be satisfactorily answered in the negative, nor successfully suppressed.

Father, son, or wholly go?

At this point we must consider the implications should Kim Il Sung formally hand over power to his son Kim Jong Il. Various pointers seem to indicate that this is increasingly likely. This was not raised earlier, since the basic thrust of this chapter is to try to tease out system-logic first. However, questions of legitimation obviously do apply to key personalities as well as to the systems they preside over. This is especially so in North Korea, where leader and system to a unique degree have come to be virtually equated in official discourse; a fact which may yet turn out to be a fateful or even fatal weakness.

Basically, any assumption of formal state and/or party leadership by Kim Jong Il would not in my view alter the above analysis. All North Korea's dilemmas, contradictions and crises would remain. The one option which in theory might make a difference, namely the son as reformer (a line occasionally canvassed in the past, e.g., in Chongryun circles), seems to be clearly contra-indicated by all known evidence.

But even if Kim Jong Il were minded to do anything as un-Confucian as repudiating his father's legacy, it would be a very difficult act to carry off. Given the evidence (anecdotal, but cumulative) of Kim Jong Il's personal defects of character, small wonder if he chooses—or is compelled (who can say what are the dynamics and who the initiators of these processes, behind Pyongyang's palace walls) to plump for inheriting his father's charisma, rather than striking out on his own.

Or perhaps it is all a cunning ploy, like the young king Juan Carlos of Spain fooling old Franco and emerging as a liberaliser once the general-issimo was safely in the grave. Even if that were his plan, Kim Jong Il (and North Korea) will be acutely vulnerable when the Great Leader finally dies. Like others, at that point I would expect a power struggle leading to a military coup, with Pyongyang's political elite desperately seeking ways of clinging to their power and privileges. While in theory Kim Jong Il could be their front man, in practice they will probably ditch him (perhaps brutally, à la Bucharest) in favour of a strategy of repudi-ating the Kim dynasty.

Could this kind of successor regime—a North Korean Iliescu—preside over a gradual improvement of ties with Seoul, thereby saving the gradualist scenario? It would certainly try to, whether out of conviction or simply because in the changed world of the 1990s it would have no other option. But I doubt whether it would succeed. How exactly to position itself *vis-à-vis* the legacy of Kim Il Sung would be one dilemma: a total disavowal as in Romania (however hypocritical) or some curate's egg formula (good in parts) like Deng on Mao? Either carries risks.

And there is still South Korea, whose sheer facticity will in my view undermine any *raison d'être* for a separate North Korea after the Kims. However much the political elites in Pyongyang and Seoul may have come to share an ironic perceived common interest in North Korea's continued existence—the latter to save their exchequer, the former to save their skins—they both appear (all too characteristically, perhaps) to impute no power of independent agency in any conceivable circumstances to those who ultimately bear the brunt: namely, the long-suffering North Korean populace.

Granted, the proposition that these will do as they are told in any circumstances might seem a secure inductive generalisation, based on almost half a century's evidence. Yet the East European revolutions of 1989, particularly East Germany, warn us how deceptive appearances can be in such cases. While there are too many imponderables to make specific predictions, I would not rule out even a new Tonghak in North Korea: a great upsurge of rage from the grassroots, against the dynasty which promised so much but by the end delivered so little. The ideological content would of course be the opposite of a century ago; no longer keeping the modern world at bay, but demanding to be part of it and share its fruits.

Conclusion: not gradualism but turbulence

The aim of this chapter has been to argue, reluctantly, against the viability of a gradualist scenario for the Korean peninsula over the next few years. In a nutshell: the North Korean system is in terminal crisis; there is as yet little sign even of a will to seek a cure; and even if the medicine of reform were to be swallowed in doses large enough to be efficacious, the side effects would render the patient fatally vulnerable to yet other maladies. (This last is very well understood in Pyongyang, which of course explains the reluctance to reform.)

My strategy has been to tease out what I take to be the presumptions of would-be gradualists about how variables interact (or how people can be expected to behave) in given circumstances, and to subject them to scrutiny. I hope this will facilitate discussion, by enabling those who predict a different outcome to indicate where their assumptions differ from mine; and/or to point to absences or flaws in my own reasoning.

It would be nice to be wrong, because obviously my own analysis predicts a degree of turbulence. I expect continued failure to embrace serious reform while Kim Il Sung lives (whether or not Kim Jong Il takes over), leading to an elite coup and/or a Timisoara-style popular arising: certainly after Kim dies, and possibly even before if things (and people) get desperate enough. Such a prospect carries obvious risks.

Equally, my conclusion is that collapse will lead to absorption. South Koreans, government and citizens alike, had better brace themselves for a role and a task very like the former West Germany has had to shoulder— only harder, because the relative gaps are that much bigger. That prospect should be concentrating minds in Seoul.

For the longer term, nonetheless, I am an optimist for Korea and Koreans (what other countries make of it is not my concern here). After the turbulence of collapse and absorption, reunification will bring obvious benefits to both individuals and the nation. It will, after all, be the fulfilment of a long-cherished dream, which only yesterday seemed impossible—yet has now become inevitable. So a happy ending, yes. But the play begun in 1945 has yet to conclude; and the story so far suggests to me that the final act will be pretty dramatic, not smooth.

THE DEPARTMENT OF INTERNATIONAL RELATIONS

PUBLICATIONS

STUDIES IN WORLD AFFAIRS

The Department of International Relations is producing a new series of monographs which are published in association with and distributed by Allen & Unwin Pty Ltd, 9 Atchison St, St Leonards, NSW 2065, Australia. Titles are:

Ethics and Foreign Policy,
edited by Paul Keal, 272pp, $24.95

Korea Under Roh Tae-woo: Democratisation, Northern Policy, and Inter-Korean Relations,
edited by James Cotton, 367pp, $24.95

Asian–Pacific Security After the Cold War,
edited by T.B. Millar and James Walter, 152pp, $24.95

The Post-Cold War Order: Diagnoses and Prognoses,
edited by Richard Leaver and James L. Richardson, 288pp, $24.95

Dependent Ally: A Study in Australian Foreign Policy,
by Coral Bell, 205pp, $24.95

A Peaceful Ocean? Maritime Security in the Pacific in the Post-Cold War Era,
edited by Andrew Mack, 232pp, $24.95

Asian Flashpoint: Security and the Korean Peninsula,
edited by Andrew Mack, 188pp, $24.95

CANBERRA STUDIES IN WORLD AFFAIRS

Distributed by: Bibliotech, Reply Paid 440 (no postage required if posted in Australia), ANUTECH Pty, Ltd, Canberra, ACT 0200, Australia (Fax order: (06) 257 1433).

22 *The Changing Pacific: Four Case Studies,*
   edited by Coral Bell, 68pp, $10.00

23 *New Directions in International Relations? Australian Perspectives,*
   edited by Richard Higgott, 218pp, $10.00

24 *Australia and the Multinationals: A Study of Power and Bargaining in the 1980s,*
   by Neil Renwick, 135pp, $10.00

25 *Refugees in the Modern World,*
   edited by Amin Saikal, 125pp, $10.00

THE AUSTRALIAN FOREIGN POLICY PROGRAMME

PUBLICATIONS

Australia's Alliance Options: Prospect and Retrospect in a World of Change,
Coral Bell, 104pp, $15.00

Selling Mirages: the Politics of Arms Trading,
Graeme Cheeseman, 85pp, $15.00

Australia's Human Rights Diplomacy,
Ian Russell, Peter Van Ness and Beng-Huat Chua, 179pp, $15.00

The European Community in Context,
John Groom, 47pp, $15.00

Coping with Washington: Players, Conventions and Strategies,
Davis Bobrow, 28pp, $10.00

*The Search for Substance: Australia–India Relations into the Nineties
and Beyond*,
Sandy Gordon, 107pp, $15.00

Protecting the Antarctic Environment: Australia and the Minerals Convention,
Lorraine Elliott, 94pp, $15.00

Australia's Taiwan Policy 1942–1992,
Gary Klintworth, 150pp, $20.00

Australia and the New World Order: Evatt in San Francisco, 1945,
W.J. Hudson, 160pp, $20.00

The Beijing Massacre: Australian Responses,
Kim Richard Nossal, 80pp, $15.00

Prices exclude postage and packaging.

Publications can be obtained from:

Bibliotech,
ANUTECH,
Canberra ACT 0200 Australia
Fax No: (06) 257 1433